A Brummie in Search of a Talent

A Brummie in Search of a Talent

Fred Stonier

The Pentland Press
Edinburgh – Cambridge – Durham – USA

© F. Stonier, 1999

First published in 1999 by
The Pentland Press Ltd
1 Hutton Close,
South Church
Bishop Auckland
Durham

All rights reserved
Unauthorised duplication
contravenes existing laws

ISBN 1 85821-715 6

Typeset in Bell 11/13
by Carnegie Publishing, Carnegie House, Chatsworth Road, Lancaster, LA1 4SL
Printed and bound by Bookcraft (Bath) Ltd.

I wish to dedicate my book to the following: my mother Elizabeth Stonier for my longevity gene – she lived to be ninety-seven and was a clever and good mother. My father James Stonier who persuaded me to join the Police and was a good father. My uncle Jack Croft MBE who offered me the chance to take up ARP, later civil defence, and my first three commandants. Major General Bruce, he was like a father to me once I had passed the test. Major General Matthews, who had confidence in me to allow my new and rather explosive material to be given as a solo effort; no small risk at a top government establishment; and Major General Cooke who followed and encouraged me to continue with my rather unconventional approach. Finally my late wife, Rose; we were married for fifty-four years, she was pretty, a good wife and mother, better educated than I, she helped both me and my two daughters in our frequent studies and exams. During the War, when we were hard-up, she got a part-time job as a machinist at a factory making Lancaster Bombers. She became so efficient that they offered her full-time on more wages than I was getting running a Civil Defence organization of 5,000 people. She was loved and is missed by her family. She was a good mate.

Contents

Illustrations		ix
Foreword		xi
Acknowledgements		xiv
Introduction		1

Chapter

I	The Family	3
II	The Farm	23
III	My Early Days	27
IV	The 1920s	60
V	The Police Force – Early Days	80
VI	Police Duties	99
VII	Motor Patrol Duties	118
VIII	Promotion	129
IX	Head Wardens	147
X	Civil Defence in the Blitz Period	165
XI	Promotion	173
XII	Return to Duty	191
XIII	To Sunningdale	211
XIV	End of Police Service – A New Life Begins	251
XV	Changes	274
XVI	Warning Signals	286
XVII	Random Recollections	300

Illustrations

CL. Supt. P.D. Peterson, West Midlands Police.	xi–xii
My Parents.	9
Just before losing my curls for ever at about 5 years old.	28
Aged 7, nursing our cat.	52
A Party at the Farm.	57
At age 20 (1927).	85
Wolverhampton Borough Police. 1931.	110–13
Visit by HRH Duke of Kent (Prince George) 1931.	125
PC Chettar standing, me sitting. Our MG – Circa 1953–4.	127
'The junior Sergeant takes the parade.'	130
Two stalwarts all through the War.	137
1937 anti-gas training in Magistrates' Court.	138
It was the time when the country thought it was about to be bombed with possibly gas.	140–1
Recruitment Parade along Penn Road about 1938.	142
New Cross Hospital about 1940.	142
Rose and Norah with the first respirators – from 1938.	144
Molineux, the Venue.	152
Plotting.	155
An increase in the Report Centre.	156
Two new W'ton Police Inspectors.	175
At the Palace to receive BEM, 1945 with Rose and Norah.	177

The First Instructional Staff at Ryton-on-Dunsmore 1946.	181
My first recruit course 1946.	183
I stage a demonstration for the Home Secretary.	183
My class at Ryton 1946–8.	184
2,000th Recruit Parade, Sept. 1947.	186
Wolves coming home with the FA Cup.	199
With my grandson, Sunningdale in background.	211
Police Staff Officer, Lecturer for UK 1954–57, 3½ years.	212
Main Hall, Sunningdale.	214
Sunningdale, house and grounds.	215–16
Lt Col Baxter; Major Andrews; Mr Coulson; Mr Brandis and Major Gen. Bruce.	224
Royal Procession, Windsor 1957–68.	226
My parents 'Diamond Wedding' Anniversary, 1954.	234
Taymouth Castle 1993.	244
My mother at 90, she went on to make 97.	280
North Lodge – my home at Sunningdale for over 8 yrs.	282
Rose and me in the 1960s, with our Triumph Herald.	284
At Sunningdale with Course Members, 1962.	310
Carole and Ken's wedding.	317
Norah and Ted's wedding.	318
Our cottages in the 1960s.	327
The garden at Redhill 1960s, before my occupation late 1960s.	328
Completed cottages at Redhill, Avon.	328
My bungalow in Alness, my home since 1989.	331
Granddaughter Rosemary Ward.	332
Lucy Sitton-Kent.	332
Grandson Christopher Kent and wife Dominique.	332

Foreword

When I joined the Police Service as a particularly youthful member of Wolverhampton Borough Constabularly in January 1937, Fred Stonier was already a seasoned officer of some ten years standing and I knew little of him until the establishment of the Civil Defence section following the outbreak of war in 1939. He was one of the few police officers chosen to train members of the force and the public in the various responsibilities known as 'Air Raid Precautions'.

In the rank of Sergeant he qualified as an Instructor, First Class, and became the Chief Instructor with the widest responsibilities in that new and vital field. His personality and confidence springing from a detailed knowledge of his subject and the ability to impart it to others, made him an outstanding instructor.

Following the end of hostilities and the slow return to some normality Fred's abilities made him a natural selection as an instructor on the staff of the Police Recruit Training Centre and brought the promotion to Inspector. His talents were there applied directly to the benefit of young officers just commencing their careers.

On his return to the force I was priviliged to work frequently under him in my new rank of Sergeant and I retain unforgettable memories of the lessons learned from his merticulous preperation of operations in connection with the then Betting and Gaming Laws.

The knowledge and experience gained by Fred in the field

This page and previous: *CL. Supt. P.D. Peterson, West Midlands Police.*

of Civil Defence was kept up to date against an international background still unsettled and it was whilst he was away attending a course that I ensured he was aware of an opportunity arising in the Civil Defence Staff College at Sunningdale as the Police Liason Officer in the rank of Superintendent. His record and ability made him the obvious choice and once again the new challenges were accepted with enthusiasm. As he was about to leave the force in Wolverhampton I was offered the many pages of handwritten notes on Police Law made by Fred for his own use whilst at the Training Centre. With great pleasure and appreciation I accepted the offer, made, I knew, out of friendship and generosity.

Such was Fred's value to the college that, on the termination of the post to which he had been seconded, he retired from the Police Service and was retained on the Instructional Staff with appropriate ranking in the Civil Service.

On two occasions I attended courses at the college and had the pleasure of renewing the old friendship. I also learned at first hand how highly he was regarded and experienced the effect on the students of his abilities.

On his eventual full retirement we both determined to keep in touch and this we have achieved although he has never returned to live in his native Midlands. He has the ability to look back on a long career devoted to "Service" in its widest sense. His influence has been spread over a particularly extensive field from the youngest Police recruits, through more seasoned officers and the general public in their execution of wartime duties to the highest ranks of the Police, Government and Armed Service Officers.

The award, quite early in his career, of the B.E.M. was a very well deserved recognition of his contribution to the good of the public of this country.

The story of Fred Stonier's life and times is difficult to condense into a single volume but I hope these words will help form a base upon which the following pages can adequately be built.

P.D. Peterson QPM
Formerly of Wolverhampton and
West Midlands Police 1937–76.
Chief Superintendent from 1966.

Acknowledgements

I wish to record my thanks to:

My late wife Rose who committed all my spoken words, and not so easy to understand handwriting, to paper in a very readable longhand, a formidable undertaking.

An equally long task was carried out by my eldest daughter, Norah, pounding away on her portable typewriter to produce the final manuscript.

To Ted and Rosemary, my son-in-law and his daughter, for their efforts in photocopying four complete copies of the manuscript, a total of some 1,000 A4 pages, and to typing my correspondence.

Lastly my thanks to the Managing Director and his Staff at the Pentland Press without whose help this book may not have seen the light of day.

Fred Stonier, Alness 1999

Introduction

My justification for penning these lines is simply that I have lived and survived through a period of time that has probably brought more changes than any other comparable period in history.

I can faintly recall the leisurely pace of life prior to the First World War, an age that seems so unreal today, and like so much of the past, is inclined to be rose-tinted in retrospect.

During the course of my life, I have lived, worked, fought and played with people from all levels of society, from the back streets of a Birmingham suburb, to the corridors of power in Whitehall.

It gives me considerable pleasure to recall these experiences, even the painful ones that hurt so much at the time, can be seen now as part of life and part of the pattern which ultimately forms character. It is, I'm afraid, only when one reaches the 'sere and yellow' that this philosophical view becomes acceptable. In any case, my main reason for this work is not that it may have any literary merit, but that it will interest my descendants.

I have always regretted not knowing more about my ancestors, few people of my generation and class can go back any further than their grandparents, occasionally perhaps, great-grandparents. This is probably the result of the upheavals of the Industrial Revolution, and perhaps the general illiteracy of most people of those times. I like to know 'what makes me tick', and heredity has much to do with this.

Chapter I

The Family

The Family

A brief description of the family is a pre-requisite to any life story; what one is, and does, is I believe greatly influenced by heredity. The genes have to answer for a great deal!

I never knew my grandfather, Walter James Stonier, he had died of cancer four or five years before I was born, which was 1906. It was generally felt that injuries received in the pit when he was a collier, had led to this fatal illness. The story was that he had wandered into the mining village of Chasetown, in Staffordshire, as a boy. He was befriended by the Bickley family who were well established in the village, and he eventually married a daughter of the family, Adelina, my grandmother. He worked as a miner, became a stallman or overseer; for much of the time he also kept a public house. I never knew from whence he came, except that it was from somewhere 'up North'. This was no uncommon thing in the mid-nineteenth century; many youngsters, boys and girls, were turned out by poverty-stricken parents, to fend for themselves.

He was undoubtedly a man of character and ability; my father always spoke of his parents with the greatest respect. When he died, he left an estate valued at about £10,000, a lot of money at the turn of the century. He had shares in Lichfield Gas Works, and in a brewery, and owned some property; he finally retired to live in one of the best houses in Chasetown, so by worldly standards, he was a successful man!

My grandmother was old and arthritic by the time I was old enough to take notice. She got around with the aid of a stick, always wore black, and a man's type of cap, which she kept on her head by the use of a hat pin.

She had been dark-haired when younger, with an aquiline nose. In her later years, she was severe and spoke with a gravelly kind of voice. She was looked after by a young woman named Lily. Lily was well treated, but kept on her toes by my strict grandmother. 'Ma', as we called her, never showed any recognizable sign of affection for me, but that was the code of her generation: treat children strictly, never show signs of affection. She herself had been in service at seven years of age, with the local doctor. She seemed to treat my mother a trifle distantly too, but this was probably due to her disapproval of the 'Crofts' clan, of which more anon.

The best story of my grandmother was that of the early years of her marriage, on the occasion of grandfather being brought home from the pit badly burned. He was lying on the bed, and when the doctor came to examine him, he tried to turn him over with his walking stick (to avoid handling the burned flesh presumably). Grandmother, in a rage, caught hold of the doctor saying, 'Don't you dare treat my man like that,' and promptly pitched him down the stairs. When they kept a public house, and remember, this was in a tough mining area, my grandmother was most often the 'chucker out', a very strong, very determined woman!

Her house, Ivyleigh, was kept scrupulously clean; it was furnished in the Victorian style with expensive mahogany furniture. Downstairs there was a scullery, a kitchen, in which she mainly lived, a lounge, and a front room. I have only a vague idea of the rooms upstairs, as when I visited the Chase, I slept at my Auntie Clara Gibbs' house; young children were not generally allowed upstairs at Ivyleigh, it was out of bounds!

She died around seventy-six years of age, and on her death the estate, which she had held in trust, was divided. The bulk went to Alice, the only daughter, and a very small proportion was divided among the sons. As Alice did not long survive her mother, her children, Florence, Edith and Mabel French shared the proceeds. The three girls had been well educated at college at the expense of the estate, and to finally collect the bulk of the residue seemed most unfair to the sons and their children, and rankled for many years. However, as Alice had been deserted by her alcoholic husband, leaving her with three young children, and as she nursed my grandfather in his final illness, I suppose he thought he was doing the right thing. My father gave me five pounds as my share of the estate!

Florence, Edith and Mabel French were schoolteachers, and surprisingly, our family kept on friendly terms with them; they often came visiting. I have a feeling that my mother and sisters admired their well-educated nieces and cousins. Mabel in particular, who was a dark beauty. I remember the breathtaking description my two sisters, Edith and Florence, gave of Mabel's exploits at the British Industries Fair at Bingley Hall, Birmingham, where apparently she created quite a stir among the menfolk. All of which was quite incomprehensible to me at the age of eight or nine. I remember her best for the gift of half-a-crown, and chocolates when she visited us.

But to return to Ivyleigh. There was a large garden, about half an acre, with a carriage house, stables, and two summer houses. The carriage house was used as a store, and the stables were used as fowl-houses. The garden was utilized to the full, with many apple trees, and all the ground was cultivated to grow food – no foolishness about using good soil to grow flowers (shows the peasant origin). A gardener came in weekly, and everywhere was beautifully kept. I was forbidden to pick the fruit, but this never stopped me helping myself to an apple or two in due season, and throwing the cores over the hedge. I cannot understand the meanness practised by a grandparent to a grandchild; I would and do lavish goodies on my own.

Later, when I was about eleven or twelve, I was on a visit to the 'Chase Wakes', a great event in those days. I was instructed to call and pay my respects to my grandmother. I duly called and did my duty, and on leaving was given a half-crown, a not inconsiderable amount in those days. I rejoined my Holland cousins, Bill and John, and went to the fair, where I promptly lost the half-crown on the 'Jazzer', a machine which jerked you in all directions as you tried to walk on it, designed, I was convinced, to jerk the money out of the pockets of boys like me! So my only present from my grandmother did me no good whatsoever.

Uncle Will Stonier

He was the eldest son; I never knew him well. When I did encounter him, he seemed to me a kindly man. He was rather short, compactly built, and worked as a craneman at the Saltley Gas Works. He had joined the Army as a young man, and I never understood why; it seemed that no man joined the Army in those days except as a last resort. He was in a Hussar Regiment, and my mother always said how handsome he looked in his tight-fitting uniform. How proud she was to dance with him at some Chasetown function, until the tight trousers split, and he had to stand by the wall for the rest of the evening. (She never spoke of my father like that, perhaps he was a poor dancer.) He was in the Egyptian Campaign under Lord Kitchener, was in the Battle of Omdurman, and I heard my parents say that Lord Kitchener described

Uncle Bill as the finest scout in the British Army. He came home and married. I never knew this aunty, 'Biddy', although I saw her once or twice. My mother described her as 'common', and would have nothing to do with her, hence the drift apart. There was a son, William, and a daughter who became a nurse. William I saw only once, during the First World War, when his father had brought him to our shop in Bamville Road. He was in uniform, ready to go to France. He was a fine-looking chap as I recall, in his Coldstream Guard's khaki; Uncle Will was very proud of him. He went to France, and like so many others, did not return, his body was never found. From linking times and places later, it appears that my brother Walter's unit, and Will's must have passed each other on that last journey, as Will went into the line, and Walter came out. They never met. This sad event, repeated so often in almost every family in the land, broke poor Uncle Will; he was never the same again, though he made a ripe old age. He refused the paltry War Office pension (about 7/6d old money), saying, 'If that is all they think my lad is worth, they can keep it.' Illogical, but understandable. My father and Will kept in contact during their lifetime.

Alice French

She was the Stoniers' only daughter. She made an unfortunate marriage. Her husband was a tea taster. Sadly, he took a fatal preference for tasting whisky, becoming an alcoholic. They split up in America, where my aunt was left with three young children. I don't know just what happened, but my father, who was little more than a boy, was in America at the time, with a good job, and looked after the family for a time. Eventually, Alice came home to her parents where she remained. She nursed my grandfather in his last illness, and benefitted in his Will to the extent I have indicated, and inherited the bulk of the residue of the estate on the death of her mother. About 1920, Alice came to live with us at 'The Farm' with her eldest unmarried daughter, Florence, who was by then the headmistress of the local school. They remained with us until moving to a house in Ward End. I helped move their bits and pieces. Aunt Alice was a nice, dignified person; Florence, my cousin, was, I suppose, fourteen or fifteen years older than I, and I always had to call her and the other French girls 'Auntie'. I did not mind, but I always had the feeling that she did not like me very much. Children are very perceptive of these things, and I disliked her intensely, a very 'vinegary old maid',

I thought. This was perhaps a little unfair, for it was whispered that she had suffered a broken love affair. That did not concern me – like most children, I responded to how people treated me. When Aunt Alice died, Florence sold up, and went to live until her death at Ivyleigh, which she had inherited.

James Stonier – My Father

He had been promised by his mother, at some stage in his early life, that he would be trained as a dentist, his great ambition. The promise was never fulfilled, and father was always bitter about it. He went to America when quite young, in his early teens, and obtained a good job at Streeter in Chicago. He worked at a large store as a salesman and night guard, but left the job to look after Alice and her children, and bring them back to England, a large responsibility for so young a man. He brought them home expecting the promise of dental training to be implemented but for some reason, obscure to me, it all fell through. He then worked at the pit at the coalface until he married my mother. They set up in a public house in the town – my mother said that everything looked so rosy, their own home fully furnished, and £90 in the bank. Then started the bad luck which seemed to dog my father all his life. No sooner had they set up in the pub, when a coal strike was called. It went on for twenty-six weeks, and they lost everything. When the sole source of income dried up in a mining community, this result was inevitable. So my parents, baby sister Edith and Uncle Will Stonier set out to improve their fortunes in America. My father felt that it would be lucky for him. They could not have chosen a worse time, for when they arrived in New York, there was a general depression, and no work of any kind. My mother could not even get a job washing up. They stuck it out until all their money was gone. Uncle Will worked his way home on a cattle boat; the others were sent the fare home by my grandparents.

On arrival home, towards the end of the nineteenth century, my father joined the Birmingham City Police Force. My mother hated the idea of this, and all her life never learned to like the Police Force.

My father's police career was a mixed bag. He certainly was a good policeman, a good 'thief taker', which is really the acid test. He was a very strong man, about 5ft 10 inches tall, and broad, a typical collier build. My mother often told me of how he used to perform feats of strength, like bending iron bars etc., at the Miners' Institute, where all Chasetown's concerts and entertainments took place.

He was quick tempered, and this combined with his strength, made him a formidable adversary, as many a tough prisoner found out to his cost. It also, inevitably, landed him in trouble from time to time. On one occasion he was travelling in a train with a brother of my mother's, Sam Crofts. They became involved in a fracas in the carriage, and father hit a man who turned out either to be a friend of the Chief Constable, or connected with some important dignitary in Birmingham. I never found out what really occurred, or why, but Mother said that it effectively barred father from promotion as long as Charles Rafter was Chief Constable of Birmingham. Father obviously felt this was so, because he became particularly allergic to Irishmen. Rafter was Irish, and saw to it that Birmingham recruited many of its men from Ireland. There was a tale, current for years, of the Harbour Master at Liverpool asking the captain of a ship from Ireland, 'What is your cargo?' The captain replied, 'Two thousand pigs, and the Police Recruits for Birmingham.' Untrue of course, but indicative.

I suppose the big event in Father's police life, and one which reserved for him a tiny niche in history, was his changing clothes with Lloyd George on the occasion of the latter's escape from Birmingham Town Hall during the famous riot of 1901.

Lloyd George, a Liberal, had come to Birmingham (a Tory stronghold at the time, and Joseph Chamberlain country) to denounce our war in South Africa. The Birmingham Press saw to it that the public was duly whipped up in anger, to give him a hostile reception. He got it alright, thousands assembled and the Town Hall was besieged. The Police ringed the building, and kept most of the crowd at a distance, but the audience inside got out of control, and Lloyd George was urged to leave while there was still time. The difficulty was, how to get him away through the mob. Someone had the brilliant idea of disguising him in a police uniform, and marching him out as a member of a relieving unit. How father came to be chosen, I can only assume, was because he was there nearby, and was, at 5ft 9–10 in., a shortish man by police standards of the day, so that Lloyd George, who was a short man, would not look too incongruous in his uniform. The change was effected, and Lloyd George got away. Father found a telegram in Lloyd George's pocket, it was in Welsh, obviously wishing him well; father later showed it to Welsh-speaking people, but none could ever translate its meaning. Father got away from the Town Hall without much trouble – he did not look much like Lloyd George, anyway. Apart from the

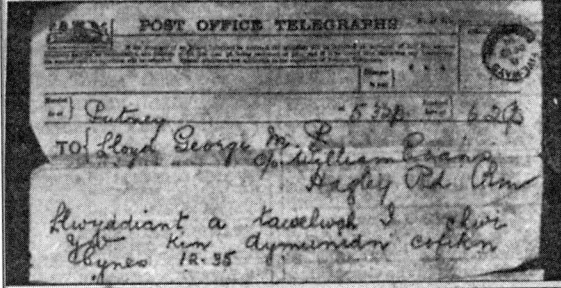

My Parents.

telegram, he also found a cigar and a shilling in the pockets. Later, he saw Lloyd George, and offered him the shilling back. Lloyd George asked him to keep it, but father refused, saying he wouldn't mix the silver with his coppers, but that he had smoked the cigar – end of incident.

During the course of the riot, baton charges were made, people were badly injured and one was killed. At the subsequent enquiry, Rafter, who was in command that night, denied giving the order, but Father, who was standing near, plainly heard him say, 'Draw your staves, men.'

I remember my father saying that whilst they faced the mob, a policeman standing in line next to him fell after being hit by a stone, he later died. *Many* years afterwards, I was on night duty as an Inspector, walking with one of my men named Thomas. We were chatting about the Birmingham riot when it transpired that it was his father who stood next to mine, and was killed by the stone – a strange coincidence.

Father was transferred to the Criminal Investigation Department shortly after the riot, and remained there for the rest of his service. He should, by my knowledge of the Police Service, have made Superintendent. He was far better educated than most of his colleagues; he wrote a beautiful copperplate hand; he headed the detections in his department for years; he often wrote or vetted his Inspector's reports, but to no avail. Every time he went up for promotion, he was stopped, probably by the Chief Constable, who, of course, had the last word. So, whatever it was my father did to earn his dislike, it dogged him all his service.

I know how easy it is to earn the dislike of a superior in the Police Service, and therefore jeopardize one's whole career. It was some years ago before men had representation, this did not come about until around 1920. As soon as father completed twenty-five years service, and became eligible for a pension, he retired. He could have remained at that time for a further twelve months and earned a somewhat higher pension. I asked him why he didn't, and he replied that they were always looking for a reason to try and fire a man during his final years of service, to avoid paying him a pension. I don't know how true this was as it did not occur in my day, but in his time it was a very likely possibility. If so, what a terrible indictment of the moral conscience of a society that could take the best years of a man's life in a dangerous, poorly paid, but vital public service, and then when he was past his best, try to rob him of his only reward – a paltry pension. Thank goodness we have progressed beyond that! He retired about 1920, having taken no part in the famous Police Strike of 1919, although he sympathized – he was too close to pension to risk losing it, as he most assuredly would.

By this time, we had left the milliner's shop in Bamville Road, which my mother had profitably run during the First World War, and moved to the farm in Alum Rock. We had to leave the shop because the Police found out, and although it was my mother's business, we had to go because no policeman or his wife was allowed to run any business. Had we stayed, my father would have lost his job and pension.

When we settled in at the farm (of which more anon), father obtained a job as a painter in a railway-carriage works in Saltley. He always fancied himself as a painter. After about twelve months, work ran out, and father was laid off. He then tried to go back into the licensing trade, had a number of interviews, and had the offer of an 'outdoor', but my mother turned it down. Eventually, he took over a milk round which he worked for my Uncle Philip Holland. This uncle had about five milk rounds, which he worked with his sons, and was able to accommodate father quite easily. After a few months I was out of work, and I joined him. Shortly afterwards, he turned it over to me.

He kept pigs at the farm, just two, which were eventually slaughtered, one sold, and the other salted down and used by us. He also tried keeping poultry in a fairly large way, but disease, and particularly rats, soon brought that to an end – more of father's bad luck! We then purchased a pony and float (a small cart), and he and my mother spent many happy hours riding into the country nearby. Eventually, the farm was sold for building development. We moved out into a council house for a short time until my parents took up their abode in a small house they had built at Four Oaks, Sutton Coldfield. There were two small houses together with a large piece of land. The other house was occupied by my sister Edith, and her husband.

During the course of the building operations, the builder went bankrupt, and father had to look round for another builder (at extra expense) to complete the work – more bad luck! They did eventually move in and lived happily there for some years.

My sister Edith and my mother were always very close, and when Edith decided to move to Solihull, a high-class suburb of Birmingham, Mother would not rest until she got a house nearby, at Olton. Edith moved because her husband, an accountant, had being doing rather well, and she thought they could afford to better themselves; in addition, a neighbour with whom she was friendly had moved to Solihull for the same reason. Father hated the idea of moving, he had spent a lot of time and money on the Four Oaks property, and liked living there. My mother, as usual, had her way, and they moved to Olton. They did not sell the property at Four Oaks, but let it, a very unfortunate decision in the light of subsequent events: they were never able to get back into it as the tenants would not move. Later, legislation protected them, and also prevented any increase in the rent, which after years of inflation became little more than 'peppercorn'. Father's continued ill luck!

They lived fairly contentedly at Olton until Birmingham received its blitz in the Second World War. Their house was slightly damaged, and as they were becoming advanced in years, they let the house and moved to Yorkshire for the rest of the War.

My sister Florence lived in Huddersfield, and she found a tiny stone cottage for them at a little village named Scapegoat Hill, outside Huddersfield. They lived quietly here for a few years. It was a pretty place on the edge of the moors, Huddersfield just visible in the distance. In this small community my father was treated with great respect, and was well liked. It was, I think, one of the happiest periods of his life, at least he was being treated with respect and liking to which he felt entitled. 'A bit of peace and quiet at last' as he used to say! Not Mother, however, and again this obsession to be near Edith caused them to move back to the house at Olton, to be near her. Father's protests were in vain. One could be forgiven for feeling that any man who allowed a woman to sway his decisions to such an extent deserved all he got, and must have been rather weak. This, I think, is untrue. Mother had, during the First World War, run a business on her own, and made a nice nest egg. She hung on to this; no-one ever knew how much she had salted away, but for most of her life, it gave her a degree of freedom and independence. She had a wild temper too and this led to frequent quarrels. My father always seemed to draw back when matters reached breaking point; it was partly because he was deeply attached to her, but also because she was epileptic. I never knew this until I was over seventy years of age, and my own wife told me; my parents knew how to keep a secret! I never saw my mother have an attack, but my wife did on one occasion when they were staying with us and I was out on duty. My father asked my wife to say nothing about it. Anyway, to return to Father – he was now looking an old man, full of rheumatism, and needing a stick to keep mobile.

The Golden Wedding anniversary was celebrated with all the family present, the last occasion when all were together. By the time of the Diamond Wedding celebrations, my two sisters had lost their husbands. I regularly visited my parents at their various homes from Wolverhampton, where I was in the Wolverhampton Police Force. My father loved to hear of all my exploits, but with an unfortunate tendency to try to cap my stories. They came to live with us for a time about 1954. It did not work out. One cannot rear young children

(I had two young daughters) with two old people, one of whom (my mother) was bedridden, a husband working shifts, and a wife trying to cope with it all. The children, young as they were, resented the old folks, and they in turn, showed their grandchildren no love or affection. After twelve months, they returned to Olton to live with my sister Edith, and her daughter Margaret. At about eighty-five, father became senile and bedridden. It was impossible for anyone to look after both parents. Father had to go into Solihull hospital, where he died after a few months aged eighty-six. I visited him twice in hospital. It was pathetic. The ward was full of senile old men; they had come from all walks of life, professional man and labourer – now nature had reduced them to a common level, even before the grave made that a certainty. It left a sad impression on me to see a man, like my father had been in his heyday, reduced to this: occasionally sane, but generally a rambling old wreck. God forbid it should happen to me. He was buried in the place always dear to him, his beloved Chasetown, in the churchyard of St Anne's, where he was christened, married and finally buried.

As an obituary I would say that he was straight, a good father and husband. He could have reached the heights in his career, given a bit more luck, and the ability to curb his tongue and his fists.

George Stonier

I only met this uncle once, during the Second World War, when I visited his farm near Brownhills with my father. He gave us a welcome piece of bacon to bring home. He was the usual Stonier stocky build, and had a daughter whose husband helped him run the small farm. Apart from that I know nothing of him.

Frederick Stonier

He was the youngest of the family and was probably spoiled a bit in consequence, as far as any children were spoiled in this strict family! He was better educated than the others, and was for a while a schoolteacher. He, too, was stockily built, and was the shortest of the menfolk. He was dark, with rather piercing eyes and the gruff manner of the family. He could act the cultured man when he chose to, but generally adopted the rough, rude manners of the average collier with whom he would be familiar, although he never worked in the pits. For a time he kept a butcher's shop in Birmingham. I often visited there with the family. My mother and father had lodged with Uncle Fred at some time in their early married life. My father always had a soft spot for him, but not my mother, who disliked his rude manner. Towards the latter part of the First World War, he volunteered, and was accepted for the Army. I admire him for this – he was well into his forties, and by the time he joined, no-one had any illusions about what 'going for a soldier' meant. He did not see active service, but 'enjoyed' all the rigours of army life in wartime. I remember one remark of his: that when on cookhouse fatigue, he had a stack of washing-up to do, 'As high as Nelson's B. Monument'. After the War, he returned to the Chase, and I often took Father to see him on my day off, if and when I could borrow a car.

He was believed to have quite a fortune put by, and he always led my father to believe that he had made him his heir, should he die first. Lily, who had been my grandmother's servant, had married a fairly wealthy elderly man, who conveniently died, and left her all his money. Uncle Fred, with his eye on the main chance, courted Lily, and they were married, so he added to his fortune. They were, of course, both elderly, and Uncle Fred died after they had been together only a short time. I was sent to the funeral to represent the family. My father still believed Uncle Fred's promise. I went reluctantly, as he was a man I didn't particularly like, and I was in no doubt that we, as a family, would not benefit from his estate. In the event, this only proved too true. I went to see Lily after the funeral service. She was lying in bed – in state – surrounded by all her relatives (all hoping). She was now quite a wealthy woman, and I couldn't help thinking what a change for her from when she was the maid-of-all-work at my grandmother's house, and used to take me on visits to Chasepool when I was very small.

After exchanging pleasantries, I left, and that was the end of that chapter.

To Summarize

Uncle Bill was a good man, but by pragmatic standards, a failure, he lacked what it takes to make a success of life.

Of Uncle George, I don't really know enough to pass judgement, except to say that his poor little farm did not impress.

Uncle Fred undoubtedly was a very intelligent man. He made plenty of money, one way and another, but he lived much of his life as a lonely bachelor. He seemed to find it easier to mix with people his intellectual inferiors, rather than go to the trouble of cultivating better-class acquaintances, who might have stretched him. He pathetically hung on to the skirts of our family, as the only family he had; he came to every wedding and special occasion celebrated by us, and called on us most Sunday mornings, much to the chagrin of my mother, who was busy with the Sunday lunch.

In retrospect, I would say that he came nowhere near realizing his potential, which is rather sad.

The Crofts

Now, a look at the distaff side of the family. We start with the oldest known ancestor.

Great-Grandfather Nixon

I know nothing more of him than this – he kept the Miners Arms at Chasetown. He was my mother's grandfather and was responsible for rearing my mother, who idolized him. This came about as follows: Mother's mother, Miss Elizabeth Nixon, married John Crofts, about whose family I know nothing at all. He was a handsome man, tall, affable and a good singer. He frequently sang at local concerts. They had seven children at the rate of one every eighteen months. He was a policeman at Walsall, and according to all accounts found the struggle of rearing such a tribe on a policeman's pay too much of a burden. He abandoned them, and cleared off with another woman, to Australia and that is all we know of him.

The children were farmed out to any relation who could and would take them, and Mother was lucky enough to land up with her Grandfather Nixon. Her mother, left in this deplorable plight, at some stage went to live with a man named Butler. They lived as man and wife and started another family.

My mother *never* spoke of *her* mother. I saw her only once, when I was about eight years old, and staying at the farm with my Auntie Phoebe. She called me into the house and said, 'Here is your grandmother, Fred.' I remember a small, quiet, dignified lady, who, even at my tender age, struck me as uncommonly like my mother. Our meeting was very short, it naturally meant little to me at that age; I knew nothing of the tragedy and upset of her life. I remember telling my mother of the meeting, but she gave no visible sign of interest or feeling on the matter. I don't even know when this grandmother died, I never heard any more of her. It was obvious that her liaison with the Butler man had placed her 'Beyond the Pale' as far as my mother was concerned.

In later years, I was taken to a public house somewhere on the Chase, by my Uncle Jack, to see my cousins, the Butlers. I could not fathom who they were, and it was years later before someone told me the whole story. Secrets to the detriment of the family, or matters of finance, were closely guarded. But back to the main theme.

Mother was the eldest child, and stayed with her grandfather until her marriage. She always spoke of her days at the Miners Arms, as some of her happiest. She was obviously doted on, she catered for parties and suppers held at the pub, and played the piano as part of the entertainment. I don't know when or how old Nixon died. Mother married very young, about eighteen; she lived to be ninety-seven, and never lost her sharp mind up until the end.

She was an attractive woman with small, regular features, but all the Crofts children were good-lookers. I think I have already said that she had a quick, violent temper when roused. She was selfish, a shrewd businesswoman, and a good mother, although she had favourites, particularly Edith, with Walter probably next, me third, and Florence last of all. All her sisters treated her with caution, they never deliberately tried to rile 'Our Lizzie'. She was a terrible snob — only my Auntie Phoebe was worse, or perhaps my sister Edith. Funny how some people suffer from this, it was not apparent with my other relatives. Mother loved dancing, she often went with brother Walter when he was on leave, and after he left the Army. When he was unavailable, she took me.

Uncle Sam

He died comparatively young, through cancer of the tongue. His last visit to us at Four Oaks was painful. He could not speak, and could only take a little liquid through the side of his mouth. He died shortly after, at about fifty years of age. During his lifetime, he had been in the licensing trade, starting as a barman, then to a pub in the slums of Birmingham, and finally running the Sydenham Palace Hotel, which at that time was the largest pub in Coventry. He was small, chubby, very jolly, and wore a moustache, and was bald on top. He was very good company, even with children. We all liked Uncle Sam. His wife Lottie was a tall, gaunt woman, who always seemed to be dressed in dark clothes, fastened high at the neck. But her rather forbidding looks belied her manner, for she was kind, took notice of us children, and we all liked her. They had three children who lived, Florence, Edith and Sam, having lost their twins soon after birth. When their father died, they moved to a smaller pub, but they all disliked the licensing trade, and could not, or would not make a go of it. Anyway, Auntie Lottie's death, and the marriages of the children took them from the trade for good. I shall mention them all again.

Uncle Willoughby

Tall, good-looking, and with all the extrovert charm which was the hallmark of the Crofts family, I didn't see much of him, just occasionally from time to time. He was a barman in his younger days, as were his brothers, Sam and Jack. A bit wild, and this 'wine and women' phase of his and Jack's lives was brought to an end, when my father, who was quite a bit older, took them to task. His words must have had the required effect, because both joined the Police Force. Jack joined at Wolverhampton, and Willoughby joined at Birmingham. He was stationed throughout his career at Handsworth, a district of Birmingham, where he was eventually transferred to the CID, and retired as a detective sergeant. He was, from all accounts, a bit wild throughout his career. He married my Auntie Kate, who must have been of Scots extraction – at least she always dressed her only child Willoughby in Scots dress, poor boy, a bit out of place in a Birmingham suburb! Auntie Kate was not a sociable woman; none of my family, or her in-laws, became very friendly. She idolized and quite spoilt poor Willoughby, who in consequence grew up to be rather a 'Mummy's boy'. His father always seemed a trifle afraid of my Aunt Kate; I think she had some money of her own, for they seemed to live above and beyond what he could have earned as a detective in those days. Uncle Will outlived her. He became a District Councillor for some place in Staffordshire, to where he and his son moved. Of course, they kept a pub which young Willougby largely ran. He married, and I'm afraid Uncle Will's last few years living with them were not very happy.

Uncle Jack – John Elder Crofts

His early life was very much like Willoughby's, so I will pick it up from where he joined Wolverhampton Police. He was over six feet tall, slim, and the most handsome of the Crofts men.

He was a member of the Police Fire Service. In those days, and in fact until the Second World War, Wolverhampton, like many other towns of its size, had a Police/Fire Brigade. This was a very economical way to run a Fire Service – and all that was required was an Inspector as Chief Fire Officer, under the Chief Constable, a sergeant who needed to be a mechanic, and two or three regular firemen who did no Police Service. All the other members of the Brigade were either single men, living in barracks at the Police/Fire Station, or married men who had opted to be standby firemen, and lived in houses close to the station. All these men were paid a paltry retainer, and received extra money for turning out. If their duties clashed, the fire attendance was the first priority; and their police beats had to be covered as best they could.

Thus, a single man in those days, who was also a member of the Fire Brigade had a very restricted life. If on call, he could only go out socially if he obtained permission; this was not easily obtained. So, a shrewd young man had two alternatives, either be well in with the Fire Brigade Inspector, by for instance, courting his daughter (which was done twice in my service), or get a job which would get him out of the Fire Brigade altogether. Uncle Jack courted not the Fire Inspector's daughter, but the Superintendent's. This eventually moved him into the Chief Constable's office as a member of the Force's administration branch – this in turn enabled him to opt out of the Fire Brigade. At some point, I am not quite sure when, he jilted the girl; I was told she never quite got over it. My family, who knew her, thought it very wrong. I often heard them say so. However, Uncle Jack had got his start, and was a sergeant. I think it follows that the Superintendent, the father of the girl, must have retired about this time, otherwise I feel he might have done something about it. From then on he settled down, and married a barmaid, my Auntie Florence. She, too, came from a family of publicans. They had three children: Victoria, who was a little younger than I, Phyllis and John. They were a devoted couple for the remainder of their lives, and whatever youthful indiscretions Uncle Jack had, he became a devoted husband and father after marriage.

He made great progress in the Police Force, and was Chief Inspector and Chief Clerk in the Chief Constable's office when I joined in 1927. He was a fairly good athlete and cricketer in his younger days, but was a far better billiard, snooker and card player, probably as a result of his misspent youth.

Like everyone else, he had to face and deal with the ups and downs of life. He lost his favourite child Phyllis when she was about fifteen. He had a very sticky period when his whole career was in jeopardy from about 1928–30, due to intrigue – a power struggle on a small scale – as to who was to be the next Superintendent when the old one retired. But more of this later. He survived all this, and became the Superintendent; he nearly became the Chief Constable of Walsall, and would have, had not his opponent for the Superintendency put in for the same job. Two applications from a small force ruled them both out.

He was awarded the MBE, became Deputy Chief Constable and eventually retired with full honour and pension. He then worked for a number of years after the Second World War at the Ministry of Fuel and Power.

He looked after my Auntie Florence during her last years, when she had periods of dementia. He nursed her with love and affection until her death. He hung on for a few years after, gradually breaking up, and finally went to live with his daughter, Victoria, until his death, when he was eighty-six. He was well known, and highly respected in Wolverhampton.

Uncle Frank Crofts

I never knew him, he died of fever as a soldier in the Boer War before I was born.

Auntie Clara

She was the eldest girl, good-looking, and lived all her life at Chasetown.

At one stage, it was thought she might marry Uncle Fred Stonier – they appear to have been attracted to each other; but from what I heard, my Grandmother Adelina put a stop to it. 'One of them is quite enough in the family,' she is reported to have said. Referring to the Crofts, of course. She married a miner, John Gibbs. I remember him as being short, broad in stature, with a dark complexion. He was deaf as the result of a pit accident, was quite kindly, but has left little or no impression. He died many years before Aunt Clara. However, he had a sister who was housekeeper to a wealthy man. On his death, she inherited a considerable sum of money. She paid for the education of Fred Gibbs, the eldest of Auntie Clara's children. He was sent to Saltley College, and trained as a teacher.

George Gibbs, the next boy, a few months younger than I, was also educated at her expense; he too became a teacher. Douglas, the youngest son, was assisted as well, and became a teacher. The girls of the family: May, the eldest, died in her teens; Nellie, the other girl, worked in an office, but was given no special education.

So Auntie Clara had much for which to thank her sister-in-law. It made sure that none of her sons had to work down the pit, which seemed to be the ambition of every thinking mother of boys in a colliery village or town.

Eventually, all the boys became head teachers. Fred, too, had a distinguished First World War career. He joined the Royal Flying Corps and was credited with shooting down thirteen enemy aircraft with another one shared. He was decorated with the Military Cross, and was promoted Captain in the field. He fought for a time against the famous 'Red Baron's' Squadron, Von Richthofen.

Yet he was a quiet, refined, gentlemanly type of man, not the swashbuckling person one might have thought from his exploits.

There was one occasion which perhaps shows a little of the character of both him and my brother Walter. They were of a similar age. When they were in their early teens, they had been left playing on their own at the farm. On the return of the adults, these two boys were seen facing each other, Walter with a knife, and Fred with a chopper, Fred shouting to Walter, 'Come on, then, and I'll chop your bloody head off,' while Walter, physically much stronger, was goading him on. They were, of course, separated before any damage was done.

Walter went on to win the Military Medal in the First World War, and Fred, as I have said, the Military Cross. Not bad for two juvenile delinquents! I often stayed with Auntie Clara when my parents visited Grandmother Stonier. Quite regularly, I spent holidays at the Chase, living with Auntie Clara, where George, her second son, and I played a great deal together. She was always nice to me, and I liked her very much. She made a ripe old age, well into her eighties when she died. She saw all her children do well in life – all her early sacrifices for her sons bore fruit; they were all dutiful and a credit to her.

Auntie Phoebe

She was the youngest Crofts girl, of average height, the most handsome of the Crofts females, with a madonna-like face.

I know nothing of her early life. When she was a young woman, she came to live with my parents in Birmingham. It was while living with them she met her future husband, Philip Holland, who was the milkman.

The Family

They had thirteen children, and reared twelve of them, residing at several addresses in Birmingham, all connected with his business as a dairyman.

He was from a good farming family and had been educated at an agricultural college, with the intention of becoming a farmer. However, he was sidetracked into the dairy business, probably through lack of capital.

He had two brothers, one went to Canada to farm, but came back as a volunteer in the Canadian Army in the First World War, and was killed at Vimy Ridge.

The other brother went to South Africa, and made a fortune catching and canning crayfish. He does impinge on our story a little, because on several occasions he rescued the Holland family from financial trouble, also at the final collapse of their little empire. After the later death of Uncle Phil, he took Auntie Phoebe and two of the youngest children to live with his family in South Africa. Auntie Phoebe came home after a while, homesick, but the girls stayed on for years until they became adult.

Much happened to the Holland family, closely linked to ours, before that came to pass. Of the Holland children, Philip, called Ned, was the eldest – small, shortsighted, but wiry, tough as whipcord. He was given a technical school education; he was intelligent, not a very nice disposition, not interested in any kind of sport. I did not have much to do with him as he was several years older than I, and we had little in common.

<u>William</u> was the next son, two years my senior. He was tall, fair, good-looking, and quite strong. He was fond of sport, a keep fit enthusiast. We had much in common as I hope to recount.

<u>John</u>, the next son, was ten months my senior. He was plump, shorter than Bill, quite bright, not to say, cunning. He was no great shakes at anything sporting, but he would try. He and I were good friends, and often went on holidays together with our mothers, to the Chase, Stratford, Worcester, usually staying with relatives or friends.

<u>Mary</u> was the next child. She was a year younger than I. Being the eldest girl, she had much 'mothering' to do with such a large family, and this she discharged very well. She was dark, pretty, well built, a very straight, forthright girl.

<u>Catherine</u> was the next child, two years younger than Mary – fair, pretty, good build, but a rather sneaky disposition. She loved to tell tales about the older children, and as a result she was not much liked by them. It is strange that after her marriage she drew further apart

from the rest of the family; she was always rather an outsider, even if physically attractive as a girl and woman.

The other children were so much younger, they made no impact on my life. By the time we were adult we scarcely knew each other.

Chapter II

The Farm

To Return to Auntie Phoebe

When at last the Hollands moved to the farm, our families became more involved. The farm figures a great deal in a part of my life, so a description is required. It was owned by a wealthy family, 'the Cattels', who let it to Uncle Phil; he remained their tenant for twenty or more years.

It was situated in Alum Rock, an outer suburb of Birmingham, on the Coventry side of the city. The area was largely underdeveloped, but not entirely so. The house was Elizabethan, very damp. There was a very large kitchen with a great stone sink, a big metal stove, and a coal-fired boiler in the corner. The dining room was large, with a huge fireplace in the corner. Another room off was used by the Hollands as a nursery, the staircase leading from it. This led to three bedrooms – one on the left at the top of the stairs, the other two, a master bedroom to the right of the stairs, and the other room leading off it, so that one needed to go through the master bedroom to get to the third; no bathroom, no inside toilet. Adjoining the house was a still room, with stone settle all round the walls, and a large sink in one corner.

The outbuildings consisted of a large building, the top storey being a hay loft, with the bottom part divided into ten stalls for cattle or horses. Some of these were used for that purpose, the others were stocked with corn, meal, old agricultural furniture, and sundry rubbish. There were six pig styes, and between the styes and the stables/loft, an area covered with corrugated roofing, which served as a storage space for carts, extra hay, hen roosts, etc. There were signs that the old-fashioned type of earth closet had been there, as the structure remained, plus the smell. Long before the Hollands' occupation, a modern type of outdoor lavatory had been installed, nearer the house. There were lean-to types of ramshakle structures attached to the main buildings, and these served as additional stables and storage space.

There was a fair-sized pool beyond the pig styes. The property consisted of nine fields. I don't know the acreage, but the fields were divided by the main Birmingham to London railway line with a bridge linking the two halves of the property. On the western extremity of the fields ran a brook which divided them on the one side of the bridge from a farmer neighbour named Ray, and on the other from an area of allotments. The eastern side of the property was bordered by other fields belonging to another farmer named Dancey.

My uncle never really farmed the land, apart from haymaking from time to time. He used the land as pasture, firstly for his cows and horses, and when he gave up the cows, he let some of the fields to sporting bodies like Saltley College, who used the flattest field for rugby football. Other football and cricket clubs rented fields from time to time. The dairy business was run from here.

There was a very large garden hedged all round except on the entrance drive side. At intervals in the hedges were placed six damson trees, which gave bumper crops every few years. About one third of the garden was planted with rhubarb. There were three large russet apple trees, a plum tree, currants and raspberries. The rest of the garden was made up of vegetable plots, with a few flower beds.

There was an old well and pump, but it was never used until Hollands started the sterilised milk business. Then they tapped the ice-cold well water to cool the tanks of cooked bottles of milk.

There were laburnum and lilac trees, the latter growing almost as a grove outside the still room.

The drive extended from Alum Rock Road, and ran past the garden, house, barn, pig styes, and the pond, until it ended at the bridge over the railway line. It separated the farm property from first an allotment cultivated by a Sgt Smith (a policeman), and fields belonging to Mr Dancey.

The dairy business at its peak had six or seven milk rounds operating from the farm, and at first, horses and carts had to be kept there for that purpose. Uncle Phil, Ned, Bill and John had a round each, while the others were run by employees. Gradually they became prosperous, and eventually quite rich.

Auntie Phoebe at this time seemed to produce a new baby each year, and looked none the worse for it. Uncle Phil's oft-expressed view was that 'Stock is as good as cash'. He put the boys to work as soon as they were able, and kept them at it as long as he ran the business. In consequence, with expenses at a minimum with saved wages, the business prospered. Of course, the boys were given money, they always had far more than I, but still, the saving in proper wages must have been considerable.

Auntie Phoebe seemed happy, she was always willing to take one or other of us nephews and nieces to stay with them, and we all enjoyed this. The farm was always an attraction.

In my view, Auntie Phoebe was the only person who cooked like my mother, and I always enjoyed her food; both she and my mother were great cooks! If Aunt Phoebe had a fault, it was her unbounded snobbery. It seemed to run in some of the Crofts. My mother had it, also my sister Edith, but Auntie Phoebe was the prize one. As fortune smiled on her, she was able to give vent to it by expensive purchases of furniture and clothes, which she then proceeded to flaunt. This made my mother furious, as she could not compete. Another person who took umbrage was Auntie Florence Crofts – she would not put up with it, as after all, her husband had a good position, if not the money; she and Auntie Phoebe had little time for each other! My mother never quarrelled with her sister, they seemed too close for that, but it did serve as a never-ending topic of discussion. Mother's favourite jibe being the occasion when she said to Auntie Phoebe during a meal at the latter's house, 'Don't you think you should take that spoon out of the fruit, Phoebe?' The crushing reply was, 'Oh, Lizzie, *silver* never tarnishes.' Seems all so childish in retrospect, but they all found it stimulating enough.

Towards the end of the First World War, the Hollands left the farm. They kept the tenancy, and still ran the now prosperous milk business from there. They were now supplying sterilized milk, and doing very well. Uncle Phil bought a large mansion at Yardley, called 'West View', with a large garden, a kitchen garden and a paddock. The house had a spacious accommodation and servants' quarters.

Auntie Phoebe was now in her element – she really could swank and put on airs; her speech became more refined and she acted the 'gracious lady' very well. Uncle Phil was persuaded to stand for election as a councillor, but was unsuccessful.

I have not described him physically. He was about 5ft 9in tall, well built, strong, with a fine face covered with a beard. He wore this because working out of doors so much made him susceptible to sore throats. A beard was the answer! He was partly bald and, like my Uncle Fred, could be the cultured gentleman if he chose, but he usually adopted the opposite manner, crude and rough, much to Auntie Phoebe's annoyance. However, he never swore, which was something!

He was cruel to his animals, often working horses when lame, or with harness sores. He was mean with their food, leaving them out to graze all the year round. He skimped repairs to the vehicles, he worked his sons all the hours imaginable so that they had very little leisure when they were young. He had no hobbies except work – I've never seen such a man for graft.

There was another side to his character. The field used by Saltley College as a rugby ground was sometimes played on by the young men who lived in the houses on the other side of the brook. Of course, they were trespassing. Uncle Phil would surprise them and they would run away, leaving their jackets, coats etc. behind. He would then collect them and take them to the farm buildings, where he had four large barrels half sunk into the ground, and full of pig swill – abominable stuff, it stank to high heaven. Into this mess he would drop their clothes. When the young men went to collect their belongings, they had to fish them out of the stinking barrels! Some of them were big fellows – why they didn't set about him I shall never know, there was enough provocation. He never seemed to fear this, so he certainly did not lack courage. He was also very sarcastic, and I often got the benefit of this.

A strange man, his weakness was a liking for drink, but it never became an obstacle to his work. He reached the top, and then saw it all crumble away. After a bad run, he was declared bankrupt. He lived his last few years fairly comfortably with the help of his brother in South Africa, and died about the age of seventy-one.

Auntie Phoebe survived all this – after Uncle Phil's death, she went to South Africa, but she did not stay there very long as she was too old to put down fresh roots. After a stroke, she stayed with her children in turn, and eventually died in her eighties.

Chapter III

My Early Days

1910-20 – First Recollections

I was born on 6 December 1906, at Membury Road, Saltley, Birmingham. The road is still there. It was a place of three-up and three-down houses, respectable, but poor. It branched off Washwood Heath Road. I have no recollections of it, and we must have left there before I was old enough to take notice. We moved to Tarry Road, a similar type of road, but a bit better class – it was off Alum Rock Road and still stands. As locations become important in my story, let me fully describe the geography.

Leading out of Birmingham City Centre in the general direction of Coventry, but north of the Coventry Road, was a route variously named as it progressed outwards, which eventually led into Nechells and Saltley. At Saltley, it divided, still going in the same general direction. One route was Washwood Heath Road, and the other Alum Rock Road. Several miles further on they merged again at a place called the Fox and Goose, a large public house, which though much altered, is still there. The route went on to Castle Bromwich, Water Orton, and eventually joined the Coventry Road at Stonebridge. In between Washwood Heath and Alum Rock Roads was a very large area of partly built-up property, Ward End Park, and fields – a general diversity which indicated the spread of the rapidly expanding City of Birmingham.

Saltley and the adjacent area was heavily industrialized – Saltley Gas Works, Metropolitan Wagon Carriage and Finance Company, Wolseley Motor Car Company, Birmingham Metal Munitions, Cammel Laird Wagon Works, to give just a few examples. This provided plenty of work for the population of the surrounding areas, so one could say it was a reasonably prosperous locality.

My first recollection of life at Tarry Road was when I went for my first visit to the barber shop. I was about four or five at the time and it was thought that the long golden ringlets which I wore down to my shoulders should be cut. I have a photograph of myself, taken at that

Just before losing my curls for ever at about 5 years old. Lots of parents exposed their young sons to this treatment, I can still recall going to the photographer before having my golden curls cut off.

time. I was dressed in velvet trousers, white woollen jersey, and button-up-boots – really precious! It was the fashion for fond mothers to dress their unfortunate young sons in this manner and let their hair grow long for their first few years. I remember I was in no way upset by the loss of my curls, and clearly recall posing for the photograph before the operation.

I recall some contacts with the immediate neighbours. On one side were the Flavells; there were two daughters who were friendly with my sister Florence. We all used to sit on the dustbin brick cover between the two gardens. I expect the conversation was over my head as sister Florence was ten years older than I. I never went into the Flavell's house as my mother did not believe in being too friendly with neighbours. As an exception to this rule she did become friendly with the childless couple who lived on our other side – the Murrays. Albert Murray was a toolmaker, a small, jolly little man. Mrs Murray was a handsome woman – she and my mother were firm friends all their lives.

Every Wednesday afternoon Mother and I went to have tea with Mrs Murray. She kept a special cup and saucer for me, which she always reached down from the top shelf of the kitchen cupboard – we always had tea in the kitchen.

In their lounge, or sitting room as it was then called, there was a fire screen, covered all over with cigar bands. It looked quite pretty; many people did this, I can only think that cigars were more generally accessible than they seem to be today.

The only other recollection of Tarry Road was seeing my brother, Walter going into the garden to smoke a cigarette, my first memory of him.

Bamville Road

We moved there for some reason unknown to me. Bamville Road was an offshoot of Washwood Heath Road, in a parish called Ward End. The house was a shop, the end one of four. It had three bedrooms, the shop, a lounge, kitchen and scullery. The lavatory and coalhouse were outside and there was a small garden.

Mother opened a milliner's shop and throughout almost all of the First World War had a thriving business, not least amongst the girl munitions workers employed at the nearby Drew's Lane Munitions factory. (Drews Lane is now the British Leyland Transmission Plant.) These factory girls had little on which to spend their money as the War progressed, everything becoming short or non-existent.

They worked hard and long, and were entitled to a little self-adornment.

Father, meanwhile, was one of the CID men stationed at Washwood Heath Police Station, from which he worked. Ward End was quite a community – the shopping centre was on Washwood Heath Road, with a few shops like ours in the side roads. St Margaret's Church in Black Pit Lane, was the Anglican Church, and a fine Methodist Chapel in Monk Road (next to Bamville Road) catered for chapel goers. I don't recollect any nearby Roman Catholic Church. There was Sladefield Road School (fairly new) taking up the space between Bamville and Sladefield Roads.

Ward End Park was about half a mile along the road towards Saltley. Away in the opposite direction towards the Fox and Goose the properties finally petered out, and there were open fields. The shop next door was occupied by a family named Richardson, mainly selling newspapers. Mrs Richardson was a kindly lady, who looked after me when my mother went to occasional late night dances etc.

When the Richardsons left, the house was occupied by a family named Kelsey. Sam Kelsey was a consumptive, and spent most of his time in bed coughing; we could hear him coughing in our house. His wife ran the business. He was a brother of Mrs Hewitt who ran a draper's shop next door. Her husband worked in a factory. She had two sons: George, who was about my age, and Fred, who was five years younger. These boys were my playmates for years. Mrs Hewitt, as I remember her, was slim, pretty and dark haired. She had quite a temper when roused.

Next to the Hewitts was the other shop in our group, Burford's, the sweet shop, run by a husband and wife, with two children, George and Mabel. For some reason we seldom played with the Burford children. Although they were nice children they were older than the Hewitt boys and myself. The age difference acted almost like a colour bar – small fry were not encouraged to mix with their elders.

On the other side of our shop was a succession of private houses extending to the other end of Bamville Road. Next door lived the Paynes, then the Whittles with their three daughters, Annie, Eva and Edith (the latter being the same age as George Hewitt and myself), who was allowed to be a kind of honorary member of our gang. Her two sisters were several years older, and therefore of only passing interest.

Then came the Laws – they were butchers, with a shop in Ward End and another in Alum Rock. There was Old Man Law, the patriarch of the family, his son Frank and his daughter and son-in-law Harry Bailey. Harry managed the shop in Ward End. His son Tommy, about my age, was another member of our gang – that is when he could get time off from his busy job of delivering meat on his bicycle.

On the opposite side of Bamville Road was the Co-op Grocers' shop on the corner of Washwood Heath Road. They had storage accommodation and a yard extending along Bamville Road. Then came a family called Tickle. Mr Tickle was a tram driver, and earned eternal fame locally by having reputedly knocked down and killed a donkey with his tram. Next came the Dares who were small builders. And finally there was Sladefield Road School, followed by another long row of houses up to the end of Bamville Road.

So much for the surroundings and some of the characters in this phase of my life.

School

I attended Sladefield Road School, of course, being so convenient across the road, although I have no recollections of the Infant School.

My first teacher in the Senior School was a Miss Fox who came to Mother's shop for her hats. I got on quite well with her, I thought, but I was not surprised when she told my mother, 'Freddie can do the work, but he is idle.' So much for my stay in Standard 1. In my next class I went on much as before. I did not care for school and could not take it seriously as it was simply an interference with my much more interesting life outside. Of course, I enjoyed playing with my school mates.

In my third class, the teacher was a Miss Spencer, and it was there I gained my first academic distinction. It was to be my only one for many a year to come!

It came about like this – we had been given a reading of Oliver Twist, and afterwards we had to write an essay (or composition as we called it) on the subject. I must have written a good one – I can only remember my using the word 'unfortunately' in the text, and had quite a struggle spelling it, I recall. Miss Spencer thought the effort first rate for I remember being sent to Standard 4 (one higher), standing in front of the class, and reading it as an example of what could be done by a younger boy. Knowing boys as I did, I thought the outcome would be quite the opposite to that expected, and that they would rather think it a presumptuous liberty, supposing that any of us knew what that meant! It is strange on reflection, that at this early age of nine years, I was showing a promise that was to blossom so splendidly for me years later.

It was a year later, in Standard 4, that I first got the urge to really put my back into it, and work hard. I suddenly realized that I could go on to a grammar school at the age of 11–12 years, if I could pass the entrance examination. We would have been told this by our teacher, and urged to try. I can't think why I felt I wanted to go to Grammar School, but try I did! In due course I sat the examination, and although I did not get sufficient marks for a free scholarship, I did obtain a pass, which meant that I could go to the Grammar school, providing my parents paid a small quarterly fee, and bought my books. My parents were not very enthusiastic about sending me at some expense. My mother, whom I felt would have the final word, must have been torn between the cost on one hand, versus the increased social prestige of having a son at the grammar school on the other. Finally, I was allowed to go.

Before I embark on that depressing period of my life, let me deal with life outside the world of school. Our little gang of George and Freddy Hewitt, the ever faithful Eddie Whittle, and Tommy Bailey on occasions when free, played together whenever possible. In those days just before and during the First World War, games played by children were seasonal. The street or road was as often as not our playground. We sometimes played in one another's garden, but not if it was cultivated.

Favourite Games

Marbles

This was a great favourite. Marbles, in assorted colours, could be bought quite cheaply; the most expensive were glass, shot through with a colour, and called 'Glarnies'. We played along the gutters of the road, or in the playground at school during the break, but chiefly at lunchtime. Certain boys with entrepreneurial inclinations would set up a screw set – small screws spaced out in front, larger ones spaced behind them, and larger still behind them. They were staggered, and laid out in front of a wall. A distance was marked at which the player stood and bowled his marble at the screws. If he knocked any down in the front row, he got one or two marbles in return; the further back, and the larger the screws, the more marbles had to be given for success.

The spacing of the screws, the distance from the bowling line, and the odds the screw set owner gave were crucial. Boys would go along the line of screw sets to see which looked the easiest, and which owners offered the best odds. If the screw set owner set his stall out too liberally, he was quickly stripped of his marbles, as I found out to my cost the first time I set up my stall. I was left marble-less in about fifteen minutes. It was, of course, excellent training for life to come, learning the hard lessons of the market-place.

At a certain time of the year marbles ceased to be played.

Hoops and Bowls

This had its season. Some were made of a flexible wood, others of metal, but the favourite was an old bicycle wheel minus all the spokes. The grooved outside of the wheel lent itself splendidly for a braking system, laying your propelling stick along it, and slowing down the wheel's speed.

Tops

They had their season and were shaped like a mushroom, with a metal tip. Stuck firmly in the divisions of the footpath paving stones, the player wrapped the string of his whip around the top, and then pulled it sharply. It was a knack, and when mastered ensured that the top spun, the player then whipping it at intervals to keep it spinning. There was another type of top marketed which was called a 'frog', but it was never very popular. The drawback with this game was, if the whip was not used skilfully, it could project the top through a window, or into someone's face.

Tip Cat

This was strictly a seasonal game, played in the street. We used a six or seven-inch circular piece of wood (like the end of a broomstick), sharpened at both ends, and a stick to hit it. A sharp tap on one end of the 'cat' caused it to jump into the air, the player then struck it with the stick, knocking it quite a distance, if skilful enough. Three 'goes' were allowed, and then the non-player strode out the distance from the starting point, and the number of strides represented the score. Again, windows were in danger from erratic players!

Hop Scotch

A marked set piece on the pavement slabs, a 'scotch', a piece of anything you could push with one foot whilst hopping from point to point in ordered sequence. This, like skipping, was largely indulged in by the girls, but boys often played. Then there was a team game, in which one player hopping on one foot, tried to knock off his balance another of several players who tried to cross the road whilst also hopping. If one so charged lost his balance, then it was his turn to stand alone. Good fun, this game was played summer or winter, as was <u>Leap Frog</u> – this could be individual or a team effort any time.

Ice Slides

Naturally, a winter only game, and only on frozen playgrounds, rivers, and ponds. We seemed to be able to skate every winter in those days.

Conkers

The use of the horse chestnut fruit. When ripened and dried hard, a hole was pierced through the conker; a strong string was threaded through the hole, and knotted at the end. One player stands, with outstretched arm, holding his conker on the string, about chest high. The other player, similarly equipped, then strikes at the suspended conker with his. This goes on alternately until one conker breaks up. The winning conker then adds the total of the defeated conker to its own, this being ascertained before the start of the contest. Conkers were baked, pickled, and given all kinds of treatment, to try to make them invincible. A seasonal game, the street or road was the main playground. At the time of which I write, there was little or no motor traffic, a few horses and carts, but as the War progressed, they became fewer and fewer. Such games could not be played now, a pity – something lost, I feel.

Expeditions

We loved these; there were several favourite places. There was Ward End Park where we could watch the tennis players, the boats on the lake and the waterfowl, or visit the bird house, or the conservatory which opened up a strange exotic world of banana and orange trees, and other wonders. There was football and cricket played on the open spaces. Sometimes two of us would offer to act as 'ball boys' to the tennis players, earning a few coppers for sweets. As often as not, our help was not required, or the players forgot to pay us.

I had an acquaintance at school named Sid Avery, who lived farther along Washwood Heath Road, towards the Fox and Goose. His father was a policeman. He was poorly clad, obviously the family were hard up, but that applied to any family trying to live solely on a police constable's pay in those days.

However, Sid was a wizard at fishing. We would go to Ward End Park lake, and with a rod, consisting of a stick, string, and a worm on a pin, he could land perch at almost every cast. I took my share of the catch home, and Mother, asking no questions, would cook them, and she and I would have a cosy little teatime treat. Eventually, the Park keepers rumbled us, and after one hectic chase, we gave up fishing!

Another excursion was a long walk to 'Cobbler White Gate' and 'Cobbler Green'; these were places at Castle Bromwich and Water Orton, where horse chestnut trees grew in some profusion, and the conker crop was good.

Another trek was to Maggerty Brook, a ford across a stream in a side lane off the Castle Bromwich road. We could only paddle our feet when we got there, but it was an established ritual.

Another favourite was 'The Navigator', a place on the canal at Castle Bromwich. Some boys would swim there, while we who couldn't swim, paddled. The water here was warm for some reason.

Interspersed between these trips with my gang were visits to 'The Farm', best of all outings for me!

I remember once during the War, George, Freddy Hewitt and I went searching for coke on a tip near Cammel Lairds' works off Washwood Heath Road. Our grapevine informed us that there was coke there for the taking. We went, and sure enough there was coke, very small, but coke none the less. We had taken small sacks, and after about two hours' search, we had filled them, and then made for home. It must have been a mile and a half journey, and we were only about nine years old. On arrival home I thought the family would be overjoyed, because by now, food and *fuel* were hard to come by. To my hurt surprise, my father was furious, and threw my hard-gathered coke away. 'I'll never burn that rubbish on my fire, I never have, and I never will,' declared Father. I was very upset. Much later, I realized that Father having been a miner working to extract 'Cannock Deep' (the best house coal in the world) from the coakface, shared the miner's hatred of coke, which they saw as an inferior substitute for their prime product. Nevertheless, he might have considered my good intentions, hard work and initiative, and treated the matter with more consideration; I still feel most unjustly treated over the affair even eighty-five years later!

Bash-Bashes

There are two well-understood meanings to this. To 'have a bash' means to have a go, to make an attempt. 'I'll bash your face in,' means to strike someone violently on the face and disfigure it. We used the term in another sense. It meant to dare someone to do something dangerous or risky. We never 'dared' another boy to do a risky act, we always said, 'I'll bash you' to jump, run, climb, or whatever it might be. The acts performed were 'bashes'. All boys in our area knew the meaning of this, and if ever our gang met another band of boys unknown to us, the quickest way of establishing friendly contact was for the two opposing champions to 'bash' each other to do certain deeds of daring – jumping streams, or climbing trees or scaffolding, or over roofs, or trespassing into forbidden territory.

I was our champion at this as I could jump reasonably well, but my real forte was climbing (due to all my practice at the farm). Only Bill Holland could match, and usually beat me at it, but he was older. We performed some hair-raising feats at times. This 'bashing' word was not understood at the Chase, and when I played with George Gibbs, he still used the term 'I'll dare you'. But all boys, whatever they called it, played this challenging game!

Choir Boy

One early evening I was playing with Tommy Bailey, when he said he would have to go as it was choir practice night. I demurred, and he asked me to go with him and join the choir as there was a vacancy. I went along, and became a probationer choirboy at our parish church, St Margaret's, in Black Pit Lane. After enrolment, I practised with the other boys, but was not permitted to sing in the choir for several months, until a vacancy fell due; instead, I had to pump the organ. To do this I went into the belfry, where the bell ropes hung, and operating a wooden lever, pumped air into the organ during playing time. A piece of lead hung on a string indicated when air was required, and when the organ was fully primed, it went up to full, and down to empty, with two marks indicating full and empty. If one's attention lapsed for too long, the organ died out with a groan, and everyone in church knew about it. I didn't have any serious mishaps, and in due course I donned surplice and cassock, and became a fully-fledged chorister. There were about eight boys and six men, all of whom walked in procession from the vestry to our positions in stalls on each side of the altar, facing each other. The lady choristers had no regalia, but simply sat or stood, as appropriate, in the front pews on each side of the church. This was how each service began.

I enjoyed my two years as a choirboy. I couldn't read a note of music, all I could tell in practice was when the notes went up or down, but I had a good ear, and soon learned the tunes; memorizing words was never a problem to me, and in most cases we had the words in front of us. Our major performance was Stainer's *Crucifixion*, which we gave on Good Friday. We practised hard for this, and always gave a good performance. It is a moving piece in which to take part. I found new friends among the boys, and we had great times after practice, usually playing in the churchyard, or sneaking into the estate next to the church. This was owned by a rundown family named Chavasse. They were impoverished, withdrawn and secretive. I never knew how many there were, or what any of the family looked like. This, to us boys, gave an air of mystery and fear. The house was hidden among trees, there was a dark, sinister pool in the grounds, and one or two ruined summer houses. We would sneak over the churchyard wall, and in fear and trembling, make little excursions into forbidden territory.

The churchyard and its trees was a splendid place for 'bashes', in which we indulged a great deal. Not very respectful to the dead perhaps, but we meant no harm. We boys were not paid at first for our attendances, but we did get a share of the apples presented to the church at Harvest Festival time. When the church was dressed for the festival, we appraised the gifts on show with discerning eyes. We would do this when walking in procession from the vestry to our choir stalls. To the congregation we looked (with our scrubbed faces, combed hair, clean collars, surplices and cassocks) like little angels, but our thoughts were on more earthly and mundane things like, 'Is it a good apple crop this year?'

We must have been a good choir for we were often invited to sing in other churches, and once in Birmingham Cathedral – this was our high spot! We also did a deal of carol singing at Christmas, enjoying the hospitality offered to us.

As the War progressed, we heard that the choir boys of our nearest church, St Mark's on Washwood Heath Road, were being paid for each attendance at church. We had a meeting and decided to ask for the same treatment, or we would withdraw our services. We duly lined the path at the entrance gate, and as the Organist/Choirmaster left with the Vicar, we presented our demand. To our surprise and relief, it was agreed, and thereafter, every quarter, we received our pay of a halfpenny per attendance, in coppers, in a small envelope. My mother kept all these, and gave them to me when I left home to join the Police Force ten years later.

This was my first experience of 'collective bargaining' and the 'power of the workers united'.

One or two events stand out in my choirboy experience. During the

War, one of our parishioners became a padre in the Army; his name was Captain Peacock. When he came home on leave he was invited to preach to our congregation. After his first sermon, he was invited, whenever on leave, and always filled the church. He was quite a spellbinder, talking of his experiences in France. Most of our families had someone fighting out there. I shall always remember one story he told. 'After one heavy bombardment, he looked around him and saw death and destruction everywhere. His faith was wavering – was there any hope? Could there really be a God? As the smoke began to disperse, it hung a little longer around the remains of what had been a wood. Suddenly, to his amazement, as if in answer to his unspoken question, the shape of the Cross appeared, due to the effect of the smoke and the shattered remains of the trees. It hung there for several minutes before eventually disappearing. He felt his faith restored.' He spoke of this so quietly, with such conviction and sincerity, that we were all spellbound. We all, young and old alike, left church that night better people. It was my first experience of the power and influence of the spoken word, and I never forgot that lesson.

At the other end of the scale we had a tremendous scandal. The Choirmaster, who was middle-aged, kindly, but not particularly prepossessing, got one of the choir ladies (single and probably in her thirties) into trouble. He had to resign and she left. This shook our small community more than a little. I never knew what happened to them.

The last event of note before I was kicked out of the choir was the appearance of Betty Jerome. One Sunday night we were in the choir stalls singing away, when I noticed a beautiful girl in the congregation. She was ten or eleven years old, and she really was a beauty. I drew the attention of Tommy Bailey to her, and he was rather stricken. Before long, all the choirboys and most of the boys in Ward End were 'smitten'. I cannot think of any other word to describe our first awakening by this lovely girl!

Her father was a Canadian, and had come to England to volunteer for the Army. He brought his wife and two daughters with him. Angeline was the elder, and quite plain; Betty the younger one had that rare quality, even as a child, to turn all male heads. Mrs Jerome came to mother's shop for her hats, and for months I suffered the pangs of first love quite unrequited.

It is strange on reflection – we mixed with plenty of girls. Edie Whittle was a member of our gang; she was well built and good-looking (years later she won a beauty contest) but to us, girls were an inferior type of playmate, who could not do 'bashes' like us, so we just tolerated them. We knew they were different, as they had their hair long, and wore dresses; they could hit you, but you were not supposed to hit back, although sometimes you did. On our long expeditions when you wanted to 'pee', you stood up, girls squatted down, usually behind cover, but not always. This was considered quite natural and caused no comment. I suppose at the age of ten-eleven-twelve we were faintly aware of the facts of life. Before puberty, it does not mean very much – it was something indulged in by grown-ups, not really very nice. One hesitated to relate it to one's parents, so it was pushed to the back of the mind, rather incomprehensible!

Then suddenly out of the blue came this strange feeling for someone of the opposite sex; it was devastating. We were not physically or mentally equipped to deal with it. Poor Betty, a shy, diffident girl, must have wondered what it was all about, there were so many of us all struck in the same way. Her sister Angeline must have encountered it before as she took charge of the situation, and to our eager questions would tell us of Betty's likes, dislikes and other details, just like a form of press conference! Had Betty been given to us as a gift, we should have been completely at a loss to know what to do with her. We were experiencing our first sexual feelings, but it was all in the mind – the body had a long way to go before it was prepared to cope. I never knew what finally happened to the Jeromes, or the 'divine' Betty, except that they returned to Canada.

Finally, I left the choir when our new Organist/Choirmaster, a Mr Smith, had been in office only a few months. He had a son about my age who wore glasses, and was considered by us other boys as 'wet'. I suppose the other boys and I chivied him, and he complained to his father. He took me to be the ringleader, and dispensed with my services.

Both my sisters at this time were courting – Edith was married first, then Florence. Both had the ceremonies at St Mark's Church instead of St Margaret's. When the vicar complained to sister Florence, she said, 'You shouldn't have sacked our Freddy from the choir.' The poor vicar pointed out that this was the Choirmaster's prerogative, but to no avail, the family honour had been assailed!

The First World War

At the end of July 1914, my parents, and a host of their friends and myself went by train to Morecambe Bay for my first seaside holiday. There were Mr and Mrs Murray, their parents, Mr and Mrs Harris, Mrs Harris's sister, Mrs Ackroyd, her husband, son and daughter, and others I have forgotten. We entirely filled the boarding house on the front. At Morecambe in those days, I recall a small liner moored permanently at the pier; it was used for dances and other functions, and was quite an attraction; it looked very large to me.

While the adults went out every day on trips, I was taken by Mrs Ackroyd on to the sands where I played quite happily until meal times. Mrs Ackroyd preferred this to going with the others, and her saying, 'No, I'll go with Freddy on the sands', was a catchphrase used for years in our family.

This happy party continued for a week, then war was declared. Father, being a serving policeman, had to return to duty, so we missed our second week's holiday. On the front were horse-drawn vehicles used for conveying holiday-makers on trips around the surrounding countryside. I remember the requisitioning officers removing the horses from the carriages and taking them away.

Disconsolately, I bought my seaside rock, the circular peppermint rock sticks beloved by all children, then we came home.

I did not see much of my father during the next few years, he was working long hours, and came home only to sleep and eat. This made me closer to my mother and sister; brother Walter had been in the Army for years, and I saw him only occasionally when he was on leave.

The gang went on playing together much as before and school seemed the same – it was some time before the impact of war was felt by us.

Firstly the young men disappeared into the services, then young fathers, like Mr Hewitt, were called up. A large munitions factory was built in Drews Lane, and this employed many of the women left at home, like Mrs Hewitt. It also brought an influx of newcomers amongst whom were a large number of Belgian refugees. There were so many of these people that a large housing estate was built to house them (at the back of Ward End Park).

Allotments began to appear on all waste or unused land; Father had one in Washwood Heath Road. Slowly, food became more scarce, as did fuel, clothes, and ultimately everything else. Rationing was introduced, and I became the family shopper and forager. We changed our grocer four times during the War, looking for a bit of favour. Fortunately, Father had a good contact in this field, a Mr Honeydew, who had a shop in Saltley. He kept us pretty well supplied. I was sent each Saturday afternoon when his shop was supposed to be closed to collect our groceries. We were never short of butter, sugar and bacon. Our meat was obtained from a local butcher named James Allen. He had a shop just around the corner from us in Washwood Heath Road. My sister Florence was a friend of Allen's two daughters, Gertie and Maud, and this helped the meat problem.

To transgress for a moment, Mr Allen had started his business life as a 'humper', a labourer, carrying the meat carcases at Birmingham meat market. He came to own two shops, and at the end of the War was wealthy enough to buy a large estate, with a mansion, stables, a huge lake, and acres of land. I know this to be true, because I once joined a party which visited there, shortly after it was purchased.

But to continue, alcoholic drink began to be rationed or restricted as to quantity and hours of sale. I occasionally was sent to a little 'outdoor' kept by a widow, in one of the side roads off Washwood Heath Road. I always went in the dark hours, and brought home two or three bottles of stout, to which both my parents were partial. This was another of Father's contacts. Occasionally, shops in the village would get a delivery of butter, apples, or potatoes. On one occasion Freddy Hewitt came running to our house saying that Neale's, the local butter and cheese shop, had half pounds of butter for issue. Mother quickly gave me some money, and Freddy and I ran to the shop together. I stood just one place in front of him in the queue, and received the last half pound of butter. Had Freddy *not* come to tell me, he would have been alright!

Christmas of 1917 was very glum – the nation, so history records, was three weeks from starvation, owing to the U-Boat campaign. The local greengrocer had one barrel of apples (extra to rationed goods) to sell. The word went round like wildfire – I managed to get a precious pound.

There was one shop which stayed open during the War: Fish and Chips, owned by Mr Salloway. He spent the daylight hours searching the countryside for potatoes for frying. His daughter, Elsie, who was a cripple, fried and served. It was only a small shop. Both Florence and I had a passion for fish and chips. When she came home from work, she would give me some money, and I would go to the shop and stand in the queue, sometimes, it seemed for hours, to get some. The 'Frying Tonight' sign would be displayed in the window two or three times a week. We used to watch for it to appear; we weren't always lucky enough to get fish with the chips!

When the War started I had one halfpenny per week pocket money. It was agonizing to decide how and where to spend this vast amount of money. The cake shop sold coffee cakes and madeleines (my favourites). At the sweet shop, I could get a large bag of the bottoms of the boiled sweet jars, various flavours, or try to find a shop which sold broken biscuits cheaply. When inflation rendered the halfpenny useless, I had to ask for a rise to a penny, and augment it as best as I could.

I never had much money when young. It was largely due to my grandmother's admonition to my father, 'Don't spoil that lad, Jim, by giving him too much pocket money.' How well they all carried this out, it made me mean and miserly for the rest of my life. The shortage of sweets caused me to try to make my own — chocolate made with cocoa butter, and toffee, just about edible, but eventually sugar became too scarce, so that was the ending of my sweetmaking efforts.

To overcome the shortage of greenstuffs, Father and Mother had the bright idea of boiling rhubarb leaves to use as cabbage. The taste wasn't too bad, and we felt quite pleased, until we read in the newspaper that a family had been poisoned, and some had died, through doing the same thing. I cannot understand why my usually very careful father did it; he was the instigator of the experiment, and was always against any kind of substitute — remember his attitude about my coke collection? Anyway, we survived without any ill effects.

As the War continued our bread became a dirty white, and gradually almost black. God knows what was put in it. I remember I was always hungry, not I think because we were on short rations, but because I was growing so quickly; and being young and energetic, I burned up my food fast. So much for the food 'front'.

My brother Walter was serving in the Coldstream Guards during the War. He was wounded three times, and won the Military Medal at twenty-one, in the trenches in France. He was, at times, used as a sniper because of his proficiency. For years in my bedroom on display was a certificate certifying that he had won the 2nd Battalion Coldstream Guards bayonet-fighting competition.

Father sometimes met men on leave in the street who would tell him that Walter's exploits at the front were the talk of the battalion — he was, they forecast, bound to be killed.

His letters home were avidly read. I remember his most memorable letter referred to the historic fraternization of the Germans and English at Christmas in 1914. He said how he and others climbed out of the trenches, and walked towards the German lines, hands outstretched to show that no arms were being carried, while the Germans advanced from their lines in the same manner. They met, exchanged cigarettes, food and drink, some even started to play football together. This went on for quite some time before both sides were ordered back by their commanders, on the threat of being fired on. It never happened again! He came on leave from time to time, either in khaki or hospital blue, but never spoke about life at the front — few soldiers who had been there did.

In our cupboard we had some samples of the biscuits issued to the troops, just like dog biscuits. The famous 'plum and apple' jam too was horrible, and tasted of the cardboard in which all jam was then encased.

While he was at the front, my mother religiously sent him a parcel every week. I helped her pack it with cigarettes, chocolate, a homemade cake, socks, and other knitted comforts. I then took the heavily protected parcel to the Post Office for dispatch. They always arrived at their destination in France, and were highly appreciated by my brother and his mates. One night I remember a small crowd from Bamville Road gathered at our street corner to watch a German Zeppelin sail overhead.

Always in times of danger or on receipt of some shattering news, people gathered together like that, all distinctions and petty squabbles forgotten for the moment, and talked in hushed tones. It happened, I recall, when the *Titanic* sank in 1912, when the Zeppelins sailed over, and even when the *Lusitania* was torpedoed in 1917.

Our news of the latest happenings, in the absence of radio or television, were in special editions of newspapers. Boys ran through the streets shouting 'Special', followed by a brief reference to the news item.

I was in our local grocer's shop one day when a boy ran past shouting 'Special, *Queen Mary* sunk'. This was our first news of the Battle of Jutland; the *Queen Mary*, a battleship, had been blow up. A lady in the shop moaned, and fell to the floor, crying, 'My son was on her.' I remember Mr Salt the grocer helping her to her feet, and trying to comfort her, saying, 'Perhaps he has been rescued.'

Every night we searched the Birmingham evening newspaper. There were always page upon page of casualties listed. We scanned the lists fearfully, in case any of our lads were mentioned: Walter, or Will Stonier, or Fred Gibbs.

Before I forget – at the start of the War, anyone with a German-sounding name was suspected of being a spy: there was 'spy mania'. Windows were broken, and often innocent people were assaulted. We had a watchmaker and family in Ward End named Guggleheim, or something like that. They were of the Jewish persuasion, and they quickly put a notice in their shop window stating, 'We are Russians'. This saved them any further trouble.

It was about this time I became a cinema fan, and I have been ever since. I never missed a Saturday children's matinee at the local. I followed Pearl White in the *Exploits of Elaine*, and Eddie Polo in the *Broken Coin* (films of twenty-four episodes). I had my first crush on a film star, Mrs Irene Vernon Castle, best remembered as the wife of a world-famous dance team, but I remember her as the beautiful heroine of the *Last of the Channings* (an epic of the Mexican-American short war), and her closing line when victory was assured, and she was being praised for her efforts, quote,

'What I did I did for the flag' – Curtain.

The children filled the cinema every Saturday morning, when we all waited until the last minute to bag the back seats. The manager then announced that next week the *first* comers would get the back seats. He never tried it again: the doors were rushed, and he lost control.

It has to be remembered that by 1916 there were no able-bodied men who were not either in the services, or working long hours on war work – hardly any police, except for a few 'Specials', few fathers or older brothers at home, many mothers and sisters at work. The result was that children had almost complete freedom. We roamed about in our gangs and had a right old time; so really our poor cinema manager had to handle us young savages as best he could, but we never went so far as to endanger the show – the hero was always cheered, the villain hissed or booed; we could never have followed a 'talkie', but they were years away. The pianist meanwhile was thumping away, playing suitable music to accompany the film. We came out of the show, pondered on what we had seen, and then, going home, tried to reproduce some of it. Charlie Chaplin, everyone's favourite, was easy to copy, some of the others were more difficult. We dug a trench across Mrs Hewett's garden as part of a war scene we were playing. She came home, sent Tommy Bailey home in disgrace, and told George and Freddy Hewett and myself to fill it in again. It took us *ages*!

Friends

A word about the friends of the family, and my two sisters Edith and Florence.

Edith

She was the eldest child, was a little plump, had frizzy dark hair, and was quite good-looking. She was attending a girls' grammar school when I was born, obviously not a planned child as there were ten years between myself and Florence (the next youngest child). Because of the extra expense of a baby, Edith had to leave school and go to work. She was doing well at school and resented having to leave. Whether this coloured her attitude to me, I can't say, but we really never got on well together. She had one or two young men who called at our house during her teens, became interested in amateur theatricals, and was a member of a local concert party, being a very good pianist.

She married Herbert Lincoln. He was an accountant, not articled, but he had been with his firm since boyhood, and was good at his job, though never very well paid. He was dark, good-looking, and was always very good to his family, and my parents. He was a local lad, a member of a 'Glee Club', and had a strong baritone voice. He was not sporty in any way, but he was a good family man.

He was obviously not fit enough to be called up to a fighting unit, but about halfway through the War he was drafted into the RAMC, and was stationed at a hospital in Birmingham, where he stayed until the War ended.

Florence

She was good-looking, had long hair, a good figure, and seemed to have lots of boyfriends. She took me over as a baby, and for years was my nurse. I remember her taking me in my pushchair along Washwood Heath Road, towards the Fox and Goose on Sunday mornings, and being stopped frequently by young men chatting her up; and having to admire me, I suppose. I am told I was a beautiful baby, with blue eyes and golden curls. They said they used to wake me up to see my beautiful smile – no wonder I developed a testy temper later on. I also remember Florence taking me to the farm, and putting me on a horse. I promptly fell off and cracked my collarbone.

We developed an affection which we have never lost, even to the ages of eighty and seventy respectively, although my parents never seemed to think as much of her as they did of Edith.

Florence took lessons in shorthand and typing, got a good job at the Birmingham Metal and Munitions factory, and finally became personal assistant to the Managing Director. Towards the end of the War she was earning far more money than my father who would not have liked this – I know how he must have felt. The police that were left in the force were working very long hours, their pay had remained almost static in an inflationary time, which of course eventually led to the police strike in 1919. To see his daughter bring home more money than he would not have suited a man from his predominately masculine world.

Towards the end of the War, Florence married Cyril Bateson. He was an officer in the Royal Flying Corps, his brother lived in Bamville

Road with his wife and two daughters. They were considered a trifle 'upper class'.

Here I will digress for a moment. Ward End was predominately a working-class district, where everyone worked in some capacity or other. But make no mistake, in those days the 'class conscience' of we English was very strong, and it had its stratas even among working-class people. On Washwood Heath Road (ignoring the shops) were many large houses occupied by executives of the many firms and industries in Saltley, and even further afield; they were from the top drawer. Then there were the shopkeepers, some shops being more profitable than others – the better the shop, the higher in the pecking order was the owner. Then, probably near equal with the shopkeeper came the skilled workman, the man who had served an apprenticeship. He ranked fairly high. Into the category came train drivers, factory foremen and chargehands. It wasn't altogether a question of money, although this opened most doors – there was a status conferred by certain jobs or education. A schoolteacher was poorly paid, but the job indicated a degree of education, and this probably elevated such a person to the shopkeeper grade. My father, as a detective, ranked higher than a uniformed man, although there was not much difference in pay. This is a dangerous field in which to be dogmatic, the point being that the English disease of class distinction went all the way down the social scale, and young as I was at Bamville Road, I knew it existed, because I was discouraged from playing with some children, and encouraged to play with others, and I knew why.

To return to the Batesons, Cyril's brother was a teacher, and his family were always accepted as a bit 'top drawer'. Cyril, being a commissioned officer in the elite Flying Corps was considered quite a catch.

Florence and he were married and went to live at Huddersfield, where Cyril took back his old job of bank cashier.

They were, like Edith and Herbert married at St Mark's Church – there was a big reception in both cases, attended by all relatives. It must have cost my parents a fortune. Cyril was college educated. Physically he was small and slight, good-looking, with perfect manners. A nice man, I thought, and one with whom I got on quite well on our infrequent meetings.

Friends

I have mentioned the Murrays who remained friends as long as they lived. Another family of equally long friendship were the Colliers. Mrs

Collier was a widow, a very handsome and kindly woman. Her husband had died as a result of injuries received as a policeman when he went to a fracas at the Gaiety Theatre in Birmingham. My father took his police collar number, and the friendship began then.

Mrs Collier kept a milliner's shop in Bloomsbury Street in Saltley. Later on during the War she opened a draper's shop next door. Into this she placed her unmarried sister Lottie, who ran the shop. There was a daughter, Madge, about Edith's age, a plain, gawky girl, very outspoken, honest enough, but lacking any female charm.

Mrs Collier was always fond of me. I often went to her shop on errands for my mother, and we spent ages chatting together; she used to tell my mother that I was so sensible to talk to.

We had parties from time to time at each other's houses, always on Wednesdays, when both milliners shops closed for half day, and we indulged in music and cards. Herbert sang – I was always called upon to sing, being a treble choirboy. 'Little Grey Home in the West' and 'Alice Blue Gown' were my contributions. Father, when he was available, was good at singing Irish songs – strange, he did it so well, accent and all, and yet he detested anything Irish. Madge Collier and Edith were both excellent pianists, and there was always an undercurrent of rivalry as to who was the better.

The food served on these occasions was always sumptuous by our standards, and this always infuriated Florence because it had all been eaten by the time she came home from work – and by Father because he considered it such a waste of money. I remember he came home once when a party was in full swing, and as he walked through the crowded room he exclaimed, 'What, another old hen's party!' When the people had left, Mother really had a go at him so he never did that again. Usually he enjoyed parties as much as anyone, particularly the card games. Once, many years later, he confided to me that Mother had spent a fortune on entertaining, and I had to agree; but still, it was her chief joy in life, she earned the money, so why not?

The Coupes

They were George and Kate, a couple who lived in Monk Road, their garden abutting ours at the back. They had originally come from Derby. George, who came from a good family, had joined the Grenadier Guards, and from his photographs was a handsome, fine-looking man. He had, during his army service, been selected to be a pallbearer at the funeral of Edward VII. Then George had a serious accident which blinded one eye and disfigured his face. Kate, when young, was small, dark and very pretty; she gave up her new fiancé, and took up with George again, because, she said, she was so sorry for him, and felt that no-one else would have him now he was so disfigured. George had a relative who held a high position at the Birmingham Gas Works whose name was Mason, and he had a daughter named Rosie, who was a lifelong friend of my sister Edith. George asked this relative to find him a job – he did – as lavatory attendant at one of Birmingham's underground public lavatories. This was a source of scandal in our family ever after. Anyway, eventually George got a better job at the Gas Works, which he kept until war broke out. He then secured employment at Drews Lane Munitions Works, and, I suppose, earned good money while the War lasted. He was a bit pompous, a terrible boaster, fond of the ladies without much success; I, even as a child, thought him a bit of a fool. He was kind enough, but without any talent to do anything well. As I reflect, when older and wiser, I realize that any handsome, well set-up young man, suffering the disfigurement that befell George so early in life, with all its consequent limitations on his employment, social, and I suppose, sexual prospects, was entitled to try and combat it with some show of pride.

George and Kate attended all our family gatherings, and looked after me on Wednesday afternoons, when my mother was occupied with her social activities. I used to take an egg for my tea round to Monk Road and stay there, playing for hours with the contents of the sewing-machine drawer.

Speaking of my mother's social activities, the shop was closed on Wednesday afternoons and often she would go to the big wholesale stores in Birmingham, Rackham's, Grey's and Chamberlain, King and Jones. I would sometimes accompany her if not at school. After buying her goods for our shop, we would go to a matinee at one of the theatres; I saw *Lilac Domino, Maid of the Mountains*, and other popular favourites of the times, with stars like Jose Collins, Billy Merson, and others. Sometimes we went to an afternoon dance at the Edgbaston Assembly Rooms, and we usually finished up with a fish and chip tea at Pattison's Restaurant in Corporation Street, to the strains of a string orchestra. At Christmas, I was always taken around the toy shops by one of the family as a treat. If I expressed a great liking for something, providing it was not too expensive, I usually found it in my Christmas stocking. I remember getting a fort and tank like this. I loved those trips, of course.

Finally, before we leave Bamville Road, one last memory. I have never considered myself brave; I am as fearful as the next person, and have often avoided confrontations which might have been painful. Yet throughout my life, if anything remotely in the course or call of duty demanded my taking risks, I have almost always responded, partly because I could not bear to live with my conscience if I had failed, and partly because anything clothed with the word duty has that effect on me.

One little incident, the first of note in my life, was when I was about eleven, and had just passed to go to Waverley Road Grammar School. I have always felt proud of my reaction on this occasion.

Mother, Mary Holland (who had also passed for Waverley Road Grammar School), and myself, had gone on holiday to Rhyl. At some point we were joined by other members of our families – I am hazy as to when.

We children went on a little expedition to the water's edge. The tide was fully out, and it was a long walk to it, so we had to cross a point where the River Clwyd entered the sea; there was myself, Mary and Cathy Holland, Vicky Crofts and two very small children about three or four years old. We found a place which enabled us to cross the Clwyd just above ankle depth, before reaching a sandbank, on the other side of which was the sea. We all paddled for a while, then Mary and I noticed that the tide was coming in fast. As it came in it swelled the waters of the river, and we were not only cut off on our sandbank, the river was too high to cross. We all, even the youngest children, realized our danger. My first reaction was to run back to the point where we had crossed, hoping it was still shallow enough for a passage across, as none of us could swim a stroke. I had even started to move as I recall, when someone said, 'You can't leave the children here.' I pulled myself together, told Mary that our only hope was to sprint back to where we had crossed before, and pray that the water hadn't risen too high. She agreed, stout girl, and kept her head well. We shepherded the others and ran about seventy yards to our crossing point. The small ones in their fright kept falling, and we had to help keep them on their feet. Cathy fell on her knees and started to pray out loud.

Well, we reached our crossing point, and the water there reached just above my knees, but the current was very strong. Mary handed the small children to me and I lifted them over the river onto the shallow water-covered sand beyond. Having got the small ones over, we just helped the others by holding hands. Having got over safely, we hared back to our people, and safety. Before we reached them, such is the resilience of youth, all our previous fears had evaporated, and we started to play happily again.

I don't think to this day the parents realized the danger we had been in – they should never have allowed us to go so far, with a turning tide.

I felt I had come out of the situation with some credit, and still think so. Mary and Cathy appreciated the situation, but we never spoke of it again.

My mother had great ambitions to make me into a little gentleman. I suspect that this was partly her reason for taking me to dances and the theatre. I was picked up for slovenly speech and told all about good manners. In particular, I remember her saying that a gentleman always raised his hat when he met a lady; she forgot to add that it should be a lady he knew. So I sallied forth wearing my school cap, and raised it to every lady or adult female that I met, even those who passed some distance away. What they must have thought I can only imagine, either that I was a good-mannered boy, or more likely, that I was either insane or mocking them, 'taking the mickey'. It took me some time to realize my mistake. Then with clothes – I always wore short trousers or knickers like most other boys, and only once was I bought a pair of knickerbockers, those trousers that fasten over the knee. With my craze for climbing anything climbable from trees to builders' scaffolding, I soon wore them out. Thereafter, I was bare kneed summer and winter. The result was that in the winter I suffered greatly from chapped legs, particularly behind the knees, and I was always sporting abrasions and cuts. My reason for mentioning clothes is to show how insensitive parents can sometimes be to the world in which children live.

Mother bought me a tweed hat, a round hat, as worn by boys very much higher up the social scale than I, and the urchins I played and lived with. Any boy seen wearing such a hat was an object of ridicule to his contemporaries, and would be followed by a small crowd of them shouting 'Po hat, Po hat'. This was a reference to the chamber pot that graced every bedroom in those days, when no working-class house, and very few middle-class houses boasted a bathroom, the lavatory being outside. One, of course, did not go outside in the middle of the night to answer nature's call, hence the widespread use of the chamber pot. By the same token, decent homes had a jug and washbasin in the bedroom, for the morning ablutions. But to return to my hat. Inverted, it did suggest a 'Po', and I did everything I could to: (a) avoid wearing it anywhere my friends and colleagues might see it, and (b) not letting Mother know. I had a horrible example of what might happen if I was seen wearing it. One of my choirboy colleagues named Griffiths had one, and wore it, so the other boys tormented him unmercifully. It was ages before I managed to lose my 'Po' hat!

It is strange how any variation from the norm was attacked by children; you had to conform. Ragged clothing was alright; many children came from poor homes, which was accepted as part of the norm, but anything that might suggest ostentation was attacked. I don't know how girls responded, I am speaking only of boys. Today, of course, children wear or can wear anything they like, but even here one might detect the same feeling in the universal use of jeans — it is after all, conformity with the norm.

Mother's efforts to make me a little gentleman were never likely to succeed, because I spent more waking hours with my friends than with her. As a group we boys were not gentlemanly — quite the reverse. Nevertheless, I did know how to behave when it was required, and the lessons were not lost or forgotten. It was part of the dual standard I had to adopt, and at which, as I matured, I became quite adept. An ability to mix at two levels has much to commend it.

Changes

By the time I was ready to go to Waverley Road School, things were changing. Tommy Bailey, with his family, had left Bamville Road. They had, like most butchers, made a lot of money, and they moved to a large house about a quarter of a mile away. This broke our long friendship, and I did not see any more of him. The Hewetts, too, moved away; their draper's shop had not functioned as such all through the War. About this time Father received his ultimatum from the police to leave our shop, or lose his job. The shop had prospered during the War, and Mother was naturally angry, and reluctant to move, but as Father was approaching pension time, it was not worth losing that.

I left Sladefield Road School with no regrets, except one: I had only to cross the road to get there, whereas my new school was four miles away. I had achieved no scholastic success. I was good at learning poetry by heart, in fact, anything which required memory, such as dates etc. I wrote a good essay, liked geography, history and natural history; at maths I was hopeless, and I detested grammar. Not the type of mind to benefit from a higher education! But of course, this is only obvious with hindsight. At the time it promised a change, a new kind of life, and I was keen to go. In the bad weather I went by tram to town, and then on another tram along Coventry Road to Small Heath. I then walked the rest of the way. In good weather I had to walk all the way, as did the other boys who attended from our area. Four miles walk to and from school was not thought out of the way in those days. Few boys had bicycles. I palled up with a boy

Aged 7, nursing our cat.

named Leslie Enderberry who lived near the Fox and Goose and we did our daily walking together. I did this for about twelve months, until we moved to the farm.

Physically I went through three phases up to the age of eleven: a pretty baby and young boy, rather slight in build. I have a photograph, taken when I was seven, of myself nursing a cat, a sturdy boy with strong legs and reasonably tall. By the age of eleven I was growing fast, and was much slimmer. Like my sister Florence I followed the Crofts side of the family, whereas Edith and Walter favoured the Stonier-Bickley side. We were fair – and they were dark. At this time Edith had her only child, a daughter, christened Margaret. As Florence had left home, and Walter was still in the Army, Edith, Herbert and baby Margaret lived for a time in Bamville Road. I often nursed the baby, it was quite a novelty for me; hitherto everybody in my immediate family was so much older. Here was someone younger, and when being nursed, dependent on me – a new sensation.

Herbert idolized his daughter. They left after a while, and went to live nearer the hospital at which Herbert was stationed, so for a time we saw less of them.

School

Waverley Road was a good mixed school. There was a fine gymnasium, a chemistry laboratory, a wood workshop, and a cookery room for the girls. Our headmaster was a fiery Scot named Frew. Cousin Mary Holland started there at the same time. On our first day we both felt a little lost, and met at break-time at the railings which separated the boys and girls. We exchanged a few words, which gave each other some small degree of comfort, and returned to class.

I started in Form 1 and remained at the school for two and a half years. I shall not waste much time describing my abysmal progress there. From Form 1, I went to 2B, then to 3C, down – down – down. I could not follow the teachers – most of what they said was over my head. I lost interest, and was largely wasting my time. I took part in the sports (we had a good sports ground) and played cricket which I loved. At football, I was either right wing or right halfback, was always getting offside, and could never kick a ball with my instep, but only toe-poke it.

It was a period when I was always hungry. I was sent from home with some sandwiches, and coppers to buy my school dinners. They were good dinners, cooked by the girls as part of their training.

But I also had, and still have, a craving for ice cream. There was a shop opposite the school, and I'm afraid, on occasions, I spent my dinner money on ice cream! The result was that by the time school dismissed, I was famished, and had to face a four-mile walk home. Sometimes I saved a penny, and on my way home bought the biggest bun I could, for the penny, and staved off starvation that way. It was not a good diet for a growing boy, and I probably paid the price later on.

The PT instructor in the gym was ex-army. He took a dislike to me, and while I enjoyed playing in the gym, he made it unpleasant at times.

The Farm

While all this was going on, we finally left Bamville Road and the milliner's shop, and went to live at the farm. The Hollands, as I have said, went to a much grander setting, at West View, Yardley. As the farmhouse was now vacant, and Uncle Phil still wished to retain the outbuildings and land, it was an ideal arrangement for us to go and live there.

I was in a second heaven over the whole idea. I had spent a lot of time there with my Holland cousins, and we always spent Christmas there. I usually stayed overnight, next day going on one of the milk-rounds and helping to deliver the milk, usually with Uncle Phil.

The prospect of living there with all the fields to play in, those massive trees to climb, the pool to play boats, the brook to jump over, the huge garden with all its fruit trees, the animals to help look after – well, it would be any boy's dream. This was the part real, largely make-believe world that I loved – they could have school for me! Going to school now was slightly different. The farm was about one mile nearer to school. A different group of boys went from Alum Rock to those who went from Ward End.

Father bought me a bicycle, second-hand, but a nice little 'New Hudson'. It had belonged to Ned Holland who no longer needed it. This gave a new dimension to life! I went to school on it, and so began my love for anything on wheels.

The farm lived up to my expectations in every way, and once the Hollands had packed up for the day, and left for home, I had a free run of the place.

Armistice

Strange to say, I have no recollection of the impact of this at school or at home. All I do remember is that I was going home from the cinema, and had reached the road at the bottom of our fields, where I saw a bonfire in the street. A crowd, mostly women and children, and a few men had gathered, and a piano was being played in the roadway. I had never seen anything like it before, and I stayed to watch for a short time as the crowd danced and sang, and in a few cases, cried. I also have a slight recollection of the terrible 'Spanish Flu' which swept the country. No-one of our acquaintance died, but many others did – and I *do* remember seeing a whole procession of hearses lined up in Great Francis Street in Saltley waiting to take away the dead. The stories of the undertakers running out of coffins were probably true. It was an anxious and frightening time for everyone, and as is well known now, the epidemic killed more people in twelve months than the war had killed in four years.

When nearly fourteen years of age, I was riding home from school on my cycle when I had an accident. I was tearing down the hill in Alum Rock Road from St Anthony's School to the factory of Southalls, when a girl suddenly ran across the road in my path. I struck her, flew over the handlebars, and was knocked out. I vaguely remember being carried in a horse and float to the doctor's surgery about a mile from home. I remember regaining consciousness, and the doctor gently shaking me. I felt so beautifully drowsy, like floating gently down a stream, and just wanted to be left alone. This apparently is what you are *not* allowed to do at this stage. The shaking continued, then I was promptly sick. I have realized ever since that day how easy it can be to die under certain circumstances. Well – they got me home, and I was put to bed. I remember the doctor telling my mother that the food

I had vomited had been eaten too quickly, not properly chewed – the possible cause of my lifelong indigestion!

As I took a few days to recover, a thought that had been with me for some time hardened into a resolution: I had to leave school as I hated it. I broke the news to my parents, who at first would not countenance the idea. However, I persisted, and taking a lesson from the more melodramatic members of my family said, 'I would rather die than go back.' This apparently convinced them, so Father went to school and told them I was leaving.

I know now that my instinct was right – I have always been blessed with a fair share of pragmatism. Young as I was, I knew that further schooling for me *at that time* was a waste. I needed to sample real life, like so many of my contemporaries. I had to find out what I was good at, if anything, and then pursue that line with a newly aroused interest. This would come, but in my case, it was going to take another nine years before the path became clear. I always rather envy youngsters who like school, and realize that it is an irreplaceable phase of life, that if neglected, for whatever reason, cannot easily be repaired by anything done later on. But late developers like myself have to adapt differently.

Brother Walter

So far I have only mentioned in passing my elder brother. I remember when I was very young being taken to the bedroom window by Florence, to see Walter leave to join the Army. Thereafter I saw him only occasionally, when he came home on leave. He was about 5ft 10in. tall, dark, with curly black hair, good regular features, but like sister Edith, with a rather full mouth, and thickish lips. He was broad, and compactly built, and very, very strong. In build he resembled my father and the Bickley clan. During all the years he was away in India, and later on in France, I heard stories of his exploits, and he became to me and the Holland cousins, something of a hero. His appearance when on leave only added to this – he was so big to us children, and so splendid in his uniform.

He had been very troublesome as a boy – my father found him thirteen jobs in twelve months after he left school, and he lost them all, mainly through fighting. Father was always afraid that Walter would land himself in some serious trouble, and jeopardize his (my father's) job. No amount of punishment inflicted on him by my father made any difference. To such a youth the Army or the Navy was the best solution, so off he went. Even there, he was in trouble. He joined the Worcestershire Regiment, and received his training. During this, he earned the dislike of his sergeant. The Regiment was ordered to India, and after embarking, the ship moved away. At some point Walter decided he was not going on such a trip, to be at the mercy of the vengeful sergeant, so he jumped overboard – deserted.

The story goes that he was in the water many hours, but he was a strong swimmer and managed to reach land. He then tramped from the coast, I'm not quite certain where, to Leamington, where he was befriended by an elderly lady for a time. I don't quite know what happened next, but poor Father must have been out of his mind if he knew of it. The idea of a serving policeman having a deserter son did not bear thinking about. Anyway, Walter joined the Coldstream Guards, and somehow the authorities never rumbled. It was years later before the matter came to light, by which time he had an army record that ruled out any further action. The next I knew of him was when he went to France, and somehow, despite being wounded three times, managed to survive. He had shrapnel in his leg, the ends of his fingers on one hand had been blown off, and he had the scar of a bayonet wound on his forehead.

He seemed to master quickly anything to which he turned his hand. He would be full of enthusiasm for a short time, and then lose interest, turning to something else.

Immediately after the War, he was a Warrant Officer and Physical Training Instructor in a crack regiment. He moved among such characters as Jimmy Wilde, the flyweight champion, Johnny Basham, the welterweight, and other famous sportsmen. He gave physical training and boxing instruction at Eton and Beaumont Colleges; I saw the presentation cigar case the Eton boys gave him. He was riding high in a career which had come to fruition and which he loved. Then the blow fell. He was reduced to corporal for some breach of discipline. He went out one evening from barracks, without permission, during a time when troops were standing by in some industrial dispute, a rail strike, I think. This finished Walter with the Army, he obtained his discharge and came home to the farm.

He had a few jobs before he settled, for a time driving a lorry hauling milk from outlying farms to Holland's Dairy.

He often went dancing, which he loved, usually to the newly opened Palais de Danse in Birmingham. From there he brought home the woman he was to marry. I remember she came one Sunday. Mother had prepared a fine tea, and we were all introduced. She was called 'Billie', though her real name was Hilda. She was tall, thin, with no

My Early Days 57

figure, and dark, with a sharp nose. She was a dance instructress at the Palais. This was really a euphemistic term for the men and women who could be hired by patrons at a fixed price per dance, or as the Americans would say, 'Ten cents a dance girl'. Young as I was, I was not very impressed. I thought my brother could have found someone a bit more prepossessing. My family shared my disquiet. However, Walter was quite infatuated with her, and they were married. By this time we had met her mother, a big retired chorus girl type of woman. Billie's father was dead. The mother of the bride is supposed to provide the wedding breakfast, but Billie's mother made it quite clear that she was not footing the bill. My mother, determined that her eldest son should have a proper send-off, arranged everything, the wedding breakfast being laid out at the farm.

I have a picture of the group: Walter in hired morning suit for the occasion. I was wearing my school cap. Meanwhile, we still retained a

A Party at the Farm.
[L-R]: Back Row: *Herbert Lincoln, Edith's husband; Mrs Murray; my brother Walter; Mr Murray; Miss Collier; Lottie Seamon; the two Squires Girls; Mrs Collier; Mrs Squires.* Middle Row: *Sister Edith and Baby Margaret; Mother; Father; Sister Florence and husband Cyril Bateson;* Front Row: *Claud Squires; Author and dog 'Scamp'; Ruby Parkes.*

link with the Bamville Road shop. Edith, Herbert and baby Margaret moved in, and Edith tried to run the shop. She had assisted my mother during the war years, and knew the business – but things had changed. No longer were there girls on munitions with plenty of money, things were tight, and Edith could not make a go of it. She gave up, and they came to live at the farm. Walter and his new wife then moved in, and Billie tried for a short time to run the business. She, too, had to give it up, and they left, and went to live in rooms for a time.

This finally broke our link with Bamville Road.

Meanwhile, at the farm, changes were taking place. When the Hollands left us the house to live in, Uncle Phil rented space to various people to establish businesses on the nearby land.

Two brothers, George and Frank Griffin, were allowed to run a coal business there. They built stables, corn store, pig styes, and the odd shed for harness, coal bags etc. They carried out all this construction work themselves, chiefly using railway sleepers. They were tough, short, chunky men, who would have made ideal pioneers. They drew their coal from a nearby railway goods yard, and sold it around the district.

Frank, who had only one arm, was married to a rather superior type of woman – George had married a widow with three children, Alec, Harold and Dorothy. Alec comes into my story later.

There was Bert Dexter and Jack Gardner who built a large shed which they used as stabling for two horses, and storage for the fruit and vegetables they sold from their carts as hawkers.

Bert was a dapper, sharp little man, an ex-officer. He had a very resplendent wife, and he always dressed respectably to go home after work. He kept his fruit and vegetable hawking well away from his residence, thereby retaining a degree of respectability he would have lost, with such a lowly calling.

Jack Gardner was more plebian; he never bothered to dress up to go home but he was shrewd and worked hard. Both men loved racing and often took a day off to go to nearby race meetings. All these parties got on well together, and we boys became very friendly with them.

It was about this time that Father and Walter tried their hand at chicken rearing. It was a dismal failure, mainly due to attacks by rats which overran the place. We had a rat hunt one day in the Griffins' corn store. It was properly organized with ferrets, dogs and us boys armed with sticks. We killed over one hundred and fifty rats in this one store, counting, of course, the young in nests. Meanwhile, I was enjoying life at the farm. I had three trees, large oaks or elms, where among the upper branches I had erected a kind of house, with sacking and wood. I could climb into this, sit in my house, and be invisible to the world. I must have spent hours in this desirable seclusion.

The Holland boys had left behind a trunk full of boys' magazines, *The Gem*, the *Magnet*, *Sexton Blake* and *Nelson Lee*. I became familiar with all the characters, and spent hours reading these, to me, gripping stories. Life was also enlivened by the various football matches, rugby matches, and in summer, cricket matches, played in the various fields hired from Uncle Phil by the various participants.

On some Sunday mornings, there were whippet races using live rabbits occasionally. These races were organized by a local character named Ratty Smith, who was a professional rat-catcher, and ran whippets for a hobby.

At home, Mother continued to entertain – Colliers, Murrays, Coupes, and others came quite frequently to roam around the fields, or play outdoor badminton, which Walter had introduced, and which we continued to play thereafter. There was always a good spread on such occasions. I took pride in displaying my charges – two pigs which I kept scrupulously clean, and whose diet I varied with apples, acorns, and slack. I trained them to beg and this went down well with visitors. I also kept ducks; they were usually on the pond in the daytime, and spent the night and came for food to a shed we kept at the bottom of the garden, about one hundred yards from the pool. One of my show pieces to visitors was to stand by the shed door and shout, 'Ducks, Ducks', several times. The ducks heard me, and to loud quacking, came tearing over the grass in single file towards the shed, and food. They looked so funny, and on arrival at the shed just collapsed, as they literally shovelled their food down. But it was the immediate response to my call which was the high spot. I caused hilarity on one occasion when describing the state of health of my ducks, I said, 'Of course, they have good constipations!' This was a family joke for years – happy days.

Chapter IV

The 1920s

First Job

When I recovered from my injury, my father quite rightly wanted to know what kind of a job I fancied. In 1920–1, jobs could be obtained, but I didn't know what I wanted, of course! My problem at school had been that I could not see my way ahead. There was a prospect that I might go to the Solomon Islands, of all places! The difficulties, however, were too great (the offer had come through a solicitor friend of Herbert's, whose brother had a plantation there). Being constantly pressed, in desperation I said that I had been pretty good at woodwork at school, so perhaps I should try a carpentry job. To my father's credit, he did his best, and found me employment in the body-building shop at the Metropolitan Carriage, Wagon, and Finance Company in Saltley. I was not exactly an apprentice as there were no articles – one served seven years learning the trade, became a journeyman for experience, and could then demand a skilled man's wage.

So, off I went to my first real job. I had been equipped with a brown boiler suit, and carried my lunch in a pudding basin. I had to walk about a mile and a quarter. I left my pudding basin at the mess hall with dozens of others; there was a large boiler into which the pudding basins were placed, in time to be picked up nice and hot when we broke for lunch or dinner (as it is known in working-class circles). We then sat down at mess tables and consumed our food. It was a very big factory, and there must have been several hundred men messing. There was an alternative: further inside the factory was a kitchen and meal room where one could buy a lunch/dinner quite reasonably. This was mainly used by office staff, but workers could use it.

I reported on my first day to the Body Shop Foreman, Mr Lane, a nice, gentlemanly, elderly man. He was well dressed, and wore a hat – no overalls – this was his badge of office. He took me to my gang. This usually consisted of six men, one of whom was the Chargehand (or Bummer). Then there was the boy of the gang – me – the next boy who would be about two years older, and then the senior boy who would be eighteen upwards, nearing his time to go out as a journeyman. The Chargehand was Bob Massey, about forty-five years old, I would say, smallish, a bit waspy, but a nice enough man. Next was Teddy Sartorious, good-looking, a bit of a joker, a good tradesman. Then Arthur Brooks, ex-navy, an immense man, young, curly-haired, good-looking, of Welsh extraction, who thought all English were bastards, and said so. He was an explosive type, and nobody mixed it with Arthur. The other three adults were men passing through, not permanent hands. The boy next to me was Billy Overton, a tall, thin, weedy youth. he looked like a probationary Bible-thumping preacher to me. He was a great moralist, and was always warning me about 'Cod Bilson', the eldest boy, who, he said, would try to lead me astray. 'Cod' got his name from his physically large mouth, and his unbridled use of it. He was a large, sturdy youth, ignorant, loud-mouthed, but not really vicious. That was our gang. There were five such gangs in the Body Shop. We each had a whole bay of the shop as our patch, and running the length of every bay was a length of railway track. At capacity, each gang would be constructing three railway coaches as its stint. When completed, they would be raised high enough to allow a bogie (the chassis or wheeled frame onto which the coach body was fixed) to be run in along the rail track. When secured, the coaches would be moved out of our shop into the Paint Shop next door, for the next stage, after which the finishers and trimmers would put in the fancy woodwork, seats, and upholstery. At all stages, the purchaser would have inspectors going round examining the work. If he was dissatisfied, the work would have to be done again, no matter how much it cost. I once saw a completed Glasgow and Scottish SW Rail Coach have a beautifully painted side panel torn out, and replaced, despite the efforts of staff all the way up to the Works Manager, to persuade the Inspector to pass it – there was a hairline crack across the panel! The 'Met' was a very efficient firm, miles ahead of its time in some respects.

The firm had a profit-sharing scheme whereby the work force had a share of the profits put in their wage packets every month. This was based on output. The result was that we in our shop, anyway, worked at top speed; the factory motto was, very rudely, 'Tear Arse', 'Get a move on'! It was worth working hard, the harder you worked as a team, the more you got in your wage packet, and it wasn't filched off you in punitive taxes. The only time I saw anyone slack at our factory was when orders were running out, and men were trying to make the work last.

As 'boy' of the gang, I had to make the tea. Every man had a 'billycan' which I looked after and kept washed. Every day the men brought tea and sugar, or more often, tea mixed with condensed milk into a sticky mess, screwed up into a paper bag. This was handed to me, and I went across the Wagon Shop to the hot water urns on the other side; there I filled the cans and made the tea. Boys came from all the other shops, 'The Smithy', Foundry, Trimmers, Paint Shop etc., on the same errand. I remember Teddy Sartorious was always forgetting to bring his tea, and asking me to pinch a little from all the others, to make up his can; I did this many times for him. Christmas came, and all the men gave me a Christmas box for making their tea. Teddy wanted to give me only a shilling; I told him he should give me *two* shillings because of all the tea I found for him during the year. The argument went on all afternoon, but I would not give way – a principle was at stake, eventually he gave me two shillings; I expect he was only teasing really; the 'kid' of the gang was always fair game.

The tool kit of a 'bodymaker' was a carpenter's set, valued in those days at over £100. As a 'boy', I started with a few, intending to add to them each year. The first essentials were a large 'Jack' plane, a smoothing plane, ratchit brace and bits, hammer, chisels, set square, and a few others. Father bought me two new planes from a tradesman friend of his. I took them to work, and was allowed, as was the custom, to go to the foreman of the Paint Shop, who immersed the two planes in a huge storage tank of linseed oil for a week. They were then removed, and after a period for drying, were ready for use. This was a concession to all aspiring tradesmen, a very nice thoughtful gesture by the management.

I was allowed to do certain work which I will describe. The three coaches allotted to our gang were laid above the ground on wooden supports about eighteen inches above the ground. First, the side and cross members were positioned, and onto these were laid the floorboards; these were measured, and any requiring sawing lengthwise, as opposed to crosswise, were marked, and laid on the sidewalk. From three coaches there usually numbered about twenty. I had to collect these and take them to the sawmill for sawing. I carried them on my shoulder, taking three or four journeys across the Wagon Shop (distance about 300 yards). We used pieces of felt on our shoulders because the heavy wood rubbed the shoulder sore. Even with the felt, my shoulder was sore as the weight was quite considerable; it was hard work!

When the floorboards were in position, Billy Overton and I had to bore holes in the ends, countersunk, in the top, and screw them down.

This job spread over several hours made my knees very sore. No wonder I staggered home some days completely exhausted.

As the sides of the coaches were positioned by using prepared shaped and machined members, another lousy job was presented. Before the side members could be erected, the partitions between each compartment of the coach had to be perfectly level. Billy Overton would check with a large wooden leveller, and shout to me where it was necessary to prop up to level; to do this, I had to crawl under the floorboards in the eighteen inches of roof space, negotiating the cross member, lugging a five-pound hammer, and several pieces of different lengths of sawn-off floorboard, and when I reached the compartment partition cross member, I had to drive the wooden piece of floorboard sufficiently to level the cross member to Billy Overton's satisfaction. The chargehand would be watching this operation, which was vital, before further construction could take place. The floor along which I crawled was dusty, full of shavings, sawdust and tea leaves – no wonder, when I emerged at the other end, I was giddy, sweaty, and rather 'fed up'. However, it wasn't always like that. I had to fetch our work supplies, screws, white lead, ventilators, door handles, hinges etc., from stores; to do this, the chargehand made out a chit which the foreman signed. I then took a trolley (there was a network of trolley rails throughout the works) and went to the stores for the supplies.

Another job was taking the panels, usually mahogany, to the corner of the shop for reinforcement. This was done by gluing a stringy support to the back of the panel. 'Ernie the Gluer' was the character who ran this corner of the shop. Dressed in a filthy overall and apron, he supervised his large cauldron of glue like a being from another world. He was a little eccentric, but was always kindly to us boys, unless we were cheeky. I did not know then, but in view of the present-day craze in some circles to sniff glue for 'kicks', I often wonder in what kind of world Ernie lived, who sniffed it all day and every day. One last job before I leave this subject was the boarding of the roof. The boards were longer and thinner than the floorboards, but I had the same boring, painful job of carrying them on my shoulder to the sawmill and back. When the boards were secured to the frames, Billy Overton and I had the quite dangerous task of levelling off the joints of the boards with our large and cumbersome 'Jack Planes'. By this time the coach was some twelve or fourteen feet from the ground with scaffolding around it. One only had to slip, and a nasty fall would result. It has to be remembered that the convex slope of a railway carriage roof is not the safest place to be perched, wielding a heavy 'Jack' plane. My climbing experience was paying off!

Lavatory arrangements

These are worth a comment. There was a section of the works sealed off with only one entrance and exit. At this entrance, in a kind of cubicle, sat a clerk operating a turnstile. If you required to go to the lavatory, you had to pass through the turnstile, and give your clock card number to the clerk, who booked the time you went in. When you left, he completed the entry. I forget now how long one was allowed, but it was under ten minutes, probably five. The lavatory arrangements were crude, but hygienic, I suppose. There were rows of wooden seats, separated from each other by a wooden partition, but open at the front. A channel ran underneath the pedestal seats, with running water carrying away the excreta. It was difficult to use this place if a person wished to have a 'scrounge', as he was always under the scrutiny of the clerk.

Wages

My starting wage was 18/9d per week. When the monthly bonus period arrived I went home with £3–10 (old money), which was a fortune to a boy of fourteen in those days. I gave it all to my mother, who gave me pocket money – I forget how much but it sufficed at that time. On reflection I cost my parents nothing from the age of fourteen, in fact, they did quite well out of me.

About this time my mother bought me my first pair of long trousers. In those days you only aspired to these when you went to work – no jeans and long trousers for youngsters then! We went to Foster Brothers Clothing, a firm still thriving today! I was easily fitted off the peg and felt very grown up!

I remained at the 'Met' for twelve months. During that time we constructed coaches for Glasgow Scottish and South Western Railways, really beautiful jobs, and an order for South Africa and Zambesi Railways. The construction of these latter was quite different in many respects. Firstly, to combat the effect of ants, the wood mainly used was teak. This seems to contain some poisonous substance, so that whenever a splinter entered the skin, invariably the part affected turned septic.

The interior was not upholstered as in Britain coaches, but was largely wicker. The fittings were quite luxurious in the First Class, the coaches reserved for the coloureds had wooden seats only, and were very spartan.

I remember, when the first batch was completed and ready for dispatch, it was suddenly realized that they were too tall to go under some of the railway bridges en route to the embarkation port. This naturally created a terrible stir – all the top management assembled to try and solve the problem. Eventually, they managed to tilt the bodywork sufficiently to give the coach bare clearance.

It was when this order was nearing completion that we realized there were no more orders on the books. We hung on for a week or two, but eventually the redundancy notices were given, and all but a skeleton staff were laid off, myself included. It was a strange feeling – Mr Lane came to me and said he was sorry but I must finish that night. I gathered my tools together, and whilst hurrying, I tripped over a rail track and fell against a large trestle, hurting my left shoulder. When we left, having drawn our wages, Billy Overton and I decided to try and find another job together the next day. We met, and walked for some hours trying various carpentry works looking for work, but with no success; had we known it, this was the beginning of the famous 1920s slump, which eventually, by 1930, led to 3,000,000 men on the dole.

I was in considerable pain from my shoulder, and on returning home, I told Father. I took off my jacket and shirt, and as I stripped, I was so thin my ribs stuck out, drawing from sister Edith some comment that I looked like a skeleton. Father touched my shoulder, then I fainted. At the hospital next day, a fractured collarbone was diagnosed. I was duly strapped up. Father then insisted that I go to the 'Met', and report that I had received the injury during my employment there, and was therefore entitled to wages until fit again.

I saw Mr Lane in the now nearly depleted Body Shop; he was sympathetic, and told me what to do. I eventually saw the works doctor every week for the next five weeks until my injury healed. I remember how hard he tried to make me say I was fit before I really was, to try and save the firm expense. However, I got my five weeks pay – in those days there was no unemployment pay for such as I.

To return to my physical appearance. From being a sturdy nine-year-old, I was now fairly tall and terribly thin. Over fifty years later, I discovered I had been tubercular. No-one knew then or later. It was only after a very comprehensive X-ray whole body examination in the early 1970s, that the doctor drew my attention to four or five dark circles around my trunk and said, 'This is as fine an example of caleined tuberculosis that I have ever seen.' Then he asked me if I had ever lived on a farm when a boy, and had untreated milk to drink. I told him that I had, and he said, 'Well, you obviously had tuberculosis, and cured yourself naturally, but don't worry about it now, it was a long time ago.' It must have been about the time I was at the 'Met' that I was in this condition. Also, at that time I developed foot sores, probably from working on wooden floors. These 'Gauls' were very painful. Father had a sovereign remedy: he obtained a bottle of carron oil, probably from a tripe and cowheel shop. I poured this into my boots and wore them soaked in this oil. In no time at all the sores healed, and I never had any further trouble.

The Milk Business

While my shoulder was strapped up, I accompanied Father on the milk round that he was working on commission for Uncle Phil. It was a good round, bringing in £3 to £3–10 (in old money), covering part of the Saltley area, where Father was well known from his police days. Some Fridays, after finishing the round, we would go with Uncle Phil in a pony and trap to Coleshill Market. Here, eggs could be bought cheaply for sale on the milk rounds. It was always a pleasant trip for me as I liked gently jogging through the countryside. When I was fully recovered, I took over the round from Father who slipped back into retirement. I worked this round for the next three years and earned a steady £3-£4 per week. I augmented these earnings with sales of rhubarb from our large stock in the garden and also sold large bunches of lilac when in season.

With the help of Bill Holland and various friends I had made in the neighbourhood, we gradually formed a cricket team. Herbert, my brother-in-law, helped by supplying me with a fine cricket bat and other accessories. These he obtained from a firm in London which was in liquidation, and to which he had been assigned by his firm of accountants to help wind up.

What a band of enthusiasts we were! Cricket was almost an obsession. We gradually built up an expertise until we were able to challenge other teams in the area, and of course, we always had a field available on which to play. Bill Holland and I became quite good bowlers. I remember one match we played against some Methodist club when I took all ten wickets. On the return match, Bill Holland did precisely the same thing. After our evening practices we would troop across to a nearby ice cream shop, and that I think was the limit of our dissipation!

Keeping fit, and following all the activities of sports celebrities, was our hobby. Bill and I started to take an interest in Birmingham Football Club, and went to their home games when we could. We also paid rare visits to Edgbaston cricket ground to watch Warwickshire County. Here we saw such characters as Hendren, Holmes, Hobbs, Quaife, and the Hon. F.S.G. Calthorpe, and many others.

Walter started taking us to the swimming baths at Nechells. We got up at 6 a.m. and went to the baths which opened at 7 a.m., but we had to get back on time to start our milk rounds at 8–8.30 a.m. Quite a rush! Walter was a very strong swimmer – I could never aspire to that, although I did learn in time and always enjoyed it.

The milk business in and around Saltley was very competitive in those days. The area was heavily populated, and many firms and individuals competed for business. There was the Midland Counties Dairy which dealt in bottled milk; Wathes, Cattell and Gurdon, a large firm dealing in loose and bottled milk, with very smart turnouts; Gearings, a firm dealing only in sterilized milk, and dozens of small one-round men who operated as individuals. Periodically, some pirate would start up, and sell at cut price, which would cause havoc for a time, but eventually they all seemed to fold up and disappear. Later on, the Co-op started up in a big way, with a great deal of publicity and extremely smart turnouts. They took a lot of the trade, as many people in and around Saltley were Co-op members. I should say that Hollands' turnouts were most disreputable – how we kept any trade was a mystery. Of course, many people imagined that operating from a farm, the milk must be much fresher. It was just an illusion. Uncle Phil had not kept cows for years, and even then had never kept more than six. We never informed our customers to the contrary!

It is worth mentioning the drill before we set off at about 8 a.m. delivering the milk. We first had to catch our horses. Uncle Phil kept them out in the fields summer and winter. During winter they were easy to catch – in fact they were usually waiting at the gate to be brought in, and fed. During wet weather they would come into the stables covered in mud, which could not be cleaned off their long winter hair. They looked terrible! In frosty and snowy weather we had to frost nail them before harnessing. This entailed knocking special nails into the shoes to give the horse more grip on icy roads. Our floats, and later, flat carts, were a bit ramshackle. Uncle Phil did not believe in paying to have them painted! We did our best to keep them washed, but nothing could disguise their squalid appearance. In icy weather it was no unusual thing to have to lead your horse all the way, to prevent it slipping down, and to keep the weight down. When I started we sold only loose milk carried in seventeen-gallon churns; we filled our two-gallon buckets from the churn. Around the rim of the bucket was a fitting to hold the half pint and gill measures. Using these, we measured out the milk to the customers into their jugs, basins, or whatever receptacle they offered. There was a lid to the bucket, of course. The whole business was most unhygenic, and looking back, I wonder there was not more sickness caused by unclean milk than in fact there was.

Carrying those heavy buckets full of milk, sometimes for quite a distance, and for many hours, was quite a strain, until familiarity made it seem easy.

I have mentioned catching the horses in the winter when they were hungry. It was a very different matter in the summer when there was plenty of grass. The horses knew they would have to work when caught, and they often led us a fine chase before being finally cornered. This sometimes took up to an hour, those whose horses had been caught early gave help in catching the others. This threw the whole business late, and we started out on the rounds physically exhausted from our chases around the fields.

None of these problems existed for other milkmen, nearly all of whom kept their horses in stables. Our horses were characters and we became attached to them. There was 'Ted', a large chestnut, a good, steady worker, which never had tantrums, and would jog around all day, but never very fast. 'Hero' was an ex-army horse and a biter. He had been ill-treated at some time, and only Bill Holland could handle him without getting bitten. He was a big, dark-coated animal, strong, a good worker, but nasty. 'Doll', a black mare, was very fast, not so strong, but a real flyer! My horse was 'Betty', a plump little mare, a good worker, but rather on the slow side. For a time we had a young stallion, 'Snowy'. Uncle Phil kept him until he was about two years old before having him castrated. During that time he managed to serve 'Betty'. Foolishly, I thought, Uncle Phil worked the mare until the last week, and she lost the foal. Shortly after castration 'Snowy' was sold.

My relations with my customers were very good. I presented a cheerful friendly face to them, and was willing to chat to those who felt in need. I seldom lost a customer, but unfortunately, I was very shy, and found it difficult to canvass for new customers. When I did pluck up enough courage to do so, I had quite good success.

The biggest bugbears of the milk business in those days were 'bad payers', and sour milk. Bad payers could mean the difference between making a living, or getting into debt when working on commission, as I was. There was, therefore, a code between milkmen, bread men and coalmen, to let one another know of any bad payers.

During a hot summer, loose milk soured very quickly, and had, in many cases, to be replaced. This led to difficulties when trying to adjust at my purchasing end. We tried all kinds of dodges to keep the milk cool, storing with ice around the churns before delivery, keeping wet sacks around the churns when delivering. After I had been on the round for about twelve months, Hollands decided to go in for sterilized milk instead of loose milk. This meant converting some of the outhouses into a plant capable of treating the milk. The milk passed through a machine which mixed the cream and milk together until it was all of uniform richness. The milk was bottled, and part-boiled in large tanks, cooled off, and the bottle tops fastened. This process made the milk safer, but it had rather a peculiar taste which took some time to get used to! Ned masterminded the project from the installation point of view, while John took over the running of the plant, and Bill stayed on the sales side.

We had to change from our floats to flat carts which were more suitable for carrying crates of a dozen bottles of milk. There was a high seat in front of the cart, leaving the driver very much exposed to the weather. We also had to convert our customers to the new milk. Surprisingly, we achieved this fairly quickly, but we always carried some loose milk for the diehards. I cannot leave this period without a mention of the driest summer in my memory – the summer of 1921. For months there was no rainfall, fields cracked and our pond dried up for the first time ever. We had a large consignment of sterilized milk bottles delivered which were wrapped in straw, and in large canvas bundles; the result was a plague of fleas which infested us. I remember waking in the night, removing my shirt, and killing the fleas on my shirt and body. My parents in the next room were doing the same thing. It seemed to go on for weeks, and then they suddenly disappeared.

The business rapidly expanded and new rounds came into being, largely as a result of appointing a canvasser. A few men with rounds of their own bought Hollands' milk, and even hired their horses and carts from them. This meant a rapid expansion of the labour force, boys and men for the plant, and extra roundsmen for the sales.

Gradually, the ubiquitous model T Ford motor lorry began to take over from the horse and cart. We youngsters could see the way things were going, quickly adapted ourselves and took every opportunity to learn to handle the internal combustion engine. Walter had three different motorcycles within a couple of years, starting with a 'Levis' two-stroke, locally made at Stetchford, then changing that for a 'Triumph' belt-drive. This he bought at an army disposal sale at Bingley Hall which I attended with him. There were dozens of such machines, all new or nearly so, and they were knocked down for £87 each, quite a lot of money then. Finally he bought a large American twin-engine 'Indian' motorcycle, a very fast, heavy brute of a machine. I often rode pillion with him, sitting on the carrier (no sprung seat then) and nearly had the stuffing knocked out of me!

When Bill Holland started to work his round with a Ford lorry, I went with him whenever I could, and quickly learned to drive. One Saturday I had finished my small round at about 2 p.m. Bill wanted to go to the football match at St Andrews Ground, and he asked me to finish his deliveries for him. I was delighted with the idea, and duly took over. He had a huge load of bottled milk. The brakes on these early vehicles were not too good, especially when the vehicle was overloaded. I had one call on a steep hill; we always made this stop by turning the front wheels into the kerb, to hold the vehicle. I made the delivery, and on coming out of the shop, saw that the lorry had mounted the kerb, and was held by the rear wheels against the kerb, with the front of the vehicle touching the shop wall. I managed, after a hair-raising few minutes, to get sufficient reverse power to back off and continue but first I had to unload several dozen crates of milk to reduce the weight, then reload them again.

However, I was gaining the experience required to take over the new form of transport.

I had disposed of my 'New Hudson' cycle, and bought a new BSA three-speed cycle for £18. I kept this for a couple of years, and then, having saved hard, bought a new 'Rudge' four-valve 350c.c. motor cycle for £55 – not bad when I think of it: I was doing all this at seventeen years of age, keeping myself, doing a man's job, and able to buy a new motorcycle! I could not drive it on the day I went to collect it. I had played about on motorcycles, but never actually driven one, so Walter picked it up from the centre of Birmingham. He gave me half an hour's instruction in a back street near Birmingham centre. I took over, and was sailing along beautifully, when a policeman on point duty signalled me to stop. I was unsure of the controls and shot past him before I could do so. He came up to me, gave me a dressing down, but I looked and felt so woebegone, telling him almost tearfully that I had only just bought the machine, that he let me off. Well, I arrived home safely; of course there was not much traffic in the early twenties, and what there was was rather slow moving. I wouldn't recommend any such foolhardiness today. So I was ready for the transition from horsepower to motor power.

About this time, it was decided that John and Mary Holland and I should be confirmed. We attended the instruction on Sunday afternoons at Yardley Church, and I had tea at the Hollands' new house, West View. The great day duly arrived. We were blessed by the Bishop of Johannesburg, whose name I have forgotten, but I do remember quite a thrilling sensation when he laid his hand on my head, saying, 'Oh Lord, defend this thy child with Thy heavenly grace.' I still remember part of the prayer, and have used it ever since.

Louie Baggott

I mentioned earlier that the eldest boy of the Griffin clan was Mrs Griffin's boy by her first husband, who was called Alec Cank. He worked one of the Hollands rounds and we became friendly; he was tall, spare, with quite good features, but quite undistinguished. At seventeen I was beginning to feel the biological urge. I could not stay home in the evenings; I would leave the comfort of our house and go out into the foulest weather with Alec to meet the opposite sex. We used to go to Birmingham town centre and parade along New Street, Corporation Street and Snow Hill. The usual drill along these 'Monkey Runs' was for two boys passing two girls who attracted them to stop and engage them in conversation. If the vibes were right you made a further appointment on parting, for another meeting. If both girls turned up you were in business; if nothing came our way, we always had a 'faggot and peas' supper in Snow Hill for a few coppers.

One Sunday night Alec and I were patrolling New Street, when I met my first regular girlfriend. We met again and started to go out regularly together. This ended the partnership with Alec, whose girl did not turn up for the second meeting. My girl was called Louisa Baggott, and she lived in a road off Alum Rock Road near its junction with Washwood Heath Road. She was tall, well built, with a lovely face. If she had a fault, it was an aquiline nose, perhaps a trifle sharp. She had blue eyes and brownish hair. I felt very flattered that such a lovely girl could be interested in me. She worked in a factory (at Typhoo Tips Tea). I suppose she was what my mother would have called 'common', her speech was very 'brummy', she had no social graces, and dressed rather flamboyantly. But at seventeen I was quite oblivious to all this, to me it was a new and wonderful experience.

We went out sometimes on my motorcycle, sometimes to the cinema, or just walked. She took me to her home and introduced me to her parents. Her father was a tall, good-looking man, a railway guard. Her mother was very dark, and had been quite handsome – it was obvious that Louie could hardly help being a good-looker.

We went on quite happily until she went with her factory friends to see Ivor Novello in the *Rat* at a Birmingham theatre. She became infatuated with him, and I had a traumatic time for weeks as she kept on about how wonderful he was. I was made to feel so inadequate and never forgave her for that. I also gathered, as time went on, that she had been going out for quite a long time (before meeting me) with a boy from Great Francis Street. She often mentioned him. He was eventually accepted for the Metropolitan Police in a time of high unemployment, and I was told all about this. I never heard why they had parted – I guess that he gave Louie the 'brush off'. He didn't last long in the police, and was back home in less than twelve months.

When I was between seventeen to eighteen years old, I went on holiday to Blackpool on my motorcycle and stayed alone at modest digs on North Shore. One morning, early in the holiday, I was wandering rather aimlessly on the North Pier, when I was joined by a man of about 30–35, who engaged me in conversation. He was of medium height, well built, quite good-looking with a good head of hair. He was cultivated in his manner, and I felt rather flattered when he asked me to join him for lunch. He told me he was single, and owned a motor coach business in Bradford. We had lunch at the Tower Restaurant, which was way beyond my means, but he insisted on paying. For the next few days I saw a lot of him. He seemed to know a number of 'Show People' in Blackpool and had an entree to the back stage of many of the shows. He was staying at the County and Lane's End Hotel, one of the most expensive on the front, and had a front room to boot! There was nothing in his behaviour that was at all strange, except that being good-looking and well-to-do, many of the stage women we met rather fawned on him, but he treated them very casually. After a few days we were in his bedroom chatting when he asked me to go to London with him as he had business there. I pointed out that I had paid for my digs for the rest of the week and didn't like losing that; I also had my motorbike. He said that money was no object, he would pay all expenses. My alarm bells rang, this sounded a bit fishy! I knew little or nothing of homosexuality, but this did not seem right to me. I staved him off, but eventually he said that he was leaving the next day, and if I changed my mind, I could let him know. We continued to chat in a friendly fashion, with no ill-feeling. During the conversation, he told me that women did not interest him – he could, he said, get more satisfaction from lying in bed with his arms around me than from any woman. He explained, to my obvious ignorance, that his condition was often brought about by a mother's strong desire (while the embryo was in the womb) for a girl to be born. If a boy, instead of a girl was born, then often the instincts were reversed. I wasn't very interested, really. I liked him, but not like that, so we parted. I can't even recall his name now. This was the first of two homosexual approaches made to me in my younger years. I *must* have been a *pretty boy*.

The End of the Farm Era

After we had been living at the farm for about two years, we heard that Uncle Phil's lease expired in another twelve months, and was not to be renewed. Birmingham Corporation needed the land for a building project. This gave us time to make our arrangements. Father had bought a sizeable piece of land at Four Oaks, Sutton Coldfield, which had always been a favourite place of my mother's, and she often took me there on the bus in summer, when I was young.

While the arrangements were being made for two houses to be built on the land, Father bought a large army hut-type of shed, and erected it on the rear boundary fence. Uncle Will Stonier and I helped to put it up. It was a fine structure, and quite large enough to act as a home, which it did on many occasions.

Father had a lot of trouble getting the houses built. The building firm, as I said earlier, went bankrupt, and he had to find another builder to finish the job at a reasonable price. Sister Edith, her husband, and child Margaret, were going to occupy the second of the two houses.

Meanwhile Father spent what time he could getting the garden into shape (which was very large). For years, only three or four houses were built on the enormous piece of land of which ours was part. The site was well out in the country, and only about half a mile from the Four Oaks entrance to Sutton Park, altogether a delightful place to live. Meanwhile, at the farm, Hollands were moving their plant out to a factory they had bought in Fazely Street, Birmingham, near the town centre. No fields here, just space for the plant, offices, and parking space for the vehicles. About this time, brother Walter, who could never keep out of trouble, broke a man's jaw, and was summoned by him for assault.

It appears that Walter was riding his motorcycle home one evening, with his wife, Billie, on the pillion. As he negotiated a corner in Birmingham, a man coming out of a public house aimed a blow at him with his stick for no apparent reason. Walter instinctively ducked, and it struck Billie. It didn't hurt her much, but Walter stopped, went back, and laid the assailant out with one mighty blow. This case caused some anxiety in the family, and a solicitor was hired. Walter got off with a farthing damages. There is something to be said for 'instant justice'; I'll wager that man never tried that sort of caper again!

Before Hollands left the farm, all the rounds were being worked with Model T Ford lorries. Rounds were being merged and added to – I lost my profitable little Saltley round, and as I was going to live at Sutton Coldfield, I took over a round there. Before I finally leave the farm, there is one other little anecdote. Hollands had partitioned our large lounge, and used one part of it as an office. In our part, we had the new 'wireless' installed. It had headphones, and you moved a cat's whisker around a crystal until you got reception. Walter, who was clever with anything like this, bought the set, which gave us hours of fun. Behind the wireless set was the partition and Hollands' office.

Once a year Uncle Phil had visits from the farmers from whom he purchased his milk. They came individually, and worked out the wholesale price of milk to be supplied for the following year. Uncle Phil always primed them well with whisky, and it was great fun listening to the half-drunken bargaining that went on. I was often torn between listening to the *new* miracle – the wireless – or listening to the old-as-time bargaining of the two shrewd old farmers.

Well, eventually, all dairy equipment and staff had finally left. The council found Mother and Father a new council house on the Perry Common Estate, until such time as the Four Oaks property was ready for occupation. I stayed for a time with George and Kate Coupe in Monk Road, and rode to Fazely Street on my motorcycle to pick up my load of milk for delivery in Sutton Coldfield.

For some time past, Father had been asking me to seriously consider joining the Police Force when I was twenty. He had tried to persuade Walter to do the same when he left the Army, but Walter said that he had had enough of discipline, and eventually wanted to be his own boss. It was surprising Father took the line he did, considering how badly he had been treated. For the first time I carefully took stock of myself. I was nearly six feet tall, very slim, very tough, my outdoor life had seen to that. I had no trade. I could see no great future in the milk business, the Sutton round was hardly providing a living because of too many slow, and downright bad payers. The competition was tremendous, particularly since the emergence of the Co-op. Employment was diminishing, money was tight, jobs hard or impossible to get; we were moving on towards the General Strike of 1926, and eventually 2–3 million unemployed.

I was half-educated – that was my fault – had learned to handle money, and people, and could drive motorcycles or motor lorries, which was not so common a skill then as it is today.

I began to see merit in the idea. My fear was that I would be too slightly built to be accepted. I knew how keen the competition would be to get appointed in such an overweighted labour market to a job for life, a pension at the end, and possible promotion. I decided to try and build myself up in the time before I was old enough to apply.

I joined the YMCA in Dale End, Birmingham, taking part in all PT activities. I did everything I could to improve my physique, which I don't think had much effect, but it kept me fit and out of mischief.

Meanwhile, we moved to Four Oaks, and I was allowed to load my lorry the night before and keep it at home ready to start early in the Sutton Coldfield district. It was a nice round in many respects, with a nice class of people and nice country, but it never paid.

In desperation, Father and I decided to try selling potatoes, buying them wholesale from the farms around Sutton, and taking them into Birmingham to greengrocers, fish and chip shops etc. To do this we had to use the milk lorry, which could easily carry a ton. Hollands were not supposed to know of our use of their lorry. We excused ourselves on the basis that they were paid for the milk we sold, whether there was any money left over for us at the end – and we were entitled to live! Walter had given us the idea – he was still hauling milk from farms to Hollands Dairy, and he had been selling potatoes as a sideline for some time, but he was using his own lorry. By the way, he and his wife were now living in Four Oaks, in a cottage about 3/4 mile from our home.

All went well for a time. Father canvassed in Birmingham among old acquaintances for customers, while I picked up the potatoes from the farms, drove the lorry into Birmingham, and delivered them. There was all the physical jerks I needed in this work, handling one hundredweight bags of potatoes!

A strange thing about Birmingham people. In those days they had a great liking for Lincolnshire King Edward potatoes. These always fetched top prices at the shops – if the Lincolnshire crop was good, you could not sell locally grown 'spuds', or only cheaply anyway. So we would hope that the Lincolnshire crop would fail, as it sometimes did, with disease, then the price of local potatoes shot up. Of course, the farmers were as aware as we were of the fluctuations of the market, and varied the price accordingly. We had to monitor the wholesale prices which varied weekly, and sometimes daily. Sometimes we had a stock of twenty tons in store, the price would occasionally shoot up £7 a ton, and you would make a handsome profit, but you had to watch that you were not caught the other way round.

This went on quite well for about twelve months, then the market dried up. Father could not get orders as the big operators were taking over. Walter continued to do well, but when Father asked him to put a few orders our way, he refused. Considering the favours he took from my father a little later, this was very mean, because he was working twelve or more hours a day to meet his commitments, and must have been earning £40-£50 a week, at least. But finally we had to stop when Uncle Phil objected to us using his lorry.

Without any delay Father and Mother went to Wolverhampton to see Uncle Jack, who was now Chief Inspector and Chief Clerk of the Wolverhampton Force, to ask if I could join there. They had not chosen a very good time apparently. It appears that Nellie Gibbs, Auntie Clara's only daughter had married a miner named George Chapman who had preceded me in an application to join the Police Force via Uncle Jack. He recommended him to the Chief Constable of Dudley, Mr Campbell, a friend of his. George duly turned up for his examination and failed so dismally at the education test that Mr Campbell had said, 'He should have his backside kicked.' Naturally this made Uncle Jack a trifle reluctant to expose himself again! Father fought hard and said I would not let the side down. They came back home with a promise that when the Borough of Wolverhampton gained its boundary extension due in 1927, I could apply to join. More to the point, Father had been briefed as to the education standard required. This gave me a few months to study as I had done no school work of any sort since I was fourteen. I had handled money, of course, and was an avid reader of news and current events, but my weakness was maths! I dug out my old Waverley Road books, and got down to it – I could work when the incentive was there.

It was at this time in 1926 that a policeman named Willetts was shot dead in Wolverhampton by some absconding delinquents from a home. This was, of course, headline news, but it did nothing to diminish my new-found enthusiasm to be a policeman.

Meanwhile, life went on. I worked my round and saw Louie Baggott nearly every night. One night I was going home via Castle Bromwich, and saw in the darkness a number of red hurricane lights across the road, indicating some excavations. Unfortunately I drove between the wrong two, and fell with my bike into the trench. I shall never forget the horror of suddenly seeing a hole open up in front of me. The trench was too narrow for the bike to fall in, so it remained perched along the top, with me in the trench. I got out, largely uninjured, rescued my bike which was alright, except for a bent handlebar, and carried on home. During the whole incident I never saw anyone else – if I had been injured, I might have lain there for hours undiscovered.

I was so annoyed at damaging my precious machine, although not seriously, that next day, after work, I took it out onto the Stonebridge Road, where there was a two-mile straight stretch, and opened it fully out for the first time. To my surprise, it only reached a maximum of 55 m.p.h. I had expected more!

Eventually, in early December 1926, I was called to attend an examination at Wolverhampton, to fill some twenty vacancies which would be created early the following year.

I set out on what was to be for me a momentous occasion and reported with some fifty or sixty others at the Town Hall. We were addressed by someone, then herded into one of the courtrooms for a written examination. It was morning time, and we had to answer papers on maths, geography, English and general knowledge. It was not particularly difficult. When we had finished we had to wait while the papers were checked. About twenty had passed, and we were told to report after lunch for the medical exam. I had passed the first hurdle! I had made friends with a tall youth who was a lorry driver and we went looking for food. We found a restaurant in the town centre called the Cafe Royal and went in there. I later found that this was the classiest and most expensive in town. We had an excellent lunch, which was far too dear, but we didn't mind, after all, it was a big occasion.

We reported back to the police station ready for the next stage – the medical. I felt I might fail this, as height, weight etc., as well as physical fitness were considered. Most of the other applicants looked as if they could give me one or two stone in weight – I was only eleven stone. Came my turn to be examined. The doctor was interested in my papers, and asked me about one of my referees, a retired Trade Union official of the NUR, who was a JP, whom I had served for years as his milkman. The examination was completed and apart from a slight varicosele, I was declared physically fit. I learned later from Uncle Jack that the doctor told him that I was a trifle lighter in weight than he usually liked to accept, however, I was through to the next round. My short-acquaintance friend had failed the physical as he had varicose veins in his legs. The next and last hurdle was the interview with the Chief Constable.

We were now reduced to twelve only and were marched in by the Chief Constable's Office Inspector, Mr Martin. We lined up in front of the great man.

David Webster, the Chief Constable, was a short, stout man of florid, Jewish appearance, who wore rather flashy clothes and a buttonhole flower.

We were ordered to stand to attention as we were addressed. The men were asked their names, jobs and why they wanted to join the Police Force.

Most of our little crowd had just left the Army, the Coldstream Guards, Grenadiers, Argyle and Sutherland Highlanders etc., and this force liked servicemen. Only two of us were civilians, I a milk and potato salesman, the other, a bread roundsman.

The Chief wanted to hear that we were giving up jobs to become policemen. The Argyle and Sutherland Highlander was out of work. The Chief told him to leave the room, he did not want out-of-work men joining his force. The Inspector pleaded for him, saying that he had written good papers, so the Chief relented, and Onions (the name of the man) was allowed to stay. Little did anyone guess that within five years Onions was to marry one of the wealthiest girls in Wolverhampton, and leave the Force a rich man.

However, we all passed muster, and went to the library for a final briefing before going home. We were all elated of course. I was now able to assess a little my future colleagues, as we waited for someone to come to address us. One made it clear that he hoped another application he had made to join Staffordshire as a mounted man would be successful. He later succeeded and we never saw him again. Another was speaking of his experiences in the Royal Engineers, on the Indian North-West Frontier. Others were talking about their service in the Army, another of his in the Royal Air Force. Several of them had served as Special Constables in Staffordshire during the General Strike of 1926. I felt that silence was the best course for me to take in this unfamiliar atmosphere. 'Hear all, and say nowt' as the Yorkies say.

After a short while Chief Inspector Crofts and others came to address us. He told us we were all accepted, congratulated us, and detailed a few to report on 19 January 1927, the rest to report at the beginning of the month. We were then dismissed.

He asked me to accompany him home to see Auntie Florrie and cousins Vicky, Phyllis and John. On the way to his home he asked me why I had not contacted him earlier, as lunch at his place had been laid on for me. I said I thought it better if I did not make it too obvious that we were related. He seemed surprised at this. I told him where I had taken lunch, and this highly amused him. I stayed for a short time at his home, then departed in great spirits for the train to Birmingham. I called on Louie Baggott first, and we spent the evening together. I think Louie began to hear the distinct sound of wedding bells, now that I was on my way.

On arrival home, the family were of course delighted. The rest of the time left to me was used to teach a new man my milk round, and say goodbye to my customers. It was a very happy time, and at last I could see ahead a little; it was quite something to land a plum job like the Police Force in those days.

I have passed over the period of the General Strike of 1926 because it had little or no effect on me and I cannot remember anything about it.

Before I leave Four Oaks, just one last incident. I took Louie Baggott home. My parents received her hospitably, but poor Louie was not very comfortable. We had a nice home, my mother saw to that, and it must have struck Louie how different it was to her own humble abode. We went for a walk to a nearby lake, and she voiced her disquiet by asking me if I loved her, in view of the differences; of course I said I did, and believed it at the time.

Father must have thought that I would go into barracks because I took in my suitcase, knives, forks, spoons, and towels, some tags on my clothing etc. Came the great day, and off I went by train to my new life in Wolverhampton.

Chapter V

The Police Force – Early Days

I can remember now standing in the corridor as the train drew in to the platform. I carried my case, walking the half mile to the Town Hall which incorporated the police and fire stations, and reported, as instructed, to the Charge Office. I was sent for by Chief Inspector Crofts, and told that I was to lodge with a retired army sergeant major and his family, who kept a restaurant on Dudley Road. PC Fletcher would take me there and introduce me.

I went with Fletcher, who was the Warrant Officer's assistant – Sgt Griffiths was the Warrant Officer, Fletcher later his successor – to my lodgings. I asked him about my colleagues. Some had gone into barracks, and so became firemen as well as policemen, others had gone to lodgings in another part of the town. I felt a bit out of it, being as it were, on my own, but as it turned out, I was better off in the long run.

The Sloanes

My home for the next five years was to be 547 Dudley Road. By and large I was happy there, and a brief resumé of the family seems appropriate.

The head of the family was ex-Captain Quartermaster 'Tod' Sloane MC, and a host of other medals. He had been a regular soldier, served pre-war in India, and in France throughout the First World War in the 6th Battalion, South Staffordshire Regiment. At the end of the War, he was put in charge of the local drill hall which was the Territorials' Headquarters. He was there engaged in catering on a large scale for dances and other functions. It was a sinecure of a job. Tod, however, was an alcoholic, who had frequent bouts, and would drink anything, even Wincarnis wine. Then he would sober up, become contrite, and go on the water waggon for a time until the next outbreak. This lost him his job at the drill hall. He had taken the restaurant in Dudley Road, and catered for the factories and offices in the vicinity as a means of supporting his large family. Lunches were supplied in two rooms downstairs for the workmen, and a room upstairs for the management.

The house was very large, three storeys, and he was able to let lodgings on a small scale. I was to be given a small bedroom, and use of a large lounge which acted as a dining room as well. A barman, Arthur Brookes, also lodged there, but he slept with the Sloane boys, Terry, Buster and Jimmy, on the top floor, and had his meals with the family. Other people stayed there for short periods from time to time.

'Tod' was portly, very red faced, had all his hair, and when sober had a commanding manner as befitted one of his previous calling. He was a top man in the RAOB, an Inspector in the Specials, and was generally respected throughout the town. His outbreaks were put down to the trauma of trench warfare in France, and hence, largely forgiven. He must have been a very good soldier.

Mrs Sloane had been a handsome woman, but had gone to seed, understandably in view of her large family, and the ups and down of life with Tod. She kept such business as there was together, was an excellent cook and caterer, and deserved better of life than she received. She was like a mother to me, and I did not, on the whole, do much to repay her. The young can be very cruel and thoughtless.

The eldest boy, Terence, was about my age, and a little shorter, but sturdier. He was dark and good-looking, very intelligent, and apprenticed as an engineer at Smith and Wellman of Darlaston. We became friends and often went out together. I remember he was keen to have a trial of strength with me early after my arrival. We wrestled on the floor of the lounge. Father had shown me about four Ju-Jitsu holds before I left home. One of these, a foot and leg hold soon stopped Terry, who had to give in.

About thirty years later I met Terry on a London platform as we were both going to see the Wolves play Charlton Athletic. I was taken aback by the close resemblance he bore to his father. He had grown stout, and his voice was even similar to the departed Tod's. He was a serving soldier, like his father, a Captain Quartermaster. He saw me to a stand seat at Charlton where he had some pull, and there we parted.

To return to the family. The eldest girl was named Evelyn, who was about twenty, tallish, with a rather sweet face. Unlike Terry, she was a churchgoer, very prim, proper and correct. She helped her mother with the cooking and looking after the younger children.

Norah the next was about fourteen, plump, very dark, and a bit of a tomboy.

Buster was the next in line, tall, dark, very clever at school, he died most tragically a few years later. The cause of death was a heart attack, unbelievable in one so young who had made rather a fetish of keeping fit. Then there were Eileen, another clever girl at school, Mary and Jim, the two toddlers.

This then was the family I joined.

My first impression of the house was 'what a shabby hole', but I got used to it, and eventually took my meals, like Brooky, with the family downstairs.

Training

Having been installed at the Sloanes, I had to report every day at 9 a.m. at the Central Police Station with the others for instruction.

We were the first and last men to be trained locally. Previously, men only joined in ones and twos. I was told that they were given a copy of the bye laws, put into uniform, and sent out with an experienced officer until they knew all the beats, picking up what knowledge they could on the way. After us, men were sent to the newly opened training school established by Birmingham City Police, where they took an intensive course lasting for many weeks. All small Midland forces eventually did this, and paid a fee for the privilege.

But we were to be trained on our home ground. Sergeant 'Dusty' or 'Tommy' Smith was in charge of us. He was an ex-Scots Guardsman, had obviously been a drill instructor, was kindly in a gruff way, but was no fool. He eventually, as is often the case in such circumstances, took a liking to us, and afterwards always referred to us as 'his boys'. We copied out standard reports on bye law offences, accidents, and a host of other everyday occurrences.

We had our copies of the bye laws, and had to buy the then standard police text book *Moriarty*, named after the Birmingham Chief Constable who published it, and a very fair guide book it was.

We had lectures from the various senior officers who were department heads of the CID, and Chief Constable's Office. We had regular drill, every day, in fact, and more if we misbehaved. Accident scenes were prepared in the police yard (I have a picture of one) and the local press were invited to write about our progress. As we applied ourselves to our task, we started to ask the kind of searching questions our superior officers found difficult to answer – after all, they had no experience of instructing. They came to see us less and less often.

First aid instruction was given by two local St John Ambulance Brigade officers, and we all passed, and gained our certificates within a few weeks. Of course, before all this took place, on the morning of our arrival, we were marched to the magistrate's court, and were sworn in as constables. We received our warrant cards and collar numbers. We were quickly fitted with uniform, and attached our St John Ambulance Brigade badge (a metal disc embossed with the Maltese Cross) to the upper part of the arm. 'Well, you got your first medal,' said Dusty Smith playfully.

The Squad

There were eleven of us to begin with, starting our collar numbers from 96–106 inclusive, then others joined us 107, 108, 109, 110. As I look back, two things occur to me: (a) How few of us survived to pension time; (b) How the civilian recruits did far better in the promotion stakes than the ex-servicemen.

96 Butcher, was a tall, gangly youth, grammar school educated, rather clever, but with a fiery temper. He managed quickly to get into the CID, where he was doing very well until he got into some scraps, and he and another officer were dismissed or forced to resign. Either way, he was out before 1939.

97 Gribben, an ex-Royal Engineer. Dark, with a lot of thick hair. An excellent clerk, but no great shakes in any other branches of police work. He managed to survive to pension time, but never made the promotion grade.

98 Dineley. An ex-cabby from Manchester, had also served some time in the Army. He was really too short to meet the exacting height standard of 5ft 10in. minimum. He was sturdy, but there must have been a bit of pull from somewhere to get him in. He was also married, and it was unusual to take on married men. He did, of course, come from the same city as the Chief Constable, which may have been it. He was a stormy petrel from the time he joined until he retired prematurely, was in the CID within a few years, and out of it after a sensationally short career. Then he became a motor patrol officer for a few years, then back to the beat, and eventually got a job as Reserve Constable, a job usually confined to men getting on in years, or not very fit. He left the Force after the Home office enquiry in about 1942–3, in which he was a key character, and of which more anon. He was shrewd, and leaving the Force on a very reduced pension worried him not a jot. He was a born businessman, always buying and selling something at a profit. He made quite a lot of money, and eventually became Deputy Mayor of Margate.

You would not trust him far, but you could not help rather liking him.

99 Lear, an ex-temporary constable from Staffordshire. He lasted a year or two, then left because of woman trouble.

100 Bailey, another ex-temporary constable from Staffs. Strongly built, slow, deliberate, precise, a good scholar, but completely lacking personality, that was our George. He served for many years, then rather surprisingly, suddenly packed it in for no apparent reason, just tired of the job. He was an ex-guardsman.

101 Windsor, a good-looking, tall, fair, well-built man, ex-Guards. Very quiet, he lasted until 1941–2, when he committed suicide in circumstances I will recount later, as they affected me to some extent.

102 Onions. He was the Argyle and Sutherland Highlander who nearly lost his appointment because he had been unemployed. He was a dapper, neat, good-looking man, going prematurely bald, but that did not seem to affect his appearance detrimentally. He was witty, and highly intelligent. He was quickly in the CID, but gave it up when he married his heiress, a Miss Sherwood, of Sherwood Estates, large property owners. I carried the first message from Miss Sherwood to Onions. She became quite infatuated after observing him on point duty as she travelled to and from the town centre.

103 Rivers. Tall, dark, good looking in an Italian way, rather vain. A fair scholar, he had been a bread roundsman, and then joined as a temporary constable in Staffordshire in the 1926 strike, before he came to Wolverhampton. We were friends on and off during our service, although we quarrelled quite often, but there was no malice in him. He managed Inspector's rank, but retired at twenty-five years, fed up with the job, and his health was indifferent.

104 was myself.

105 Phillips, ex-Coldstream Guards. Well built, not particularly good looking, and suffered all the time I knew him with a pimply face. The strange thing was, he stripped beautifully, not a blemish at all on his body. He was my first friend in the force; we went on our first leave together in October 1927 when we spent a week at Blackpool. Where else?

He became a keen Police Federationist, a kind of shop steward. He never achieved any rank, but got his time in satisfactorily, and married a girl from a well-to-do family.

106 Mosely. A very large ex-RAF man, had all the characteristics of a conman. He lasted only about two weeks, and was dismissed for some scandalous behaviour in the Grand Theatre, where he upset some

At age 20 (1927).

friends of the Superintendent – Mr Haynes. He was replaced by Brothwood, a simple Shropshire lad, big and rather soft, but a nice man. He was pure constable material, no desire, and no hope of ever being anything else. It is the way of contentment, but pretty boring. He got his time in alright. Dennis never did enough to get into trouble, or to get any recognition.

107 Marsh. A broad, sturdy lad from Gornal, near Dudley; had been either a lorry driver, or lorry driver's mate. He had a pleasant open manner which concealed a shrewd, calculating mind. Not well educated, but he overcame all that, as did many of us. He had a successful career, and attained Deputy Chief Constable's rank.

108 Clews. An ex-soldier, and married. He was tall and thin, a good plodding policeman. He completed his service as a constable.

109 Edwards. The type of man one can hardly remember. Nothing to distinguish him. He never got in trouble, never did anything out of the ordinary. He served for many years before, I believe, he died, but he may have resigned.

110 Williams. A clerk from a Welsh colliery. He was over six feet in height, with hardly any neck. This gave him a peculiar appearance in uniform, as though his head sat straight on his shoulders, with nothing between. He was fairly well educated, a clerk type who was quickly taken into the Chief Constable's Office, which dealt with the force administration. He came back into uniform as a Sergeant, and then Inspector, but was always happiest on administration, preferring this to practical work. However, he finally achieved Superintendent rank.

111 Bill Marshall. He joined towards the end of our training. More of him later.

112 O'Leary. Similar in build to Marsh, he came from outside Dudley. He was a smooth talker, full of 'Blarney', quite shrewd, never quite achieved promotion, and ended after a mixed career as Coroners Officer.

Our training was to be completed before April 1927, when the extension of the Borough took effect. This had been the reason for our appointments. With the new districts to be taken over, Wolverhampton was to have two police divisions. Supt Haynes was to be in charge of A Division, which included most of the town centre, and Mr Crofts was to be Superintendent in charge of the newly formed B Division, which covered Bushbury, Low Hill, Fordhouses, Cannock Road, Wednesfield Road, Heath Town and Stafford Road areas.

Of the men from our squad earmarked to go to B Division were 96 Butcher, 97 Gribben, 98 Dinely, 99 Lear, 100 Bailey, 101 Windsor, 103 Rivers, 108 Clews, 109 Edwards, 110 Williams. I was rather pleased not to be going to B Division as I wanted the opportunity to make my own way unaided.

Meanwhile we continued our training. I was keen to put in the first report, anything so long as it exercised my newly acquired knowledge and was therefore delighted when an accident occurred outside Sloane's one evening. No-one was hurt; two motor vehicles were involved. I went to the scene and took all particulars which had to be done from memory. There was no aide memoire to help, and there is an awful lot of detail required even with the simplest accident. I came back into the house, and started roughing out my report – no proformas then, it all had to go in the right sequence on a miscellaneous report. I handed it in to 'Dusty' Smith next day, he read it through and congratulated me on my first effort; it was then processed in the usual way.

But to my disappointment, I was not the first. Dinely had just pipped me. The night before he had reported someone for using obscene language outside his lodgings. Our drill, by this time, was first class, so much so that a special parade was called on Friday afternoon at Yeomanry Riding School, and we gave a display to all the Force on how precision drill should be done. I can imagine the feelings of the spectators dragged out of bed for this. All went well, back and forth we went in fine style. 'Dusty' Smith was enjoying himself, showing off his lads. Unfortunately, the floor had been french chalked for a dance the night before, and on one spectacular 'About Turn', some slipped, and fell into a heap, to the delight of the spectators. However, a few threats from 'Dusty' on the likelihood of them staying and doing an hour's drill themselves soon stopped that!

This recalls an earlier incident when 'Dusty' was asking us what previous experience we had in drill. 'Coldstream Guards', 'Grenadier Guards' etc., as the experienced ex-servicemen replied in turn. I, of course, had to reply, 'No experience', but Rivers, ever naive, said that he had drilled in the 'Wolf Cubs'. This so shook 'Dusty' that he retired to a corner behind the bar of the canteen, and as he drank his pints, was heard to moan to the old bartender, 'Wolf Cubs, bloody Wolf Cubs.'

Our last stage of training was going to the courts to hear cases presented and evidence given. We were sent out on day beats with experienced men.

We had one memorable trip to Winson Green Gaol to learn how to act as escort. We were in plain clothes and sat in the back of the van taking the prisoners. One turned to me and said, 'How long have you got, mate?' I might have replied, 'Thirty years,' but I didn't think of it in time. He, poor chap, was going down for maintenance arrears. We were taken into the prison and everything of interest was explained to us.

On Parade – Night Duty

Came the great day. B Division came into being, and off went most of our squad. The rest of us were posted to night duty, to be shown around all the beats, of which there were twenty-four in A Division. It was still cold in April and greatcoats were the order. I should mention that our uniform, the serge and the topcoat had a tunic neck which was held together with a hook and eye so no shirt collar and tie were needed; all ranks wore this. I liked it far better than the later open front with collar and tie. It was much warmer, also you could wear warmer clothing underneath. One has to be out all night in wintry weather to realize how important that can be. Unlike today, you could not wear waterproof trousers, or a scarf, even rubber boots were frowned on, and you were not allowed to change from topcoats into tunics, and later from tunics into serges without a General Order from the Chief Constable authorizing it. The result was, as the seasons changed, one was either too hot, or literally frozen, as our fickle climate varied. It was good for uniformity, but uncomfortable for the out-of-doors men.

We paraded in the Parade Room on the Sergeant's whistle at 9.45 p.m. In came the Duty Inspector. 'Produce your appointments,' the sergeant would order, and we would produce a pair of handcuffs, and a staff from our pockets (the trousers having a special pocket made to hold the latter). The appointments would be held out in front, and the Inspector would cast a glance along the line, noting that every man was properly dressed and sober. 'Return your appointments,' he would say, and we would do so.

First, the sergeants would be detached, usually two of them to cover One and Two Sections. They would then make a note of who was detailed to their section, his ringing-in times, and the time he was due to return to the station for coffee break.

Next, the plain clothes men, usually two, whose job it was to visit and book the jewellers, banks, and pawnshops in the division. They were not subject to the same supervision as the beat men, and were usually middle-service men who could be trusted.

Next, we were detailed to our beats. The man's number would be called, say PC 51, he would reply with the beat or beats he was to work, say, 'one', or 'one and two', if working two beats, which was often the case if we were short of men, so it went on consecutively until beat 24 was reached. Ringing-in and coffee break times were given; the former was usually three times a night; the coffee break, 12. 45, and 1. 45, for half an hour.

The items of interest were read out, recent crimes, local persons wanted and so on. When all this was completed, came the order, 'Right Turn', and out we marched from Red Lion Street to Queen Square, before breaking off to the beats; some men broke off to visit the Charge Office to check on 'Special Attentions' – property requiring a visit during the night. Some places were always on 'Special Attention', jewellers, banks, pawnshops for example. Large houses would go on the list during the summer months when the occupants went on holiday. This usually applied to the beats on the fringe of the country. Times of visits had to be entered in the pocket book.

The 'Ringing-In' was done through a chain of pillar telephones spread throughout the whole of the Borough. There was a fire alarm for public use, and a telephone which could be reached by opening a door to which we all had a key on our whistle chain. Three pushes on a plunger, and we were in contact with the Charge Office, which was the operational centre in those days. All requests for any help had to go through the Charge Office – the telephone switchboard was manned day and night. On the bottom right hand side of the call box was a glass circle. If the station wanted a beat man, it was possible to drop a silver tab behind the glass circle, 'dropping the tab' we called it, and it indicated that he was required to call the station. Heaven help the man who took longer than half an hour to answer the tab. In an emergency, all the tabs would be dropped, and the information quickly passed. It was a good system before wireless was available. All beats had a call box or boxes.

To return to our first night. We recruits were allotted to a beat man, and remained with him all night, learning all there was to know about the beat. We new men all came off duty, exhausted after nearly eight hours walking and wearing the heavy uniform. Each night we would be allotted to a different beat until we had been around and learned them all. This was our first chance to get to know the older men who formed this force.

The Men of the Force

Most of the men were First World War veterans. Any man who saw active service in that war and survived carried the mark in some form or other for the rest of his life. They were tough men, hard, often brutal, and seemed so much older than we new boys. We were not received with any display of enthusiasm on their part. They generally considered showing us around was a nuisance, in many cases it interfered with their drinking. They had to show us the beats properly because it would rebound on them if they didn't, so any inclination to idle an hour away in a warm bakery, or pub, or any other place that offered warmth and company was fraught with some risk to them when showing round new, raw, unknown youngsters. The result was we were walked off our feet for a time. However, when asked if we drank (meaning beer, of course) we quickly learned that to maintain workable relations with the majority, it was better to say 'Yes'. We then saw the many devices used to get into certain pubs, always one or more on every beat. The time between 10.45 p.m. until after midnight was the critical period – the licensee would have washed up and balanced, the streets were becoming deserted, most of the trouble with drunks and family disturbances would have quietened down.

A gentle tap or taps on the right door or window, and we were in. Then a few quick drinks and chat, then away. Like everything else, some men took advantage, and overstayed their welcome; some did not like paying for their beer. I often wondered what the licensee got out of it. He sold a drop more beer, he kept well in with the police, but he took considerable risk too, if caught. When first dragged into this, I had great difficulty in drinking even half a pint. I'd never tasted beer before and didn't much care for it. Then we had to drink so quickly. I can truthfully say that most of our squad felt the same – they disliked this at first, but gradually got used to it, and even eventually liked it. This was how the whole sorry business was perpetuated.

Drink was an obsession with a lot of our men, always beer of course, ten pints during a session was nothing to them; I have heard figures quoted of up to twenty on a night off duty.

How this widespread police habit of beer drinking came about I cannot answer, it had been the case apparently almost from the inception of the service. It was certainly a widespread evil in our force at that time.

Countless numbers of good policemen, good thief takers, lost their jobs or missed their promotion through their addiction. It went on in the higher ranks too. The Superintendent frequently visited a French businessman who was famed for his fine cellar, and would stay there for hours, but at least he was off duty.

In a large pub one night the Inspector was drinking in the front bar, and two of his men, unknown to both, were drinking in the back bar. The whole town at that time had a reputation for drunkenness.

Even so, I never left any beat I was shown over, without knowing all there was to know about it. Apart from drinking, men usually worked their beats conscientiously. The Force was full of characters; we were only about 130 strong, but a more mixed bunch of men would be difficult to find. Not all drank, some were very sober, even religious in some cases.

Apart from the bulk of our men who were war veterans, there was a handful of men of all ranks who were pre-war entrants.

The Super, George Haynes, was a Boer War cavalry veteran. He retired about 1929–30, by which time all the pre-war men had gone.

He was a remote character, and I never heard him ever address the men, although he attended our famous dances, but never mixed. I encountered him once.

I was being carpeted, I suppose. It was in my first year. I had been on duty at midday in Princess Square in the town centre. A local character named Annie, an elderly drunk, was making herself a nuisance there. I went up to her and persuaded her to go home as she lived nearby in Charles Street. She thought at first I was going to arrest her, and was prepared to be very awkward, however, she agreed to go home quietly. I took her there with some difficulty for she was very drunk. Later, I reported her for being Drunk and Incapable. This simple action caused such a stir. 'Why had I not arrested her, whoever heard of a person being summoned for "D & I"?' I said I was instructed 'That when the ends of justice can be met without apprehending a person, proceed by summons'. 'Who told you that?' asked the three Inspectors who were debating what to do about this strange new procedure. I thought hard, and declared that I thought it was Chief Inspector Martin (who was now Chief Clerk) who had given us some instruction. They went away and consulted some more. Later I was instructed to present myself to the Superintendent's office. 'Dusty' Smith, who was now an Inspector, took me in. I don't think I was on any charge as the usual formalities had not been followed. The Superintendent was quite kind, really, and made a profound statement which I never forgot. 'You have to decide in a few minutes what a judge and jury may take days to decide.' I was then told I should have arrested her, and brought her to the station. That was my first and only appearance before my superiors for any misconduct, if that is the right word.

But it was the panic caused by an unexpected and unusually simple action that stayed in my mind – after all the long history of police procedure, I had to find one that had not been tried before.

To return to our manpower, apart from those I have mentioned, a few others had joined well after the War, but before we were appointed. These would be men making good losses through retirement, death or dismissal.

After working six weeks on night duty, we were to work 6 a.m.–2 p.m. and 2 p.m.–10 p.m. day shifts, before returning to night duty for another month. This was to be the pattern for the next few years.

I had my first case while working a night beat, in fact it was my first night alone. I found a motor lorry parked in a side street, with no lights showing, at 11 p.m. A simple enough case, and yet it had some repercussions. I went to great trouble to describe the condition of the lamps on the lorry; they were candlelamps, and the candles had burnt down, no wick left, only a little grease. The lampholder was stone cold etc.

Instead of waiting until 6 a.m. before reporting off duty, I went into the station at 5.30 a.m., and stated that I had come in to make out an offence report. Again the establishment was dumbfounded – you did not in those days leave your beat to make out reports without authority; usually you had to make them out in your own time. However, Inspector Hayes was kindly, put me right, and sent me back again. The case came to court a few weeks later. I gave my evidence (which I had learned by heart) and went into some details about the condition of the lamps. The Stipendiary Magistrate was impressed, fined the poor chap rather heavily, and commented on my detailed evidence. The Staffordshire County Superintendent was also in court as Staffordshire cases too were heard by the Stipendiary. He later spoke to Jack Crofts of how impressed he was with the evidence of 'that young man'.

The first spell on night duty gave all of us our first taste of traffic control point duty. There was a crossing in the town centre at Salop Street, which took traffic from the west towards Birmingham and Walsall. It was always very busy and we worked it for an hour from 10 p.m. – 11 p.m., Saturdays until 11.30 p.m., or until all was quiet. Saturdays was the drunken revelry night when the men went home drunk and beat up their womenfolk, particularly if the 'Wolves', the local football team, had lost. It was known that a police officer was available at Salop Street, and invariably on Saturdays, the man there would be called to some family disturbance in the near vicinity. The area on the south side of the point was very rough indeed and the same people usually caused the trouble. But to return to my first point duty experience. We all knew we would have to do it, so we watched the professionals at work, and practised it in our training. I was made to don the white coat, and took up my position in the centre of the road. The traffic at night was not heavy, just intermittent. I raised my hand in the approved manner, to stop one line of traffic in front and behind, whilst I beckoned on that which was to proceed. To my surprise, the traffic signalled obeyed. Did they not realize I was only a new recruit – evidently not – my confidence grew. This was power and authority if you like. I was never the same again. I was at last realizing that I carried authority, it grew on me, and as the years rolled by it became part of me, so much so that even after I retired, I still found myself taking charge without thinking of various situations that arose. The strange thing is that one carries this aura to such an extent that people respond, recognizing the authority. Of course we all loved this experience, the time was to come when point duty would become an unwanted chore, but not yet.

Day Duty

At last we could display ourselves in daylight to the citizens of our adopted town, and show them what they were getting for their money. We were in tunic order. This was a smart form of dress, just like guardsmen wore, except that it was blue instead of crimson. We wore helmets, except in high summer when we changed into lighter serge uniform, and wore flat caps with a white cover on fine days.

We looked very smart, and took great pride in our appearance. We paraded as for nights, but the duties were different. Points had to be covered (there were as yet no traffic signals), reliefs arranged; usually points were relieved every half hour if busy, every hour if less busy. If schools were open, children had to be seen across busy roads. Obstructions were an obsession in our force. Idlers, and there were plenty of unemployed to fit that category, were not to gather in the town centre. The railway drive was infested with a small crowd of unemployed scroungers, who pestered passengers to let them carry their luggage. With the Railway Police, we waged continual war against them, but never got rid of them. In my time we knew them all by name and reputation; it was like a long drawn-out game.

The main streets in the town centre had car parking problems then as now. Some places were forbidden to parkers, and one man was kept for years just patrolling Victoria Street, and reporting anyone parking there. My first job was to stay at the mouth of Dudley Street and Snow Hill to prevent any traffic entering Dudley Street. This was, and is, a main shopping area. I took up my position, gave my appropriate signals, and quite enjoyed it. I was a little hurt when later Evelyn Sloane said that girlfriends of hers said that every time I turned, I did a step of the 'Charleston' (a popular dance). It showed one thing, anyway – we were attracting attention. The town was small then, about 130,000 population. People knew one another. We had one old CID man who claimed that he knew whenever a stranger came into town. The influx of twenty new, young presentable policemen was bound to be noticed, by the girls if no-one else! The police were well thought of then. I went to a dance one night at the Victoria Hotel which was organized by the Butchers' Association. I went alone and knew no-one. As soon as I entered, the President, who managed a Dewhurst branch, came over and said, 'Ah, one of our young policemen, welcome.' He then introduced me to his party, who made me feel at home. It was there that Miss Sherwood, who was one of the party, gave me a message to take to Bert Onions, whom I mentioned earlier, thus beginning their romance. I, too, became interested in another member of the party – Gertie Fox. Her father had a coal business, was pretty well off, and Gertie was his only child. We kept company for a short time, she was a nice girl, but I was not ready yet for the settling down stakes, and we parted amicably.

Which brings me back to Louie Baggott. I went to see her less and less. For one thing, it was not easy when working shifts. For another, I had lost interest – getting tied up to any girl at twenty years of age, and on the threshold of a new life, became unattractive. Eventually, she sent me a short letter, asking me my intentions; she said that someone else was interested in her and therefore would like matters settled. I wrote back and ended the affair – that was the last I heard of Louie. I hope she made something of her life. She was my first girlfriend, and she taught me a great deal.

Meanwhile, I had changed my Rudge motorcycle for a BSA inclined engine job. It was a nice machine, and much faster. Shortly after I bought it I went on a short holiday to Weston-Super-Mare. The engine started to fail going up a steep hill. I diagnosed trouble with the push rod operating the overhead valves but I did not have a spanner that would fit the nut I needed to tighten. However I managed to get as far as a pub called the King William where I saw a similar machine. I went into the pub and found that the machine was owned by a young naval officer. I told him my trouble, and he came out and lent me the required spanner, with which I completed the adjustment. Forty years later, when I was at the Civil Defence Staff College, I was chatting to my Commandant, Vice Admiral Sir Nicholas Copeman about motorcycles we had owned. It turned out that he was the young naval officer at the King William. Such a strange coincidence.

Cricket

During the summer of our first year, the men responsible for running the force football team, and the cricket team, came among us looking for new talent. Cricket was the first. Those of us who expressed interest were taken one evening to the West Park, one of the town's two parks, and were tried out. It emerged that Marsh was a good fast bowler, Gribben and Phillips, fair batsmen. This culminated in Marsh and I being chosen to play in the season's key fixture, the two matches against

Birmingham City's D Division. The first match was played on the Wolverhampton Cricket Club ground at Tettenhall. It was a lovely ground, and Wolverhampton, who also had an annual fixture with us, were a very good side, mainly comprising the sons of prominent businessmen. To return to the match against D Division; this had been played for many years, and I suppose, probably still does, under new team titles. It was always a needle match, and was attended by the top brass of both forces. Birmingham batted first, and made a poor score of something like 70 all out.

We batted little better, as it was a bowler's day. I was last man in and we needed seven runs to win. Oh, the drama of it all, it reminded me of the famous poem, 'There's a breathless hush in the close tonight'. 'Get the runs and I'll buy you a hat,' shouted Jack Crofts as I went out to bat. Tommy Marsh was the other batsman. Here we were, we two raw recruits, with the honour of the Force in our hands, and before an audience that was all-powerful as far as we were concerned. We gathered the runs one by one, I probably got three, and Tommy four; he made the winning hit.

Pandemonium broke out, we were both carried off the field shoulder high – my first and only experience of this precarious method of locomotion. We were thrilled to bits! That evening, at the usual dinner given to the visiting team, we were mentioned in the speeches, and Marsh was given a small present as he had taken a few wickets as well. It was all great fun.

The sequel was, that bearing in mind Jack Croft's promise, I bought myself a new trilby hat for the enormous price of 17/6 (old money). I duly gave him the receipt in the canteen one night. He then told me that what he meant was that he would buy me a 'Wolverhampton Police Cricket Club' cap if we got the runs, not a trilby. However, he laughingly gave me the money. That was the best hat I was able to buy for years.

Football

We produced one or two men for this team too, although I was not interested. We had a good, if rough, football team, but shortly afterwards, something happened somewhere else in the county which changed matters. A policeman received leg injuries playing football, was declared unfit for duty and had to resign. It was held that men played sport at their own risk; football is hard on the legs, a policeman has to take care of his as they have to stand up to long hours of punishing work for 25–30 years. The death knell of the football team had been sounded!

Social Life

Shift work places limitations on this. We would take a girl out in the afternoon if on night duty, or in the evening if on early turn. On late turn, one only had the morning, which is hardly a period of social activity. In the winter we had a number of dances every week, organized by a host of people, either as a social activity, or to raise funds. Many of the large firms in the town held an annual dance and there was a Military Ball run by the British Legion. The churches ran dances, particularly the Roman Catholics. The Royal Orphanage ran a two-night affair, with a huge whist drive as part of the entertainment. The prizes were valuable – bicycles, suites of furniture, and so on, worth a few hundred pounds.

These dances were held at the swimming baths, which would be adapted by covering the two pools with flooring. One hall was all dancing, the other served firstly as a whist room, probably a couple of hundred playing. After the whist was finished, the hall would be made over to dancing, with another band playing. There would be refreshments and a bar, and these activities went on until 1 a.m., occasionally 2 a.m., and once until 3 a.m.

So when we finished later turn at 10 p.m., it only took about thirty minutes to dash home and change, then off to the 'Baths' for a night's entertainment, with no worries about having to get up early next day. We also went when on early turn, but one tended to get a bit tired, as it was rather like 'burning the candle at both ends'. Dances were also held at the two major hotels, the Star and Garter and the Victoria. These were smaller and usually more expensive functions.

There were the theatres, the Grand for musical comedies, opera and plays etc.; the Hippodrome which played variety twice nightly; and the Theatre Royal, a repertory theatre playing melodramas. Alas, only the Grand now survives. There were cinemas-a-plenty, eight in all. We could go into any of these in those early days on production of our warrant cards, a concession which lasted for years and was greatly appreciated. The idea was that the manager knew he had a policeman handy in case of trouble. I used all these facilities frequently and was and still am a great cinema fan.

We had our local football team, Wolverhampton Wanderers, to whom I eventually changed my allegiance from my old team, Birmingham

City, who never seemed to win anything. We had a greyhound track, and sometimes motorcycle dirt track racing. There was a horse race track at Dunstall Park.

But I suppose the greatest source of entertainment for young single men in their twenties was, and still is, girls! I had quite a few girlfriends from all sections of our society, as did my colleagues similarly placed. And it was about this time that I became involved in a few torrid romances!

Poppy Critchlow

She was the daughter of a retired and wealthy butcher who had once employed my Uncle Fred Stonier in Birmingham. The family was well known to, and friendly with my family, and Mrs Collier.

I met Poppy at a dance organized by the Oddfellows Friendly Society. It was an evening dress affair, with men wearing dinner jackets, or tails. I cannot remember how the family, the Murrays and the Colliers came to be there as we did not usually meet in those kind of circumstances. But it was a splendid affair, and having been introduced, Poppy and I became interested in each other. She was not particularly pretty, rather I would say 'striking' – tall, slim, always expensively and beautifully dressed. She was highly articulate, having been college educated, not that the two things are synonymous. It was a short and sharp affair, we were infatuated with each other and I was invited to go to her home, Milford House at Bakewell in Derbyshire, to meet her family at Christmas. This I did, taking my evening clothes as requested. I remember the journey so well, it was snowing and was altogether very Christmassy. I was introduced to her parents and met her elder brother and sister. Everyone was kindly but obviously not overenthusiastic, and I quickly realized that Poppy was more or less engaged to a local boy named Frank Nelson, whose family were in the meat trade and quite well off. I was an interloper, and a policeman's prospects were hardly sufficient or ever likely to be adequate to support Poppy in 'the manner to which she was accustomed'. My sister Ethel had apparently pointed this out to Poppy when my family could see the way things were going. Poppy had insisted to Edith that she loved me, and that was all that mattered. Edith had kindly told her that what I earned would hardly keep her (Poppy) in silk stockings.

On the evening of my arrival at Milford House, we went to a local dance, at which Poppy had intended to produce me like a rabbit out of a hat, to her girlfriends. I had a whale of a time – poor Frank was there too, but quite out in the cold.

I stayed until about midday the following day, and returned to Wolverhampton, as my short leave was over. Poppy and I had a heart to heart talk: I had apparently made a good impression, her mother thought I was a very nice boy, but she still considered Frank to be the best choice for Poppy.

We met a few more times in Birmingham, where Poppy stayed with the Colliers. It was all hopeless, of course. I had no money, and no inclination towards marriage. Poppy had a safe bet at home, she would have been a fool to throw it all away. We sadly parted in a final passionate meeting near, of all places, my old Sunday School in Black Pit Lane, Ward End.

Betty Fulton

She was a barmaid, dark, with slightly irregular teeth which I always found attractive. I met her at a dance at the 'Baths'. I was with cousin John Holland, who had come from Birmingham for a night out. Betty and I became very attached. She was married, but she and her husband did not get on too well together.

I was, at this time, a bit fed up with single girls – they always seemed to be trying to entrap a man into marriage, and I was not ready.

Our affair went on for about two years. We went dancing, or out on my motorcycle, or to the cinema. She left Wolverhampton and was barmaiding in Birmingham, so I used to ride over there to meet her. Her husband did not seem to mind what she did. She was working, and to that extent was fairly independent. She told me she was unable to have children, but twelve months later our affair ended when she became pregnant.

I saw her many years later during the War, by which time she had three children. She was living then at a farm near Wolverhampton, and knowing where I could be found, as I was an ARP celebrity, she had brought me a dozen eggs – a godsend then. So I must have made a fairly good and lasting impression on her. Well, enough of that aspect of life for the time being.

Chapter VI

Police Duties

Hollands and the Family

During the latter part of the twenties Hollands' milk business ran into serious trouble, and eventually they were declared bankrupt. Uncle Phil and Aunt Phoebe were helped by his South African brother, and put in a small farm in Worcestershire. The boys found jobs, and the girls were married, except the youngest.

At home, Walter's wife had died of an overdose of pills – she had become a heavy drinker, and had other vices too. He was now living at home with my parents, who were quite happy at Four Oaks. I went to see them as often as I could. Father loved to hear tales of my life in the Force, but he would continually try to cap my stories.

Arrests

Back at work, I had made my first arrest. One night I was working Dudley Street, when I was called to a disturbance in St John Street, a side road. On arrival at the scene – a fish and chip shop – I found a man drunk in charge of a motorcycle combination. I decided to arrest him, and brought him to the station, where he was later examined by the Police Surgeon, who agreed. The man was charged and placed in the cells until fit to be discharged on bail to appear in court the following morning, while I collected his motorcycle combination. Next day he was brought up in court. I cannot remember how he pleaded – 'Guilty', I expect, as he was not defended. I went into the witness box, took the oath, and started to recite my evidence. Suddenly, my mind went blank. I could not remember a word. The silence seemed interminable, then I heard a voice; it was the Clerk of the Court who sat just below where I was standing. 'Go on, you are alright,' said this always kindly man. I pulled myself together and completed my evidence. I doubt if anyone other than the Clerk and I knew what had happened. The man was convicted. I thanked Mr Jones, the clerk, to whom I later explained my trouble. He laughed it off and said, 'You did very well, really.'

My next arrest was quite different – it never got to court. I was on duty in Chapel Ash around 9.30 p.m. where it was fairly quiet, but it always was, there. Then I was told of a fight going on in Clarence Street, a poorish quarter behind the rather classy Chapel Ash facade. I went there and saw a large muscular man holding another man against a wall, and punching him. He looked as if he would bash him to death. I dragged the assailant off the victim, who ran for his life. We fell to the ground, struggling. Fortunately, I was sober, and he was drunk, and I fell on top of him – he was large enough to eat me. I managed to handcuff him, and whilst I was doing this, his wife, who had fetched me in the first place, knocked off my helmet and generally set about me. Then one or two passers by dragged her away and we got to our feet. It appeared that 'Bill', the handcuffed one, had found the victim (now disappeared) making love to his wife, and thought he was justified in his actions. We were now quite calm. I told Bill he would have to come to the police station, as I was arresting him. He came quietly enough. I unlocked the handcuffs, and on the way he told me that he was a brewer's drayman, employed by Banks' Brewery. He hoped I would not charge him with assault on the police, although he didn't mind the other. On arrival at the station, I explained the facts to Sgt Neal who was on reserve. He decided that in view of the provocation Bill had received, and as no harm had come to me, he would refuse the charge, and let Bill go. I did not mind greatly as I had got to quite like this genial giant called Bill. Ever after that, for years in fact, whenever Bill rode by on the brewery lorry, he always had a wave for me.

This was my first encounter with Sgt Neal. He was a smart cockney, who had worked many years in the CID. I was told that as I walked up the station yard towards the Charge Office on one occasion, he said to his PC in the office, 'Look at him, he has got more edge on him than a rag man's trumpet.' Strange that a few years later, when he was at home dying with cancer, I went to visit him, and by then we were quite good friends.

Point Duty Incidents

When I joined, we had five fixed points in Wolverhampton for about two or three years, until the installation of traffic signals, and were one of the first towns in the country to install them. At about the same period our old-fashioned tram service using tram lines changed over to trolley buses. We were, I believe, the very first town to do this. But to return to the fixed and other points.

Queen Square, Princess Square, Snow Hill, Queen Street and Salop Street were worked from 9 a.m.–6 p.m. by a small team who for several years did this work only. They were all very good at it, and were indicated to us as an example on which to pattern ourselves.

There was 'Big Jim', a giant of 6ft 7in., gentle, placid, with a dry humour. He was very popular in the town, and was one of our showpieces. Alas, as a policeman he was hopeless – I cannot remember him ever having a case. When point duty ended, poor Jim had to work a beat, his moments of glory gone for ever. He completed his service at twenty-five years, and retired to a caretaker job at Bantock House, a kind of museum. He was very strong, and jokingly picked me up with one hand in the police yard one day; it is strange how often giants are gentle. Jim did very well at Christmas time from his admiring public!

Then there was 'Taffy' Watkins, who had only a couple of years more service than us, but he had been picked for this plum job with its delightful hours of 9 a.m.–6 p.m. for some obscure reason; he was very good at it. He later courted and married the daughter of a prominent Labour councillor and alderman, who was a member of the Watch Committee and later became Mayor for one year. Despite this, and the fact that 'Taffy' was a good policeman, he never got promotion. He had spells in various departments, including the CID, but he never made it. Then there were Chance, and Dawson, who both became inspectors in due course.

Finally, Joe Tonks – a character from Walsall. He came from a fairly well-off family, but he was destined for disaster. Going bald, with a 'Charlie Chaplin' moustache, regular features, and rather a dandy dresser, Joe was a proper man-about-town when off duty. He was, unfortunately, addicted to drink. He was reported several times for drinking offences, and got away with it every time during David Webster's reign. However, on the arrival of the next Chief Constable, Joe did it once too often, and was dismissed – a pity, as he was good company. He became an insurance agent, but his path was always downhill.

These were the regular pointsmen; we others relieved them every half hour for a walk around. Other points were worked entirely by men of the relief.

We used what was then a novel method of pulpits – large, wooden pulpits, which elevated us, and gave a little protection laterally from the weather, and were infinitely superior to standing in the road. It was only very rarely that one was knocked over.

I was relieving Chance one day on Snow Hill point, standing in my pulpit, quite enjoying it all. It was a difficult place at which to do point duty as a large statue of Sir Charles Villiers (a dead and gone town luminary) stood in the way of proper control. This, at times, necessitated giving signals not in the book. For example, traffic coming along Cleveland Street, wishing to turn right towards the Birmingham Road – you had to stop three other lines of traffic, this meant a fore and aft stop signal with one arm raised, and the other out at right angles to stop traffic coming from front and back. It was also necessary to stop traffic coming from the left, which meant a separate signal in that direction. Having only two arms, this was rather difficult. The drill was to raise the right arm above the head to stop this traffic, then drop the hand and give formal fore and aft signals. I had seen it done successfully dozens of times and had done it myself dozens of times. On this memorable day, I did it once too often. A heavily laden milk lorry was coming up Cleveland Street, and the driver wanted to turn right towards Birmingham. It was uphill for him. I gave him preference and called him on. I then stopped the fore and aft traffic after I had signalled a steam lorry coming from Cleveland Road to stop. Alas, the steam lorry driver must have misread my signal, for to my horror he came 'batting on'. By this time the milk lorry had half negotiated his right-hand turn across the path of the steamer. There was the most almighty crash – steam blowing off, the clatter of falling milk churns, Snow Hill flowing with spilled milk. I stood in my pulpit and the thought crossed my mind, 'Look, all your own work'. No-one was hurt; I looked for witnesses; the first one started to tell a story the reverse of what I had intended, so I stopped halfway through his statement. I found another person who agreed with my version – so much for witnesses. I had to report the steam lorry driver for the usual offences, and the case duly came to court. I gave my version. The defending solicitor said, 'Did you not start to take a statement from a witness, and then stop?' I had to think quickly. 'Yes,' I said. 'Then why did you stop?' came the next question. 'Well, when I realized where the witness was standing, I saw that he could not possibly have seen what signal I gave,' I answered. This was to some extent true, and I got away with that. What finally sank me was when the solicitor asked me to reproduce my signal. I did so, and he rightly pointed out that it was not an orthodox signal from the book. I argued that this point could not be worked in an orthodox way. I lost – case dismissed. I left the court feeling my career was in ruins. I confessed my fears to an old grizzled sergeant who was visiting me during the afternoon; he laughed, and told me not to worry, worse things than that would happen to me. I got a lot of mileage out of that story when I was instructing police recruits many years later.

I once worked Darlington Street point, which was very busy, for five and a half hours, in the winter, without relief, or a visit from any senior officer. I was on 6 a.m.–2 p.m. early turn. The night before I had attended the 'Hippodrome Ball' at the 'Baths'. This was a popular event because the showgirls always attended, plus the stars. I went with a friend, a bus inspector named Jack Mills. He was a little older than I, but we were good friends until he married. After the dance we somehow got invited with some of the Hippodrome girls to a party at the Molineux Hotel. We remained there drinking and frolicking until about 5 a.m. – I was on duty at 5.45 a.m. A quick rush home, changed into uniform, and I just made it in time. I did the usual property checks and beat working until breakfast at 8.15–8.45 a.m. I then took up the Darlington Street point wearing my white helmet and white coat, in time to catch the 9 o'clock traffic coming into town.

I was, as might be expected, not feeling very bright, but I never expected to be left there without a relief for 5½ hours. I had never heard of it happening before. By the time 1 p.m. came round, I couldn't care what the traffic did, I was tired and fed up! However, I was eventually relieved by the late turn man at 2.10 p.m. I went home, had a meal, and went to bed, where I remained until it was time for the next day's duty.

Another small incident. I was working Chapel Ash Point, when Johnstone, of the famous Layton and Johnstone duetists, who were playing at the Hippodrome that week, came to me and asked me to direct him to Bullocks Racing Stables. I was an admirer of these two, and felt quite thrilled at having met one of them. He went back to a magnificent car, and drove off with a wave to me.

Every morning at 8.50 a.m. David Webster, our Chief, would ride in state along Tettenhall Road past Chapel Ash point, and on to town. He was driven always by his police chauffeur Sgt Franks. We had to be ready to give him a smart salute. He was often dressed in a light grey frock coat, and grey topper, always a buttonhole. He was a great socialite and a heavy drinker.

The End of the Twenties

This was a difficult period for Jack Crofts. There was a great deal of intrigue going on for the vacant job of Superintendent when Mr Haynes retired.

The job of Superintendent at B division was only a second-grade appointment, the plum job was superintendent of A division. Jimmy Aston, the CID Chief Inspector, was working hard to get the job, and had managed to convince David Webster that he was the man. The result was a campaign to make life unbearable for Jack Crofts, hoping he might be forced to resign, and make the way clear for Aston. I only heard vague rumours of this, and the few occasions when Uncle Jack mentioned it.

Also, during this period, he lost his youngest daughter, Phyllis. She contracted meningitis and died after a long and brave battle. I acted as a bearer at her funeral, along with other young police officers.

Whatever intrigues were going on at the top, Jack Crofts was generally greatly liked and respected by the Force, and by the public who knew him. The matter came to an end when Webster died of cancer after a short illness. He had a splendid funeral, and there were representatives from all the surrounding forces. We marched about 1½ miles from Police Headquarters to Jeffcock Road cemetery. Slow march was the order, to the 'Dead March from Saul'. Several hundred well-drilled men was an impressive sight, and was even more impressive to be a member of it.

The body was lowered into the grave, and I was ordered to remain behind, and stay there until the grave was filled in. All our men marched off, a few dozen morbid spectators rushed to the grave to have a last look at the coffin, and nearly pushed me in. As the grave was filled, I had a strange feeling of the futility of it all. Here was a man, a power in the town, given all the pomp and circumstance at his funeral, then left to be buried with a raw recruit as his bodyguard. I went home in a very reflective mood.

General Reflections on the Roaring Twenties

As the decade came to an end, let me give a point of view of this now distant, and often wrongly quoted period. When it began, the country was going through the false honeymoon period of plenty, following the First World War. Everything seemed wonderful for about two years, then the decline of employment began, and continued until about

1936–7. Eventually, as is now well known, the figure of unemployment reached 3,000,000 plus, and the dole queues became a familiar sight in every town and village in the country. I saw, in Wolverhampton, how men I knew and respected, good skilled tradesmen, stood in line, week after week, gradually becoming more and more shabby and dejected. The attitude of the more fortunate, as always, was 'They don't want work, useless lot', and so on. It was surprising what men would do to earn a few bob. The general standard of living was poor. I went into many houses in my early service and saw examples of the most appalling poverty. The rubbish that some people were forced to eat, such as 'cag mag', meat sold late at night on the market patch by butchers about to close down, meat they would have destroyed next day.

We had a 'Chief Constable's Poor Children's Boot Fund'. Funds were raised by an annual charity week at the Grand Theatre, organized by the Wolverhampton Operatic Society. The boots were purchased and distributed to deserving poor children, of which there were always too many.

But there was another side. At the start of the decade, dances in Birmingham were held in schoolrooms at night, with small three- or even two-piece bands. The dances were the waltz, old-fashioned style, the Maxina, Veleta, military two-step, and the Lancers.

The Palais de Danse which opened in Birmingham in the early twenties was the nearest we got to the 'high life'. It was a lavish set-up, with a dance floor surrounded by tables, cabaret style. There were two American bands, and on Saturday nights admission was five shillings – a lot of money then, and one had to wear evening dress. Between the schoolrooms and the Palais there were hosts of other dance places, church rooms and masonic halls.

The foxtrot emerged, and became the 'rage', as the saying was. Before long the foxtrot, quick and slow, the waltz, and the tango were the main dances. The old-fashioned dances were still performed, but only as novelties.

The cinema was still highly popular. In 1929 I went with a girlfriend to see and hear the *Singing Fool* with Al Jolson starring – not a dry eye in the house; the impact of the 'talkie' was quite staggering.

Football and cricket were popular, but overshadowing all was the national cancer of unemployment, which seemed to eat away at the moral fibre of the country. The dole money was quite insufficient to support families. The pressure on wages became acute, leading to strikes, lock-outs, and culminating in the General Strike of 1926.

I was too young to be greatly affected by all this, as I was never out of work, and can only speak as an observer, yet one who knew that any slip on his part could put him among that hopeless class, the unemployed; it was a good disciplinarian. This I can say: the 'Roaring Twenties' was no fun time period for the mass of people in this country. Whatever went on in London's West End was no true reflection of what was happening elsewhere in the country where it became a struggle for survival of the grimmest kind.

Wages and Conditions

My wages when I joined the Force in 1927 were £3–10, old money, 6 shillings per week rent allowance, and 1 shilling per week boot allowance. This was good pay, increments every year for five years being dependent on good conduct, and proficiency made it better. One needs to realize that the pay of an express train driver, the aristocrat of the working class, was only about £5 per week at that time. From this, one can see that the Police were a well-paid body. It was splendid pay for a single man, although it didn't go very far when married.

Promotion did not raise the pay very much – a top-grade constable earned almost as much as a first-year sergeant; in fact, a top-grade CID constable, with his allowances, received more than a first-year sergeant. Of course, in time, the sergeant's increments put him well ahead. The next stage to inspector was much the same. A source of extra income was our special duty. Police could be hired for football matches, horse racing, dog racing, cinemas, theatres, auctions of animals, and big sales of property. Some of these were regular occurrences. Night duty men did football matches and race meetings, early turn men the others. The pay was good as a day at the races would bring in about 25 shillings, a football match 12/6 to 15/-, dog racing about 7/6 (all old money). This extra money, coming as it did fairly regularly, was a godsend to a married man, but a bit of a bind to a single one. You could nominate someone else to do a special duty for you, but it was not often done.

We had a three-day flower show every year, a great occasion which was nationally popular, and was held in the West Park. We detested it. We had to do some 15–20 hours overtime and were paid only subsistence money, about 6/- per day. We were supposed by regulations to be given time off in lieu, but nobody ever got this, so it was a standing joke how much flower show time one had owing. It was exploitation which would not be tolerated today. The reason given was that if inspectors gave time off, in a small force like ours, it meant stripping the beats. This posed a risk for the Inspector, in case of a spate of breakings-in, or some calamity for which he might be held accountable because he had injudiciously stripped the beats. Thus, playing it safe, it was easier to impose on the men, than risk falling foul of higher authority.

'Time off' was always allowed for a night man to attend court – he came off duty at 4 a.m. instead of 6 a.m. to enable him to get some sleep before attending court at 11 a.m. The worst ordeal was two days' racing. Good pay, of course, but it meant going off duty at 6 a.m., at the racecourse by 10 a.m., there until 5.50 p.m., on night duty again at 9.45 p.m. The same again next day. By this time, men were so tired it was common to walk along asleep and fall off the pavement. Reasonable inspectors would give two hours off to as many men as possible, each night, but even so, it was quite an ordeal.

General Inspection

Once a year the Home Office, which contributed a substantial part of police expenditure, sent an Inspector of Constabulary to examine the force and its records, to report on the state of efficiency.

As soon as notification of the visit was received, the whole force was thrown into a ferment. Drill parades were arranged. All issued uniform had to be brought into the parade room, and laid out in neat bundles for inspection. All force records were gathered for easy collection on the great day. All members collected their pocket books since the last inspection. Vehicles were cleaned, fire appliances, always immaculate, were cleaned again.

Came the great day. Usually we paraded in the police yard, confined as it was, for drill purposes, but on my first inspection it was held at the West Park. On this occasion, His Majesty's Inspector of Constabulary was a Mr Norman de Courcey Parry. He never inspected us again, and probably took over another part of the country. I heard nothing of him until fifty-two years later when I was in the process of writing these notes, and had completed the part on General Inspection while watching a programme on the exploits of a certain Percy Topless, who was involved in a mutiny of the British Army at Étaples in France in 1917. While on the run later, he shot and killed a taxi driver, wounded a policeman, and two gamekeepers in Scotland, and threatened another police officer with firearms, in what is now, Cumbria. He was eventually cornered by the Police of Cumbria. There were three armed officers in a car at the time, and Topless died from a bullet. Some people thought that the police had shot him, but the police said Topless shot himself.

To my surprise, there on the TV screen, being interviewed as a police participant in the final stage, was Mr de Courcey Parry. He looked fit and well, and spoke quite authoritively and responsibly. Now His Majesty's Inspectors of Constabulary were usually retired Chief Constables, I never met one who was less than fifty years old. This must have put Mr de Courcey Parry at least in his nineties, probably over the century. I think the interviewer might have remarked on this! Later I realized that the man I saw was de Courcey Parry's son who was a young stripling when Topless was cornered but as he aged, looked just like his father all those years earlier.

But to return to general inspections (the next year we had a new man). We paraded, and as the great man came down the steps from the Chief Constable's Office, accompanied by the Chief Constable and members of the Watch Committee plus the mayor, the Drill Parade Inspector called out, 'General Salute'. The officers saluted and the men stood to attention. The ranks were then inspected, the HMI speaking to some of the men.

The CID were formed up separately, as were the mounted men, about six in number, and as they became a unit later, the motor patrol section.

All were inspected briefly, in turn. After my first year, all our inspections were conducted by a Lieut. Col. Allen, an ex-Chief Constable. He was a very small man of the usual army appearance, good clothes, short moustache, sharp eyes and incisive speech.

He was a stickler for drill and always had a display of it. We had a fine reputation for drill as a force, of which we were very proud. He had one foible: every year he fell out the junior sergeant and asked him to drill the men. We all thought it great fun, the junior sergeant excepted. He was usually scared to death, and unless an experienced drill sergeant would make a proper cock-up of it, to our great amusement. It always happened every year. After the parade we were told to collect our pocket books and go to the Quarter Sessions Court for the records exam, usually the toughest part of the whole proceedings. While we waited, the HMI inspected the laid-out uniforms and equipment. Eventually he arrived in the courtroom; all the CID and Admin. records and books were there, or readily available.

Meanwhile, the town was being policed by a few old-timers, and those it was policy to keep out of sight for one reason or another; either they were not very bright, or their appearance left something to be desired. It was considered to be a bit of a comedown to be allotted to duty on Inspection Day.

After we had resumed our seats, the HMI glanced around, and

perhaps looked through the Charge Book, picked out a particular crime, and followed it through the books from start to finish. Or he might pick on a day — any day — and ask if anyone had had an arrest on that day, and starting with the constable's pocket book (if it was a constable's arrest) follow that through including the visits from his sergeant and inspector, whose booking times had to agree one with the other — occasionally they did not, in which case they would be gently reproved by the HMI, with a promise of a much more severe wigging from the Superintendent, or even Chief Constable when it was all over. But it could also lead to commendation if a man was lucky and his best day chosen.

I was glad my Snow Hill epic was avoided. I was never called upon in my service to be questioned by an HMI, except on the matter of drill, of which more later on. Eventually the inspection came to an end, the HMI expressed himself satisfied and pleased with all he had seen, and we were dismissed.

Later, the Chief Constable would issue a General Order, expressing his appreciation of our efforts, and the Government Grant would be safe for another year. Occasionally when *we* thought it all over, the old fox would tour the streets, pick on some man and question him about his work, 'off the cuff' as it were, which was as it should be.

The introduction of Motor Patrol

I had, by 1929, my BSA inclined engine motorcycle, and had added a sidecar.

The Force vehicles were an ambulance and a van for collecting prisoners either off the streets or to convey them to Winson Green. We also had an old 'Clyno' open four-seater car for CID and general purposes, and an AIS motorcycle combination 8 HP twin. This latter was used for anything, CID chiefly, but also by a man patrolling on it in uniform, to keep an eye on the growing traffic problems. This was a new idea, and was pre-empting the powers to be given in 1930 to use mobile police for traffic purposes.

An officer named Sid Holland (previously mentioned) was the first. He had a good record for the arrest of thieves and good opportunities for advancement, but fouled everything up through his weakness for drink — at the Flower Show of all places!

One afternoon shortly after this, I was parading for late turn — 2 p.m. to 10 p.m. Billy Churchward was the relief inspector parading us. He opened up by saying, 'You can ride a motorcycle can't you, Stonier?'

A Brummie in Search of a Talent

This Page and following three pages: *Wolverhampton Borough Police. 1931.*

Characters mentioned, numbered from left to right:
Fourth Row: *25 Eccleston, (third from end)* Third Row: *19 Wykes* Second Row: *9 Philips; 10 Chance; 11 Big Jim Jones; 14 Rivers* Front Row: *1 Shale; 3 Marsh; 5 Granger; 6 Dineley.*

It shakes me somewhat when I realise that Wilf De LA Cour and I are probably the only two left alive today from that assembly. [1999]

Fourth Row: *27 Burge; 28 Watkins;* Second Row: *11 Brown (promoted with me); 13 Whetton; 14 Green* Front Row: *3 Jordan; 4 Ansell; 5 Balance; 7 Crofts; 8 Chief Constable Tilley.*

'Yes, Sir', I promptly answered. 'Right then, you take Eccleston, and go on motor patrol today.' That was how I began my next five years of motor patrol duties.

Out I went on the huge AIS combination with PC Eccleston in the sidecar. I forget our instructions, but they were of a pretty general nature. Out of Red Lion Street into Darlington Street, and on to the traffic signals there, which were showing 'red'. I applied my clutch and brake, both operating from the handlebars. Unfortunately, they were on the opposite side to my BSA. Before I could remedy the mistake we had sailed over the crossing against the red light – what a splendid start to my motor patrol career, I thought! Eccleston remained silent, frightened to death, no doubt. We remained on patrol all day, and had

Fourth Row: *28 De La Cour; 32 Ball* Second Row: *10 Holland; 15 Gribben;* Front Row: *1 part of Tilly; 2 Ashton; 3 Monks; 4 Churchward; 5 Dawson; 6 Franks; 7 Fire Brigade Inspector.*

a couple of speeding offenders, I recall. Our uniform was, of course, incongruous. To wear a top coat was bad enough, but a helmet on a motorcycle was ridiculous! I pointed this out to the Inspector, and asked if I could wear the flat summer cap, but adapt a chinstrap to keep it on. He agreed and so whenever I did this particular job that is what I wore. There was no issue of any kind of special gear until the Road Traffic Act of 1930 became operative when our equipment came in bits and pieces. We had to press for gauntlets, short coats, oilskin trousers and so on.

Of course, this was a time of financial stringency. The county and the town was hard up. Wolverhampton's failing motor car and motorcycle industries had been doing poorly for a long time. It was

Fourth Row: *22 the Author; 23 Balance (George)* Third Row: *17 Windsor; 19 Gwilliam; 26 'Alf Kyte'* Second Row: *7 Barber; 11 Williams; 15 Pendered* Front Row: *Mainly Fire Brigade, 2 Llewelyn; 3 Barnwell; 6 Howell*

the home of the 'Sunbeam' car and motorcycle, 'AJS', 'Star', 'Clyno', Guy Motors and Villiers mainly. Our town was saved at this time by the arrival of two great firms, who between them gave the place a blood transfusion: Goodyears and Courtaulds. They both established large plants and changed the pattern of life in the town. The Americans sent a large number of young executives and experts to teach the unskilled new labour force how to make tyres. These young men became a feature of the town's social life, and had loads of money to spend. Tod Sloane took the opportunity to invite a number of them to a champagne party. This was part of a campaign he engaged in to get his son Terence a good job at Goodyears; he succeeded, too.

Terence's engineering firm at Darlaston had no prospects for him at that time.

A Look Back on my First Three Years

As I plunged into my new role of motorcycle 'Cop', let me take stock.

I had survived my probation and knew all the beats. I had learned to pen a good report, and had a fair number of Court appearances behind me. There were no spectacular cases but I had a fair mixture, which had reasonably satisfied my superiors. I had obviously impressed the Stipendiary Magistrate favourably, for he gave me several pats on the back, and this was very important – to be trusted by the Bench was no mean achievement. With my comrades I had a good working relationship. This could have presented difficulties, as anyone related to a high-ranking officer was a little suspect.

I felt after three years I was trusted by my colleagues. I had achieved my first purpose – to be accepted as a working policeman. During this time we had lost three of our squad. I have briefly mentioned Mosely, who left after about two weeks. Then there was PC 99, Lear, who went after twelve or eighteen months. Finally, Billy Marshall. He was a tall, gingery, lanky youth who had joined the squad rather late in its training life. He was the son of a former force member who had died. He did, therefore, find quite a few of the older members who had known and liked his father. We had about six similar cases in our force, of sons who had followed their father.

Bill was a poor policeman, untidy and a drinker. He got away with it for a time, but eventually 'cooked his goose' as follows. We came off duty one morning at 6 a.m. and marched in as usual. The Inspector, Billy Churchward, checked the relief, and found Marshall missing. Now this is always a problem – has the man gone to sleep somewhere, or has something serious befallen him? One must remember that PC Willetts had been shot dead in our force in 1926 whilst on night duty, and was only discovered when he failed to report at 6 a.m. We had to wait while his beat was combed. At about 6.50 a.m., up the yard staggered Billy, helmet missing, uniform undone. It appeared he had drunk quite a lot the night before and had gone to sleep in a car in a garage he had found open. To make matters worse, it was the Mayor's car, and Billy had left behind his helmet. There was nothing that could be done to help him, and he was dismissed.

Discipline

I don't want to give the impression that discipline was lax in our force, quite the reverse in fact. Let me give some examples. There was little or no familiarity between the ranks, lines of demarkation were strictly kept. Untidiness of self or uniform was never tolerated, and men were not allowed to be slovenly off duty either – this was likely to bring discredit on the force, a wide-ranging phrase. Police trousers were not to be worn with civvies; hair had to be short back and sides. Any man caught sitting down, leaning against a building or gossiping, could be treated as a defaulter. We never sat down at football matches during the course of a match and were not allowed to wear extra outer clothing such as waterproof trousers, rubber boots or scarves. We could not marry without permission, and the prospective wife had to be vetted for respectability; usually poor old Wilf Fletcher had this unthankful job. No man or his wife was allowed to have any other occupation, nor could they engage in business. A man could not take any civil action without permission. Our chaps who had served in the Guards said our discipline was more strict. It was only on the question of beer-drinking that any relaxation was offered, and even in this, any man caught red-handed drinking on duty could expect dismissal.

Mayor's Sunday

Every November when the new Mayor was elected, he was taken to church for a service. In the procession were all the aldermen and councillors, the chief officers of the authority, and other invited dignitaries. After the church service, the Mayor was escorted back to the Town Hall where there was a specially erected platform, he took the salute of attending forces and services, the Territorials, Scouts, Girl Guides, St John's, Red Cross, Trade Councils, Volunteer Works Fire Brigades, and a number of other units. We, the Police, turned out in full ceremonial order, tunics, medals and best block-front boots. We took him to church and brought him back, and then waited in Corporation Street, by the side of the Town hall, to be the last to march past. We always had our tallest men in the leading ranks, with a contingent of Special Constables marshalled by Tod Sloane, and their quite splendid band. We always made a fine spectacle, and were undoubtedly in those days the 'Pièce de Résistance' of the whole parade. I always loved marching under those circumstances – there is a bit of exhibitionist in us all. After we were dismissed, we repaired to our canteen, unless on or about to go on duty. These gatherings on Mayor's Sunday were great occasions in the bar. Some men gave impromptu turns, and a special favourite was 'Flanagan's Band' sung by 'Ike' Howell, in which we all joined. 'Ike' was an ex-pro boxer who had been quite useful in his day, had a good war record and was greatly liked.

Shrewsbury Flower Show

Before I leave this period, there is one other affair I must mention – Shrewsbury Flower Show. This, with Chelsea and Southport, was the show of the year. It was held in high summer and we always sent a contingent. I had heard stories of what went on during the two-day show and I badly wanted to go. The men were carefully picked – they had to be trusted and to be presentable, as we were visiting another force's territory, in Shrewsbury. As Billy Churchward was in charge, and I was a bit of a favourite of his, I was chosen to go. We boarded the train in uniform, and off we went, playing cards, of course, all the way. On arrival at Shrewsbury, we marched in fine order to our hotel. We were about twelve or fourteen strong. After we had deposited our kit we reported for duty at the Flower Show. We were detailed to our various posts by about 10 a.m., usually on gate or marquee duty. There we remained for the next twelve hours. It was a long stint, but we were able to get away for half hours at a time, and go into the rear of the local pubs for a drink and some food. The pubs were open all day and we had no trouble going in the back and being served. The old hands knew all the ropes and I was taken along.

Time went reasonably quickly and eventually we marched back to our hotel where a splendid meal awaited us. After that, we had a concert in which all had to contribute. I remember I joined a chap named Leighton Jukes in a duet. We sang 'The Bells of St Mary's', which was well received. We carried on until about 1 a.m. and were all more or less drunk. Then to bed. I heard an uproar in some of the other rooms during the night, but ignored it.

Next morning it appeared that George Tongue, a big ex-artilleryman, had thrown a wash jug full of water over Roland Sutton, who was the Force champion sprinter; poor Sutton had presented himself in his sodden nightshirt to Inspector Churchward, asking for redress, which he did not get, of course. Another man got out of bed to relieve himself, and did it in Alf Kyte's boots, which he (Alf) only discovered when he put them on. For years after, there was a catchphrase in our force – 'Who pissed in Alf Kyte's boots?' So passed the night. Up early for a good breakfast which a number could not face, then another twelve-hour stint at the Flower Show. Time seemed to drag this time as many were feeling fragile. Finally when the show ended, we paraded and were thanked by the Shrewsbury Superintendent. We picked up our luggage, left the hotel and boarded the train for home. It was my first and only visit, and I quite enjoyed the experience.

Chapter VII

Motor Patrol Duties

As soon as the Road Traffic Act 1930 became law, three of us were appointed as Motor Patrol Officers: Reg Chettar, a dour kind of chap from Shropshire, and Arthur Burge, also from Shropshire. Chettar, I think, had worked on a farm, while Burge had worked for his father, a hairdresser. He was a mild-natured man, quite unlike our rough, tough, ex-war veterans. The force purchased a Sunbeam motorcycle combination from the local Sunbeamland firm. This was to be my machine, much to the envy of all my motorcycle colleagues. The Sunbeam was a very highly regarded machine. For some strange reason I was sent to take a week going through the factory. I never saw the reason for this as I was not a mechanic and we had men in the fire station to take care of that. However, it was an enjoyable experience. Tommy De La Hay was my guide throughout the week and we became quite friendly. He had won fame as a Tourist Trophy winner on a Sunbeam in the early twenties, hence his position as Competition Manager. Sunbeams were no longer a contender for TT honours; this was the era of the Norton and AJS, but they entered a number of reliability trials and did well. After the week at the factory, I took delivery of my new machine and started patrol. We had a new Chief Constable now. He was a Chief Inspector from Birmingham, named Edwin Tilley. He was ex-service and had been wounded during the War. He was a bandsman in the Birmingham Force and worked in the Chief Constable's Office. Chief Inspector was rather a low rank to obtain the top job in Wolverhampton, but the people in authority in our town were always a little in awe of their mighty neighbour, Birmingham, and its servants. He gave us a short address on his appointment. He was sparely built, very pale, and had the appearance of a rather cold fish. However, he proved to be an able administrator and soon started to make his presence felt. The Crofts-Aston friction was quickly resolved. When Haynes retired, Crofts was appointed Superintendent of A and B Divisions. There was no more divided control and an inspector took over B Division. Aston did not stay long after that, he retired, and took a job as Chief Security Officer at the Dog Racing Track. The second thing the new Chief did was to clamp down on drinking, and it was made quite clear that the 'blind eye' days were over. Any breach would be dealt with most severely. A few men carried on as before and lost their jobs in consequence. This was no light matter, with a 2,000,000 to 3,000,000 dole queue. When a policeman left the Force, then, the townspeople quickly knew, and one was always asked, 'What had he done?', not 'Why has he left?' No men ever *gave up* a secure job then except in extremis. From that point drinking declined, the old guard retired, and new men replaced them. I stayed in the service long enough to see the whole problem become almost a folklore story, and to see a force of men half of whom were teetotal.

Drink

I often pondered on why this had been so prevalent, not only in my force, but in others. The reasons are, I think, twofold.

(i) Perusal of old force records indicate that much depended on the attitude of the Chief Constable. The lot of the early constable was hard – when he had completed his tour of duty, he returned to his quarters to take the necessary rest, and he was required to remain there until he next went on duty. The average day was twelve hours, and a patrol could cover anything up to thirty miles on foot. There was no annual leave and no rest day. Uniform had to be worn at all times, even at Divine Service, which he had to attend at least once on Sundays. It is not surprising that some of the overworked men attempted to find solace in drink and drunkenness figures prominently in early misconduct books.

When I joined, the Force was only about 100 years old, five generations perhaps. For most of that time, in fact, until the Police Strike in 1919, conditions were very bad. Youngsters took their lead from their older colleagues, and so the habit was handed on.

(ii) Most of a policeman's patrol time was at night, and often lonely. Many would be tempted by the promise of comfort which a visit to a pub after hours would provide.

My duties as a motor patrol officer had no fixed pattern in those early days. I had carte blanche to work anywhere in the borough. I had to keep in touch with the station, and be prepared to go and deal with sudden emergencies, accidents, fires, sudden deaths and so on, should they arise. I was used by the inspectors as a conveyance to visit the men on outlying beats. I took the off-duty inspectors their pay on

Fridays – always in a sealed envelope, which had to be handed to the Inspector personally – not to his wife! On Sunday mornings I took Sunday papers to the Chief Constable, and fetched the Cook at 7 a.m. from Sedgley, about six miles distant, as there were no early buses on Sunday morning. I also took the night Inspector home, after collecting the early turn man.

Here are some examples of the variety of tasks falling to the motor patrol. We had a call at the Central Police Station that the caller had a fox in his garden and would we do something about it. I was sent to see what I could do about it. Sure enough, there was a fox wandering around, but unable to escape. A cornered fox is a vicious animal, as I soon found out, and could leap to an astonishing height. After about twenty minutes chasing around, I managed to smother him with a sack, and I brought him to the station where he was secured in one of the cells. Shortly after, the owner came to collect him. After my difficulties catching the animal, I gave him a dressing down for the trouble he had caused me. I should say that from this experience, a fox is untameable.

As a contrast, I was ordered one Sunday morning to take a cooked chicken and a bottle of gin to David Webster's house. I collected the chicken from the barracks cook, and the gin from the canteen, and carefully took them to the house. I had a job to avoid spilling the gravy! On arrival, I carried the articles to the house and rang the bell. Out came David in a dressing gown. I gave him a splendid salute as I handed over the chicken, and another as I left – I hope he was impressed – he looked it.

These were only diversions as the real job was main road patrolling, and enforcement of the new 'Road Traffic Act' and its attendant 'Construction and Use' regulations. I made a close study of both until I knew them by heart. I had more cases than anyone had ever had before, about 200–250 per annum with about 160–180 court appearances, the others being dealt with by caution. I made it my business to get experience in every section of both pieces of legislation as I was determined to become an expert.

My good-time years were over and I was determined to get out of the ruck. As I assessed it, the way to promotion lay through the Chief Constable's Office, the CID, or by making oneself so prominent that my superiors' attention could not help but be attracted. As the first two courses were not available, I determined to use this advantage of being on motor patrol to the full. The only way to do this was to appear constantly in court, and subsequently in the local papers as a result. This I achieved quite clinically. I never lied in court, or in any report; my cases were always fairly obtained. I worked enthusiastically and ruthlessly so that my name stank in certain quarters. A colleague who hailed from Liverpool told me that he had heard lorry drivers in Liverpool speak of that 'bastard' motor patrol in Wolverhampton. I also heard the same remark in a pub in town. I didn't care a hoot, I had acquired a hard casing as everything became subordinate to my ambition. Burge used to tell me I would 'pinch' my own mother! Ambition is a strange thing. Once bitten by it, I could not rest, whatever I achieved. I wanted to surpass it right away and was never satisfied. Ambition, it seems to me, feeds on itself.

The variety of cases I brought in sometimes puzzled and worried my Inspector, who had to check and forward my reports with recommendations. Billy Churchward, who was nearing the end of his service, and in any case was a cavalryman, was not at all happy with dangerous driving cases, or those involving faulty exhausts and brakes, or motor coaches using routes not authorized by the Traffic Commissioners, and a host of other new and original types of prosecution.

Imagine my surprise after twelve months of this, when the Chief Constable sent for me, and told me that he thought there was too much careless driving going on in the town, and that I ought to increase my efforts! I told the Fire Station Inspector, whose department serviced our machines, and he was dumbfounded. 'More cases,' he said. 'You are already infamous in the town.'

I went out fuming! That day, I had a careless driving, three speeding offences, and ended the day by arresting a prominent butcher for being 'under the influence of drink while driving a motor car!'

One evening I was pacing a sports car through our 30 m.p.h. limit town. The driver had two girls sitting with him in the front and drove at a steady 48 m.p.h. down Darlington Street, Chapel Ash, Merridale Road, Finchfield Road. I kept on his tail until, intending to turn sharp left into a driveway, he drew out to his right and stopped suddenly, without giving any indication. I collided with his rear and sailed over the handlebars into a hedge. I was not hurt, but the sidecar front was stove in. We were both shaken and cursed each other quite expertly for a few seconds until we realized that there were ladies present.

I took his particulars – he was Luis Fontes, a Brazilian millionaire, and his girlfriends were the daughters of the Mayor of Dudley – big stuff.

I drove home despondent at the damage to the machine and immediately typed my report (the typewriter Burge and I bought ourselves). I pondered on the bad language episode, how to explain the unexplainable. I had a brainwave and my report simply read at that point: 'When we became composed, I said to him, etc., etc.'

Meanwhile, one of our inspectors who had seen me come back went visiting the sub-stations, and, I heard, was jubilantly saying, 'He's come unstuck, I knew he would.' The case eventually came off before the Stipendiary — I was as much on trial as Fontes. He was a young man, good-looking, and spoke perfect English. To my surprise and relief, he more or less bore out my version of the affair. He was convicted of careless driving, but the Stipendiary dealt leniently with him because of his honest admission. I thought the Stipendiary regarded me rather quizzically when I recited my 'when we became composed' bit.

The local press made quite a story of it, the risk policemen took in discharging their duty, and so on. I had several friends among the *Express & Star* and *Birmingham Post* reporters who attended court as I was always in the newspaper and have quite a collection of press cuttings.

This was the pattern for the next two years at work, but there were other aspects of my life going on at this time. We had evening classes during the winter which I attended, as a lead-in to forthcoming promotion examinations. Our teacher was a retired professional named Cox, who was rather deaf. Among the class were a number of firemen and on occasions during class the fire bells would ring. Poor old Cox could not hear them — all he saw was half a dozen men suddenly leap up, scramble over the desks, and away. After the first occasion, he adapted well, and on subsequent alarms he would turn

---

DOWN TETTENHALL ROAD AT OVER 48 M.P.H.

TWO MOTORISTS EACH FINED £5

Two motorists who drove down Tettenhall-road, Wolverhampton, on Sunday, December 23rd, when weather conditions were very bad, at speeds of over 48 miles an hour, and with little space between them, were each fined £5 at Wolverhampton to-day for driving at a dangerous speed.

They were Urban Edward Hicken (26), of 41, Rose-hill, Willenhall, and Roland C. Longbottom (35), 135. Hall Green-road, West Bromwich.

Patrol-officers Chettar and Stonier said they followed Hicken's car, and saw it attempt to pass Longbottom's on more than one occasion. They alleged speeds of over 50 m.p.h. at certain points and expressed the opinion that neither driver could have pulled up safely in an emergency owing to the greasy state of the road.

Hicken admitted a speed of 40 to 45 miles an hour but said he had the car under perfect control. Longbottom's defence was that the car was not run in properly and his speed was lower than the officers stated.

In answer to Superintendent Crofts, Longbottom said he would think it right and proper to approach a traffic island on a main road at a speed of 40 m.p.h.

Superintendent Crofts said he would ask no more questions, in view of that answer.

The Bench described the two cases as equally serious.

to the rest of us and say, 'A fire alarm, I presume, gentlemen.' As well as this instruction, I was using a correspondence course in English, Police Duties, Maths, and Geography, and those Police Duties books were useful to me all through my service. Mr Cox, too, was a fine teacher, and I could follow his maths teaching which was more than I had been capable of at Waverley Road School. I kept my exercise books, with his methods enshrined, and found them most useful years afterwards.

The great effort for learning was triggered off by a pathetic effort I had made in some exam we had about 1929. In this exam, while not bottom, I was too near there for comfort. It was not a promotion exam, just some small internal affair, but the result had badly shaken me, and I think really started my intention to make my mark, which has a humorous connotation when you stop to think on it.

Anyway, when the time of the promotion examinations came I sat with a fair hope of success. I had worked hard. The exam took two days. It covered arithmetic up to decimals and fractions, Geography, General Knowledge on one, and Police Evidence, Procedure and Arrest on the other.

The results were eventually announced: I had passed. The order of merit was never disclosed, but one learned through various channels. I heard that I had finished third from top. Ahead was Taffy Williams, who was now a clerk in the Chief Constable's Office, and Percy Weight, a type who represented no promotion threat.

On the home front I had been taking out Evelyn Sloane. I think I was feeling lonely on occasions, and she was a nice girl, always there – I can well see how so many men marry their landladies' daughters. I suppose I went out with her for about six months before I realized I could not go through with it. I was beginning to feel the need to settle down. I was twenty-four, and a policeman does need a good home life to do his work properly. I had enjoyed my years of freedom and had had a good time, but now I was in a more serious mood.

Rose

One night I went to a small dance at the Baths; it was a Boys Brigade dance, and not very well attended. My companion was Fred Ball, the Liverpool man I mentioned earlier, a grammar school boy of very independent mind. We were looking around the female talent as is the way of young men, when I saw a girl on the stairs I knew by sight – I had seen her leave Fowler's Ladies Outfitters in Chapel Ash when I was on point duty there. She attracted me then – and did so now. She was small, dark-haired, with slanting hazel eyes, and slightly uneven teeth, which as I have said before always attracted me. I said to Fred Ball, 'I'm going to ask her to dance.' He replied, 'If you don't, I shall.' I went to ask her to dance, and that was how I met my wife-to-be.

About this time, we started the change from motorcycles to cars. The first to be obtained was a Ford, the first small car that eventually sold for just over £100. I was paired with Dinely, who had come out of the CID after an eventful spell of duty there. Chattar and Burge still used the motorcycles until we added a Morris to our outfit. My partnership with Dinely lasted about twelve months. In the CID he had specialized in street bookies, and had remarkable success. As we still had carte blanche on motor patrol, we now included this aspect of police work in our repertoire. 'Joe', as we called Dinely, was too well known to the bookies and their collectors or 'runners', to play the active role, so he would point out where the man was operating, and I would make the arrest. All kinds of subterfuges were needed – one which worked well was to take off our serge jacket and cap, change into an old macintosh, tie a muffler round the neck, and dressed in breeches and leggings (which was now our standard motor patrol dress), the victim hardly knew what to make of us. It worked well for a time, and we had many exciting chases and cases.

My vehicle driving experience had been with model T Ford lorries, but I had no experience of driving a car with a gearbox. I had to learn, and Dinely taught me, very well, too. I was grateful to him for that, although I, too, contributed something. I was a far better report writer than Joe, in fact by this time, with so much practice, I was good! I could remember all that had happened, and had excellent recall. I could also type after a fashion, so I did the drafting and typing, and I had a quicker appreciation of the moving situations which could be construed as Careless or Dangerous Driving. Together we were a formidable team.

I was not sorry to change from motorcycles for they were punishing to drive in cold and wet weather. I have been so cold sometimes I could have cried – it must be remembered that we were driving these machines sometimes until 2 a.m.

Before I leave that scene entirely, I must recall the occasion when Burge and I acted as motorcycle escort to Prince George, Duke of Kent, on the occasion of his visit to Wolverhampton to open the Technical College, and visit Courtauld's works. Nothing unusual happened, and it was an unexciting routine escort. The only other occasion when I saw royalty was in the late twenties when I was helping to control the

Visit by HRH Duke of Kent (Prince George) 1931 or 2, later he opened the technical college.
Left to Right: *Insp. Ballance. PC Burge and Stonier*

crowds in Dudley Street as the Prince of Wales drove through on his way to open the new Birmingham motorway.

My First FA Cup Final

About this time, the early thirties, I went on my first trip to London. Birmingham was playing West Bromwich Albion in the Cup Final and as an old Birmingham supporter I was keen to see the match. Someone got me a precious ticket and I went with a party that included Major Richards, the Commandant of our Special Constables, Inspector Ballance, of whom more later, and a few others whose names now elude me. As a 'first-timer' to London, the others took pleasure in taking me around the usual sights – Downing Street, Buckingham Palace, Horse Guards, the House of Commons – no doubt enjoying my open-mouthed appreciation. We had lunch in Jermyn Street, a beautiful tender steak, I remember, and then, off to the match. The only bad part of a memorable day for me was that Birmingham lost. After a meal at Lyons

Corner House, we entrained for home. On the way back, I recalled one of the fullest and most enjoyable days of my life, culminating in being part of the Wembley spectacle, which is such a thrill, no matter how often one attends.

The MG Sports Car

After about twelve months together, Dinely and I were split up. I was not surprised as the Stipendiary had said something to Supt. Crofts, who usually conducted police prosecutions; I don't know what he said, but we were separated. It was for the best – we could learn no more from each other.

The Force also took delivery of an MG sports car, and Chettar and I were designated as the drivers. We started off together, but eventually worked different shifts, handing the car over to each other as we changed.

It was a gem of a car, with good acceleration and marvellous cornering ability. We both loved it. But we could not change down from high to low gears without awful grinding noises. As we were to be a bit of a 'showpiece', this was not very desirable. The car had been purchased from Attwood Motors, and young Harry Attwood was a racing driver of some note. We called on him and explained our difficulty. He came out with us, and drove around the block. It was an eye-opener as he went through that gearbox, up and down like lightning. The secret, he explained, was that the MG was a 'straight' gearbox, not syncromesh as fitted to most saloon cars. It needed rather high revs, and very speedy gear change to coincide with each other. After a spot of practice under his skilled guidance we finally got it right.

It was an open car with a hood for bad weather. On the back was a 'Stop Police' sign that could be illuminated at night.

I drove this car for about two years, and during that time had no regular partner, but usually picked up a beat man. Towards the end of this phase of my career I was given newly trained recruits to take around and show them the ropes, and to get court experience as my witness. I liked this, and found that I had patience and the ability to pass on knowledge. Several of my protégés later on, when they achieved rank, told me what a lot I had taught them (shape of things to come!).

Before I leave motor patrol, I must mention two things:
First, I received a fulsome commendation from the Stipendiary for tracing a motorist who had injured an elderly lady, taken her home with a damaged arm, and left on it a bandage – a tied handkerchief.

PC Chettar standing, me sitting. Our MG – Circa 1933–4.

He had not left his name or reported it to the police, as he should have done. The only clue was the handkerchief with the name 'I. Hunt', stitched in the corner. I traced eight Hunts through the motor taxation office, picked the most likely, and struck lucky. At the subsequent court case the motorist was found guilty, and was heavily fined, as the Stipendiary said, 'If it had not been for the skill and perseverance of this officer, you would not have been traced.' That constitutes a commendation. I think the old 'Stipe' liked me. My friends from the local press made something of it, the article in the evening paper described my efforts as a 'Sherlock Holmes' type of investigation; not quite that good, I fear.

The other event in my life was my marriage to Rose. We had been going together for about twelve months. I had taken her to my home at Four Oaks several times, and went to her home almost every free evening. We were compatible, and suited each other admirably, as over fifty years together proves. We had a quiet wedding at St Andrews Church, and went to live in Sweetman Street, not far from her parents' home and fairly near the Police Station.

Our home was a council-built house, of three rooms up and down, with a small garden back and front. It cost £408, the deposit being

£70. By the time it was furnished, we were more or less broke. The police had a 10 per cent reduction in pay in the early thirties as part of a Philip Snowden economy budget, and this had not helped. We seemed to be hard up for the next twenty years, but the early days were probably the hardest financially. Of course, all the people we knew were hard up too, our next-door neighbours for instance. He was a Solicitor's Clerk; they had no children, and we often went for long walks as a foursome on summer evenings when I was free. We were both so poor, we could not afford a half pint of beer. Rose had three married sisters, and though their husbands were in work they were all hard up – it was symptomatic of the period. This made it more bearable, I suppose, but despite it all, we were happy enough. Our first child, Norah, was born the next year; we were very pleased of course, although it didn't help the financial position very much.

Chapter VIII

Promotion

The year that my career took another turn was 1935 when I was promoted Sergeant. An ex-navy man named Brown who had 16–17 years service and myself were warned to attend the Watch Committee at 3 p.m. on Friday, 21 November 1935. We were marched before the Committee, and the Chief Constable gave them his recommendations which they approved. The Chairman then congratulated us, and we marched out. It was all over quite quickly; of course we were both on top of the world. We went to the stores and were issued with a pair of stripes to sew on our uniforms in time for duty as patrol sergeants the following night. I went to my car and drove to my mother-in-law's house where Rose always called on Fridays. I walked in, and with a dramatic gesture tossed the stripes to Rose (who knew nothing about my attending the Watch Committee) and said, 'Stitch those on.' She was thrilled, and so was my mother-in-law; we had a good laugh together.

To get promotion at eight years service was quite unusual in those days, although it is, I believe, more commonplace now.

After the first euphoria had died down, and after I had paid my canteen bill of a free pint of beer to every person wishing to have a drink on me, I began to consider my new job and responsibilities.

Patrol Sergeant

Firstly, I had to prepare for the certainty that I should be called upon to drill the men at the next General Inspection, if Colonel Allen was the Inspecting Officer. I had never drilled men, although I had very often been drilled.

I went to the only source of learning that I knew, brother Walter. After all, he had been a drill sergeant in the Guards, among other things. On my next visit home I enlisted his help and we practised in the lounge, until I had gained a fair idea. From then on until the inspection I mentally worked on it.

'The junior Sergeant takes the parade.'
My head and shoulders in foreground.
Lt Col Allan – H.M. Insp of Constabulary
Insp Shale – Drill Officer
Supt. Crofts and five members of Watch Committee.

Came the great day and I was called out as expected. Naturally, I was very nervous. Present were all the senior officers, Mayor, Chairman of the Watch Committee, and others, but chiefly my colleagues whom I had to drill, well knowing what they were thinking. I saluted the HMI, and was told to carry on. I called the men to attention, numbered them off, formed fours, right turn, quick march, about turn, squad will advance in line and so on. As I roared out the orders, the men ably responding, the Colonel said, 'Where did you learn to drill? Have you been in the Army?' I replied, 'I learned here, Sir. I have not served in the Army.' Just as I had reached the end of my limited repertoire, he told me that was enough, so I halted the men and stood them at ease.

The Colonel complimented me briefly and I was dismissed. I felt I had done very well and my colleagues thought so too. I can well believe that drilling men could get hold of one as it gives you a splendid feeling of power. There were fifteen sergeants in our force, but after staffing the departments, there were three for the three reliefs, as Reserve or Station Sergeant, and one for early turn, one for late turn, and two for nights on patrol in A Division. They would be working to three or sometimes four inspectors.

B Division was covered by three sergeants and one inspector, but if we were short-handed for any reason, the B Division men were brought in to A Division.

Much of a patrol sergeant's work was carried out on a bicycle. The town centre men could be visited on foot, but the men working the outer beats could only be contacted either by travelling on the buses or by using a cycle. A supply of police cycles was kept for this purpose. It was customary to visit the day men twice on a relief, and three times on nights which was always hard physical graft. The strict unbending discipline never matched up to this situation of visits to the men. You were not supposed to make appointments with them, you were supposed to find them without prior notice. If this had been carried out, a sergeant might have visited his town centre men perhaps twice on days, and even perhaps on nights, but there was never any hope of visiting men on outside beats literally covering several miles in extent in this way. Yet three visits had to be made on nights. How this farce went on year after year I don't know; everyone knew that visits had to be arranged, yet for years the silly pretence was carried on. Eventually the sheer futility of it all finally put it to sleep. I mention this because it was one of those handed-on traditions going back to the foundation of the service. Founded as it was on largely military principles, many of which were excellent, others were just not applicable to the police service, but they were adhered to as though they were holy writ. Much as I loved the service, this blind adherence to old worn-out practices always annoyed me.

I cannot say I much enjoyed my short spell as a patrol sergeant – after the excitement and independence of motor patrol I found it largely futile and boring, although I went out of my way to get some variety into the work. On nights I conducted several raids on pubs serving after time, and anything else which could offer some excitement.

I should mention before I leave this less rewarding period of my life that initially I had a psychological problem to face and overcome. I was just twenty-eight years old when I was promoted, in charge of men in their forties and fifties, and war veterans to boot. They, like my brother Walter, had been through an experience in the War that put them apart from other men. I knew enough about it to believe that any man who had survived was in some way special, yet I also knew that if I showed any sign of weakness, they would immediately take advantage. I had seen how they treated incompetents like poor Sgt. Franks, who had been David Webster's chauffeur, and had been put out as a patrol sergeant when Webster died. I had not fought my way out of the ruck to risk jeapordizing my prize.

After a few short, sharp exchanges with one or two of the hard cases, the word soon got around that nobody could take advantage of me. It had not been easy. We had one inspector of whom I must say a few words. He exemplified the old type of senior officer. He was Ernie Monks – an ex-lieutenant – a quartermaster from a Scots regiment in the First World War. Well educated he had obviously been good-looking in his youth; both his son and daughter were quite handsome. However, time had taken its toll, he was very bald, and rather fierce-looking, spare in build, and very bad-tempered. Men were afraid to report anything to him when he was a Reserve Sergeant, he always found some fault. He seemed to have a chip on his shoulder – probably he considered promotion overdue, as it very likely was. His attitude could not have helped him much. As an Inspector, he would walk round with me on nights, his favourite occupation being to start with PC No. 1 and go through the whole lot up to PC 115, and find fault with all of them. He was the man who was so amused when I crashed the police motorcycle combination. Yet I knew from certain sources not related to me, that he considered I was one of the few good men in the Force. A strange man, our Ernie, he loved his family, his garden, and fishing, and that was about all.

A New Opportunity

One afternoon in 1936 I was on late turn patrol in Princes Square, when I was approached by Supt. Crofts who told me that a young sergeant was to be sent from one of the police forces in our district to a Home Office course lasting two weeks, to be trained in anti-gas precautions. He was, on return, to pass on his knowledge to all the forces of the district. Would I be interested? He could not say whether it was a good prospect or otherwise. I thought for a moment, and said I would like to be given the chance.

Some weeks elapsed, before a sergeant from Dudley was chosen. He went on the course, and on his return, gave instruction in anti-gas precautions to the local forces. He was very good was Sgt. Cooke, and we became quite friendly and co-operated a great deal a few years later. The next year I was nominated to go on the same type of course at Falfield in Gloucestershire, but before I come on to this, there are other matters on which I must comment.

Penn Police Station

About this time the sergeant who occupied the police house at Penn received permission to leave, and purchase a house of his own. Now Penn in those days was a very desirable area, partly in the country, and two and a half miles out on the southern side of the town. The police house was rented by the authority from John Fox, a coal merchant, the uncle of Gertie Fox whom I mentioned earlier. I was asked if I would like to live there. I was finding the mortgage and the rates on the house in Sweetman Street something of a burden, so the idea of living rent and rates free appealed to both Rose and I, and we accepted gladly. I wanted to move in on a Sunday, but Supt. Crofts thought this would create a bad impression, so we had to choose a weekday. We lived there quite happily for the next ten or eleven years. I never worked Penn as a district as my predecessor had but always worked from the Central Police Station. I did, however, have a police lamp illuminated at night, and a telephone. My wife, who answered many of the queries, became a good unpaid auxiliary of the force. She knew the Penn district and people far better than I.

Fascists and Communists

During the thirties, particularly the mid-thirties, I was actively concerned with these two bodies of worthies. I had taken shorthand lessons and had achieved the giddy speed of about fifty words a minute. It was thought necessary to have observers attend the meetings of both parties when they held their public meetings, which were usually held on the Market Patch opposite the Town Hall. I went to one Communist effort, and tried taking down the speeches, or at least those parts I thought might be seditious. PC Barnwell accompanied me. Now most public speakers can rattle off at least 150 words per minute. The result was that when Barnwell and I tried to read our shorthand back, it took us all night to do so. We managed to get a report from it all, but it was not easy. The value of the report, even if there were seditious statements, would have been useless – any test of our speed capacity would have rendered our evidence unacceptable. There was a case not long after in Glamorgan which was lost for that very reason. I never had to do that particular chore again. I did, however, attend many meetings of the Fascists and Communists. As soon as the one party set up their meeting on the Market Patch, the other would start their meeting a few dozen yards away in opposition. Sometimes it led to violence. I was on duty one night at a Fascist meeting, with the Communist holding an opposition meeting some short distance away. Suddenly a man rushed towards the platform where the Union Jack was flying, and as he neared the platform another man floored him with a blow. It is a strange fact that I have frequently noted – a meeting is going quite quietly, a quarrel starts, a blow is struck, and it seems as if an electric current courses through the crowd, it becomes tense, and serious trouble is on the verge of breaking out; it is as though violence begets violence. I sensed this, stepped in, and arrested both men. They came fairly quietly, the crowd quietened, and I brought my two prisoners to the station which was nearby. When I arrived Inspector Dawson was on duty. He nearly had a fit as he was always reluctant to take a charge if it seemed the tiniest bit risky. At that time this was political dynamite: 'Why have you brought them in? Couldn't you have taken some other course?' I stuck to my guns. I had prevented a possible riot, I told him. The men were charged, and bailed. Next day in court they were both found guilty, the Fascist was fined 40/- on each of two charges, the Communist, 5/- on each.

The newspapers seized on it, not only locally, but nationally, as well. It was one of the first cases (prosecutions) under the new Public Order Act. I did some other work, too, in this connection, but must not disclose its nature.

Falfield

I attended my first course away from home in May 1937. Falfield was the home of the Air Raid Precautions. It was a Home Office school and the principal was a Major Ollis, a retired army officer. His staff of about ten were all fairly high-ranking retired service officers, a Surgeon Captain, a Commander and Lieutenant Commander, a serving Flight Lieutenant from the RAF, and so on. To assist them were a number of assistant instructors, NCO types, to give drill, and assist with indoor and outdoor demonstrations. It was a most efficient set-up and the instruction was of the highest order.

We had lots of theory, also practical work on the range using real chemical warfare agents – or gas. We had to work in respirators or gas masks, and in the heavy oilskin clothing which was to some extent a protection from mustard gas.

Our respirator drill had to be perfect. By this I mean we had to instruct others how to put on the respirator, and our drills had to be word perfect – no putting it in your own words – and it was a difficult drill to master. We had to give a lecturette for fifteen minutes on a variety of relevant subjects. This was at the last part of the course and largely determined whether you passed or failed. My subject was 'The Boiling Method of Decontaminating Protective Clothing'. How to make this interesting, to illustrate it, and to sell it was the object. I practised as did all the others on their chosen subject. We worked in syndicates for the drills with the assistant instructors, and attended lectures and field demonstrations with the instructors, while in our own time, we studied in pairs of our own choosing. I worked throughout with a fire officer from Birmingham. We drilled each other, listened to, and criticized each other's lecturettes, and questioned each other as preparation for the oral and written exam. We worked very hard indeed. The rest of our course consisted of officers similar in age and rank to ourselves from all over the country.

Falfield had been the country home of an MP before being taken over by the Home Office and was situated in a delightful spot between Gloucester and Bristol. There was a mansion, a Home Farm, acres of fields and woods, a large number of auxiliary buildings for training purposes, and some sleeping accommodation.

I had a bedroom in the mansion, very luxurious, I thought, with tea in bed in the morning! Meals were served in the huge dining room, and what a spread! For lunch and dinner there was a choice of three hot dishes, or if you preferred, a buffet table with all kinds of cold meats and cheeses and smart waiters, one to three guests, with a head waiter keeping an eagle eye on everything. I had never before seen anything quite like it; it was based, of course, on an officers' mess. I was to see much of this in later life, but never again was I to see such a spread and variety of food served day after day. The difficulty was not to overeat and become dull and listless during lectures.

Finally, the day of examinations. I managed the respirator drill without difficulty. My lecturette, I felt, was good, the oral exam was easy, and finally the written paper. I completed this so quickly I was the first out. I went upstairs and relaxed in a warm bath, feeling that I had done my very best, and having no second thoughts. We concluded the course by marching in formation to the local pub, and making a night of it!

Apart from the Birmingham fireman with whom I had studied, I made the acquaintance of several people I was to meet again in later years. One in particular was a Sgt. Reg Reynolds from Worcester City Force – we were to cross paths many times in the future.

Before we departed for home, it was impressed upon us that we were

> **No. F/SPEC/ 213 (B)** SPECIAL CERTIFICATE
>
> HOME   OFFICE
>
> ## CIVILIAN ANTI-GAS SCHOOL
> (TWENTYFIFTH Course)
>
> I CERTIFY that SERGEANT F. STONIER, WOLVERHAMPTON BOROUGH POLICE, attended a General Course at this School from 18th. MAY, 1937, to 29th. MAY, 1937, and QUALIFIED AS A FIRST CLASS INSTRUCTOR (SPECIAL CERTIFICATE) in civilian anti-gas precautions.
>
> CIVILIAN ANTI-GAS SCHOOL,
> Eastwood Park,
> Falfield, Glos.
>
> Chief Instructor.
>
> Date 31st.May,1937.
>
> Qualification for SPECIAL CERTIFICATE,
> 80% or over in Theoretical examination.
> 85% or over in Practical examination.

the few who were to train the many, who were to train the mass. That was the snowball principle to be adopted.

After a week, I was sent my first-class certificate, which was amended shortly afterwards to the coveted Special Certificate – a new departure – which meant I had obtained in excess of 80 per cent on all subjects, and was now deemed capable myself of training instructors. No other local authority nominee who subsequently went to a Home Office school ever obtained a 'Special' although one person from industry in the town did.

On my return to Wolverhampton, I had to await delivery of respirators, charts, and other equipment before general training could commence.

During this period of waiting I qualified for the Bronze Medallion of the Royal Life Saving Society. The Force had entered a national competition to see which force could gain the most marks per man within a set time limit. Marks were given on the basis of so many for

Promotion

Last night nine Wolverhampton A.R.P. workers were presented with the first local anti-gas course certificates in the town. Here you see them admiring the certificates, with Sergeant Stonier (C.A.G.S. Special) in the centre.

Second left in front row, Reg Reynolds. Third left in back row Arthur May, two stalwarts all through the War.

obtaining a bronze, more for a silver, and more still for becoming an instructor. Everyone had to enter below the rank of inspector. We had to attend the swimming baths and practise for an examination to be in December of all times! We went at it, driven by Inspector Pendered, a real hard case who worked on us remorselessly. One man had to resign on medical grounds as he could not stand the pace. I was glad to be involved, learned to dive and my swimming greatly improved; in addition, it was the only winter in which I did not catch a cold, although sometimes it meant going out from the warm baths onto night duty. We did not win the national competition, coming third I think, but I received my bronze medallion.

Acting upon instructions, the Police called upon various well-known townspeople (in their own areas) and enrolled some fifty of them as air raid wardens. This was the beginning of a force of civil defence personnel which eventually reached nearly 5,000 in Wolverhampton.

My first classes started in August 1937, in a small room at the Central Police Station. My first talk was reported in the local paper, and a correspondent wrote to say he did not agree with half of what I said. I did not reply. I remember during that first lecture I dried up with nerves, but fortunately it was of such short duration that it went unnoticed.

1937 anti-gas training in Magistrates Court. My first class somewhat reduced in members as the 8 weeks course progressed.

I mixed training with police duty for the next six months, helping slowly to build up an organiztion. Public opinion had not awakened to the menace of war and the going was hard. Interest, except among the stalwarts, was at a low ebb.

Together with Chief Inspector Ballance and Sgt. Llewellyn, the borough was divided up into divisions, based on the municipal wards.

Police experience here, as it was all the way through, was of great help and we arranged warden patrol areas on the lines of small police beats.

In these early days instructors felt gratified if two dozen people came to their meetings. The paucity of official guidance on what wardens were to do was our chief trouble. I mention wardens here because they and the Auxiliary Fire Service were the first services to be formed, the others coming later. When these other services came into being we lost many good men and women, because the Ambulance, Rescue, First Aid, the Report Control Centre and the Home Guard appealed to many of them, so they transferred.

Rotary and Round Table were two of the first organizations to offer their services, and were trained as units. At that time we had no particular duty for them to perform, but many of them were later to be of great service in bringing their experience to work on such complex organizations as control room work. One eminent Rotarian annoyed me considerably. The class was always held on a Tuesday afternoon after the Rotary lunch. No-one can deny that gas training is not an exciting subject and, after a heavy meal, it was too much for this man, who every week went to sleep, and punctuated my lecture with resounding snores. The louder he snored, the louder I talked, but I never managed to wake him. I had my revenge at question time. One member of the Round Table class asked me to give him the chemical formula for mustard gas. I realized now that he was particularly interested, but at the time I thought he was trying to be funny as the formula is a terrific length. I was able to give it, and from then on I was not worried by this class with highly technical questions. I must say that they were the easiest class I had for absorbing information.

Persistent Gas

A little later, I took Wolverhampton head teachers in a class. Without thinking, I started to explain to them how one calculated the surface area of a room. Halfway through, I suddenly realized what I was doing in trying to instruct a class of head teachers in simple arithmetic, and apologized amid loud laughter.

It was about this time that one of my colleagues asked a member of his class, 'What is a persistent gas?' The reply came without hesitation, 'You don't know my old woman.'

A member of one of my classes achieved what I thought to be impossible – in respirator drill he put his CD respirator on upside down and managed to keep on breathing. On another occasion, I issued

Wolverhampton's first instalment of gas masks arrived yesterday and were speedily st[ored] in the warehouse in Raglan-street, preparatory to assembling them; 3, Mr. J. E. Birch, w[ith] quarters staff, arranging for depots; 4, Volunteer workers ass[...]

Above and opposite: These pictures are historic. It was the time when the country thought it was about to be bombed with possibly gas.

examination papers and the class was busy writing, except one elderly man. I went to him and said, 'Can't you mange it, Joe?' 'Sergeant,' he said, 'I cor write.' I gave him an oral examination, and later he turned out to be one of our best.

A Royal Parade

To give a fillip to ARP, a royal inspection of the NFS, ARP, and ancillary services was held in Hyde Park during 1939. Every Scheme Making Authority, as they were then called, sent a detachment proportionate to their size. We sent about six people, I think. Report Centre, Transport, Wardens, Rescue, Ambulance, each sent a representative,

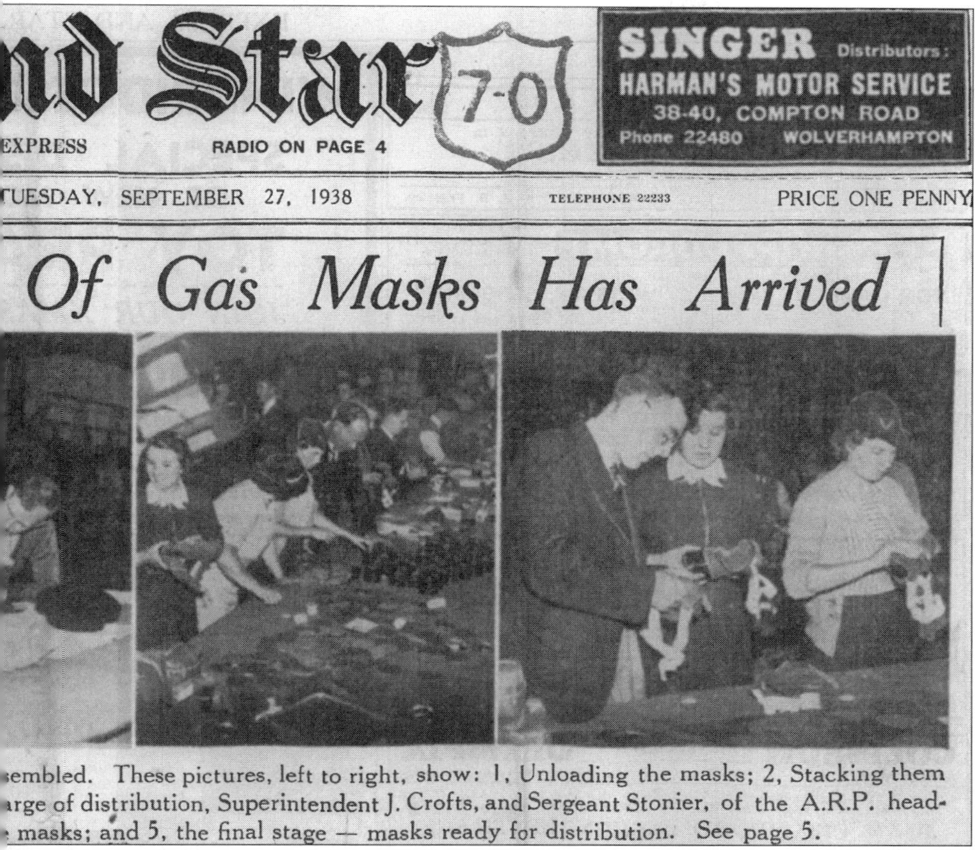

nd Star 7-0

SINGER Distributors: HARMAN'S MOTOR SERVICE 38-40, COMPTON ROAD Phone 22480 WOLVERHAMPTON

EXPRESS RADIO ON PAGE 4

TUESDAY, SEPTEMBER 27, 1938 TELEPHONE 22233 PRICE ONE PENNY

Of Gas Masks Has Arrived

sembled. These pictures, left to right, show: 1, Unloading the masks; 2, Stacking them
rge of distribution, Superintendent J. Crofts, and Sergeant Stonier, of the A.R.P. head-
masks; and 5, the final stage — masks ready for distribution. See page 5.

and I accompanied them. It was all done in one day. We travelled by train, reported to Hyde Park, were given a large sign with Wolverhampton inscribed on it, and at a given signal, we fell in. There were thousands on parade with no uniforms at that stage, only armbands.

We marched off to band music and passed the saluting base, an elevated structure on our left. George VI and Queen Elizabeth, with the Queen Mother and the princesses, plus the usual entourage were there. The King took the salute, it was very impressive and I was struck by the appearance of the Royal Family. They all looked beautiful, as if wearing make-up. After the march past, we returned to our tent, gathered our belongings and left for home. The impression left was that this really was a serious business – all that organization and expense indicated the importance that authority attached to our young and faltering organization, which is precisely what it was intended to achieve.

Recruitment Parade along Penn Road about 1938.

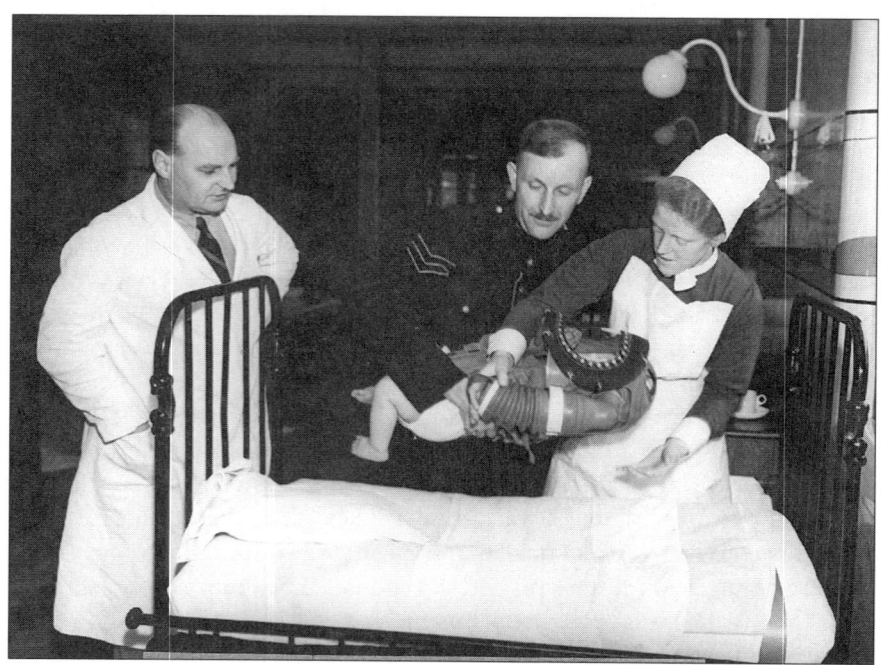

New Cross Hospital about 1940. Trying the baby respirator with nurse and doctor in attendance.

Press Reports on Respirator Census

This is taken from an interview given by Inspector Stonier to the *Express and Star* after the War, as is the report on persistent Gas.

The respirator census and fitting during the crisis of September 1938, brought events close home to the public, gave a fillip to A.R.P. recruiting, and introduced the Warden to his neighbour. I visited all cinemas and theatres to appeal for volunteers, for the assembly of respirators. Hundreds of people were mobilised, and large factory premises taken over. The work went on night and day, and there was no rest for the A.R.P. staff. We, of course, had to explain and demonstrate how the respirators were assembled. After a few hours of this, I lost my voice, and nearly collapsed with exhaustion.

We saw for the first time, how a crisis can throw all sorts of persons together in a spirit of comradeship, and it gave me a very warm feeling to see how readily our call for assistants was answered.

Recruiting went forward, and all instructors were at full stretch for weeks after.

Premises were taken over for wardens' posts, and I had the task of making these arrangements. It speaks volumes for the public spiritedness of Wolverhampton people that when we had decided that certain premises would be convenient, never once was consent refused by the owners or occupiers, often at great inconvenience to themselves.

Our wardens were then given their first public duty. It was decided to compile a record of every resident in Wolverhampton, and their size of respirator.

Respirator Fitting

A band of schoolteachers volunteered to keep the records, and a small band of unpaid wardens took on the colossal task of fitting everyone in Wolverhampton with a respirator.

We started off in Wimborne Road, Heath Town, and Alexandra Road, Penn. I and two assistants went to the first house and were well received. In fact, during the whole time there was very little trouble.

It was rather pathetic at times to find that elderly people could not breathe with a respirator on, and of course the problem of babies and

Rose and Norah with the first respirators – from 1938.

children had to be answered by vague promises of something in the future.

Once the ice had been broken, our wardens set about the job like Trojans, and great progress was made, but events moved too quickly and with the crisis of September 1938, respirators were issued, the fitting in many cases coming later. The crisis having temporarily passed, our organization began to take better shape, and training began to include incendiary bomb theory. Here at last we found a subject that really did interest people.

August 1939 saw Wolverhampton's first large-scale exercise, the largest blackout exercise held in the country up to that date. It had required months of preparation by the ARP staff as we had no precedent to work on, and were really pioneering. The programme was too ambitious, people being expected to run before they could walk properly, but war often creates this problem.

Generally it went off well, and I shall never forget that memorable night in the Civic Hall, when over 1,000 ARP personnel of all services attended at the close of the exercise at three o'clock in the morning to listen to an address by Wing Commander (now Sir John) Hodsall, Inspector General of Civil Defence, nor shall I forget the tribute they paid spontaneously to Mr Ballance and myself. It was a very proud moment and compensated for much of the hard work and disappointment previously experienced.

At the end of the month I took an incendiary and high-explosive course at Birmingham, and came back to train new classes of instructors, mostly for industry.

Red Tape

Some of my previously trained instructors went on this course too, but war was declared before they took their exam. To increase my band of fully trained instructors, I included those who had not taken the examination at Birmingham in my class, and they qualified and started instructing.

When the official in charge of the school heard about it, he created such a rumpus. Reports and correspondence passed between Wolverhampton and Birmingham on this 'unethical conduct'. At last we were told that it would be 'all right, but don't do it again'. I boiled at such childish conduct at such a critical time. I saw the pedantic person on many occasions later during the War. He never managed to achieve anything more than the rather low-grade clerical job he held at the beginning.

At Christmas 1938, I received a book from one of my trainees, a very remarkable lady. It was entitled, *Impossible People*, and to this day I don't quite know whether it was a sly crack at my trainees or myself.

Chapter IX

Head Wardens

The year 1939 was memorable for the declaration of war. We had moved to a large old factory in the town centre which had been a Chubbs Lock works. It was a huge old-fashioned building, and generously housed both the ARP and the NFS headquarters staff, and also our stores. We had taken delivery, and continued to do so for a long time after war was declared, of a variety of equipment – rubber gum boots, general service respirators, civilian duty respirators, steel helmets, light and heavy oilskin suits. These latter had to be unpacked and hung on hangers, and there were hundreds of them. We had a carpenter working full time adapting the large rooms allotted as stores for this purpose. I was put in charge of equipment, as well as training, and it gave me a bigger headache than ever the training did.

The 'day war broke out', as Rob Wilton used to say, there was a panic issue of steel helmets, rubber boots and CD respirators. No proper check was made. I had little say in how the stores were issued as the principle was 'Get it out to the wardens' posts, Ambulance Depot, and rescue depots, and never mind the paperwork.' Later, when the immediate panic subsided, we tried to get our records straight. I never achieved this and we never traced a lot of equipment despite all our efforts. As a return had to be made annually of stock held against stock issued, it proved an annual problem. It posed the same problem for the Fire Service next door who were in the same boat, as in fact were all CD authorities, as I later found out. The Fire Service storeman and I had a useful working arrangement over this which survived until such time as the government department concerned wrote off the losses. Towns which later were 'blitzed' solved their stores problems by 'destroyed by enemy action' techniques.

The Phoney War Period

The expected blitz in 1939 did not materialize and for twelve months there was little action on the war front. All theatres and cinemas had closed on the outbreak of war, but they began to reopen after a short time. Football, racing and all local sports activities ceased. People in our service felt bored and frustrated. The Rotary and Round Table had organized a flag day to provide comforts for ARP and NFS personnel and about £1,000 was raised – the question then arose, what to do with it. I had a brainwave which I put to those in authority. Why not form sporting activities among our personnel by taking over, for the duration of war, the facilities of the now defunct local sporting bodies? The idea was approved, and neither they nor I realized what a winner we had here.

I bought football and cricket equipment from local clubs, paying a cheap price for it on the understanding that it could be purchased back at the same price afterwards. I took over sports grounds on the same basis, plus the need to keep the grounds in fair repair. Any cash required, I obtained from the Comforts Fund. There was a special committee which examined and audited all expenditure. The whole idea went like a bomb. Before long we had cricket clubs, football, golf, tennis, bowls, angling, snooker, darts, all being formed and played. I found experts in the various services who had long experience in their pastime; they took charge of their own sport, became a Sports Committee Member, and came to me for the required cash. I went to the Comforts Fund and obtained what was required. Eventually over 5,000 people were associated in some way with the activities. An example was that our football team comprised nearly all the Wolverhampton Wanderers reserve team. Birmingham did the same with the Villa, Birmingham and West Bromwich teams. We had matches played on Sundays that were practically league football standard. Initially we had a deal of co-operation from the Midland representative of the Football Association who attended every match. It didn't last long as the FA raised objections to Sunday football, and that ended the high-class performances, but we carried on at a more amateur level. Of the other sports, cricket was a great favourite. We had good grounds, good equipment, and some good, if ageing, players. Snooker, and darts, too, were highly popular; we had leagues on a service basis for these. However, the most popular of all was angling – we had 2,500 members. Our expert anglers within the services had obtained the use of waters around Wolverhampton, and our fund met the expenditure.

All this was very time-consuming and could only have been organized during a period such as the 'Phoney War' allowed. The culmination of all these efforts was a presentation of the mass of cups that had been spontaneously presented by prominent townspeople. This was performed by none other than the Regional Commissioner, Lord Dudley. It was held at the new Civic Hall, which had been completed in 1939, and the attendance was a picked house of 1,100 people. To our surprise, the Chief Constable, Mr Tilley, did not attend; this was the first sign of something amiss. The commissioner said, 'If the Controller is not here, he should be,' and that was that.

It was a great night, and a triumph for a small enthusiastic body of experts in their sports, members of the Comforts Fund, and my Sports Committee. This aspect of my work gave me great satisfaction and pleasure. It was highly successful, I enjoyed doing it, it filled a great gap in the lives of many people, and went on for the duration of the War.

Penn Wardens Cricket Club

Living as I did in Penn, the Penn Wardens naturally were of some concern to me, particularly as some of them used my house as a post. I can't remember exactly how it started, but early on we formed a cricket club as a number of us were very interested. We formed a team and obtained equipment through the Sports Association, of which I was, of course, Chairman. The question of a ground was easily solved – Mrs Twentyman and her daughters were wardens. She was a member of a wealthy and well-known local family, and owned considerable land in Penn. Close to their house, which stood in its own grounds, was a paddock in which they kept a few horses. It was quite large enough for a cricket ground, ideal in fact, being very pleasantly situated with trees around it, well away from the road.

Mrs Twentyman kindly gave us the use of this when I approached her, and from the beginning of the War until I left Wolverhampton, Penn Wardens played their home matches there. We had many happy hours. There was a small pavilion, we were able to make tea and with our wives and children, quite enjoyed our summers in the Twentymans' field.

Penn Wardens Cricket Club still exists I believe. A local manufacturer who put his hand in his pocket on occasions to help us became our President. We had a fairly good minor club side and won as often as we lost. I remember later on in the War, Penn Wardens played Wolverhampton Police. I had not played for the Police for many years as I played for the Wardens.

It was quite amazing – they batted first. I was fielding at first slip when the batsman put one up in the air, between the position of fine leg and square leg. We had nobody fielding there so I ran from first slip around the wicketkeeper, and stretching to my utmost, made a spectacular catch – I can hear the applause from the pavilion now! Later, at the other end, I was still at first slip, the batsman touched a fast ball, the wicket keeper partly caught it, then dropped it, but before it could reach the ground I caught it off him, as it were. Then I went on to bowl and took three wickets, including the skipper, Jim Quinn. I made about ten when we batted. We lost by about six runs. On our return to the pavilion, many of the police players, who probably did not know that I had played for them years before, wanted me back in their team. It was a very gratifying day for me.

Carole

I had offered my house at Penn as a wardens' post. One room was taken, the front of the house was sandbagged and eventually a brick shelter was constructed at the rear. The arrangement worked very well, Rose became a warden and there was always someone in the house with her during my long hours of duty. As there was a good percentage of women in the Penn Wardens, she was not left alone with men only.

In November 1939, our second daughter was born, Carole Ann. As 'Alerts' became more frequent during the forties, I was always on duty in town, and it was always a great comfort to me to know that Rose and the children were as safe as they could be with her fellow wardens. She did not go out on patrol but made tea and refreshments for the men as they came in off patrol during those long cold winter nights.

My two daughters then and now are quite unlike each other both physically and mentally. As they now have children of their own, and may well read these lines, let it suffice if I say that they were both loved and helped in life as much as Rose and I could manage.

Gelignite and Unexploded Bombs

In October 1939 I was sent on a course with Inspector Finney of the Fire Service, and PC Quinn from the ARP Dept. It was devised to instruct us how to explode bombs which might drop and *not* explode.

We were sent on a Royal Engineers course at Rugeley, Staffs, and were taught there for a week how to use dynamite or gelignite, gun cotton and detonators, instructed by NCOs. There were no handouts. The policy at that time seemed to be, 'If a bomb drops in your area, and doesn't explode, you slap a gob of gelignite onto the casing, fix a detonator, light the fuse, and retire.' Utterly idiotic, of course, and it invites more questions than I have time to answer. But we were worried! On the way home we decided to write a paper on the course ourselves. We went to the Public Library to obtain suitable books, visited the Mining College at Cannock, and spent hours drafting out a very good paper. We showed it to the colonel in charge, who was very impressed and begged us for a copy to use as a syllabus, so we gave him a copy. It was obvious to us that this was a very scratch unit and if typical of our state of readiness, not very reassuring. On completion of the course, which included actual use of gelignite on the range, we returned home, having qualified for what? I thought. We acquired a suitable hut for the storage of explosives in Wolverhampton and awaited our next instructions in the dicey business of blowing up unexploded bombs in situ. Fortunately they never came, common sense must have prevailed at higher levels, and we heard no more of this. Altogether, 1939 was proving a busy year.

Molineux Grounds

One last 1939 event. When war was declared, the Chief Constable sent for me and told me to go and take over Molineux Grounds. He had no idea what to do with it and I had to think up some use. I took with me an architect, who like so many at that time, was at a loose end. His usual business had closed and he was awaiting government instructions. We went to the Grounds, saw the Secretary, Jack Howley, and told him our instructions; he did not seem surprised. We looked over the premises and I decided that the showers and bath facilities, with some alterations, would make a splendid gas cleansing station. My architect friend took the required details and measurements, later produced the drawings and the work was carried out quite speedily. This began an association with Molineux and its staff which lasted throughout the War. As well as Jack Howley, there was the trainer, assistant trainer, masseurs and groundsman. It made a nice little team; I trained them and with the use of the facilities in our exercises, they became expert cleansing station operatives, and I had a real showpiece for visitors. If gas was ever used, they were my nucleus on which I could build a service. The stands I intended to use for airing contaminated clothing. I managed later in the War to prevent their call-up by enrolling them in the Rescue Service. This enabled them to keep the famous football club ticking over. At the end of the War I went to take charge of policing a league football match at Molinuex, and lined up in the

Manager's office was Jack Howley and his team. Jack made a little speech of thanks and gave me a bottle of gin. He also saw that I got Cup Final tickets later on when the Wolves were involved.

Training Developments

During the next two years training went on apace. I had trained a team of instructors, formed an Instructors' Association, trained them to act as umpires in our large-scale exercises. I also published a 'Questions and Answers' booklet on gas, incendiary bombs and high explosives. I will not go into details, so much happened so quickly. The chief item of interest was the falling value of gas as a war threat, and the growing danger of fire and incendiary bombs as the destroyer of cities and war potential. The emphasis began to switch to methods of dealing with them which was more interesting as people could better understand fire, instructors could set up fire situations and volunteers could tackle them with the newly issued stirrup pump. We took over a yard and old stables off Darlington Street and made it our fire practice ground. We obtained vast quantities of magnesium swarf, which when ignited, acted as an incendiary bomb did. We occasionally used real incendiary bombs of which we accumulated a number.

The enemy put an explosive pellet in the bomb which scattered the burning material over a wider area, so we had to adapt the training again. Then an explosive head was fixed to the bomb which was a lethal contraption at close range. We were one of the first towns to have this type used against us. It was only a desultory raid, with not much damage, but a dozen people lost their lives tackling these bombs at close range, so the technique had to be changed again, all of which necessitated vast training programmes. I was sent on a course to Falfield in 1942 and qualified again with a Special Certificate as a Fire Guard Instructor. It was fairly easy, for we had been doing this training for quite a time by then.

How Falfield had changed! Strict austerity, food poor or indifferent, hardly any sugar — we knew we were at war alright!

The term Fire Guard was now the one in popular use. Almost everyone was a potential Fire Guard, either in his or her own street and/or at their place of work. Even we ARP personnel had to do our stint of fire watching at the Central Police Station at night.

The town centre was divided into blocks and the people working there had to provide night cover. This was compulsory; in 1940, PC Quinn from our department was promoted sergeant, and had the task of enforcing this regulation. Outside the town centre street parties were formed, a party to six houses. They were issued with stirrup pumps and given instruction.

George Windsor – a Tragedy

Our training of volunteers usually took place during the evenings, and was held either in the Magistrates' Court, or the Sessions Court Room in the Town Hall. We always had respirator drill during the session, and it was a standard practice next day to disinfect the respirators (inside the facepiece of the mask). A weak solution of Izal was used for this.

The work was carried out in a tiny office in the corner of the police yard, which was always kept locked when not in use by our small staff. It was stocked with respirators, cleansing materials, and a small poisons cabinet in which I kept Bromine in liquid form in a bottle, and a little hydrochloric acid also in a bottle. The Bromine was used in a demonstration to illustrate the heavier-than-air properties of gas (chemical warfare agents), together with the hydrochloric acid. George Windsor was a PC who had joined the force with me in 1927. He was a good-looking, well-set-up man, an ex-Coldstream Guardsman. He was the quiet, unobtrusive type that never seems to attract any attention, a good steady plodder.

He had attended a rather nasty suicide. The person had cut his throat, and sat in a chair, head back, revealing a gaping wound. This had so upset George that it preyed on his mind and he became withdrawn. As a result of this rather strange behaviour he had been taken off regular duty and posted to our department for odd jobs. It is not easy to find work in a specialized job such as ours was, for a uniformed outsider. However I showed George how to disinfect respirators, and he did this job in our little corner store. Unfortunately, he had some kind of brainstorm and drank the liquid Bromine and hydrochloric acid from the bottles. He was seen staggering round the police yard before he collapsed. He died very painfully, poor chap. It was said that the corrosives had burned through from his stomach to the outside. The inquest returned a verdict apportioning no blame to anyone. I wonder if the poison cabinet had been locked, whether the tragedy might have been averted, although if a person is determined to die they will find a way.

I found that attending suicides was often distressing. I went to a bookmaker who had blown the top of his head off with a shotgun. There he sat, with half a head, and his blood and brains scattered around the ceiling.

Drownings, if the body had been in water a long time, were a horrible business, particularly when the limbs came away from the body.

Railway deaths, when a person was smashed into little pieces were also horrifying. On the other hand, gas poisonings leave the body intact, and a pink flush to the face – they are not so bad to deal with.

There is always an element of shock in attending such cases. I found that I went off my food for a day or two, and one did have a tendency to brood on it for a short time.

The nasty side of police work!

Department Personalities and Changes

In charge of ARP was the Chief Constable, who was Controller and Fire Guard Officer. Chief Inspector Ballance was the Deputy Controller, and in charge of our department. This consisted of myself and a number of constables which varied as the War continued, but was never more than six. Quinn was promoted out of the department in 1940. We had two typists and a schoolteacher who was a great friend of Ballance. He collected her every day from school, and she would come to the office which she shared with him as a kind of unpaid personal assistant. There was naturally a lot of gossip about this but it was shrugged off. Ballance

Plotting. Myself, Gribbin and Ballance. Gribbin joined with me and held the 'India Frontier Medal'; he never got promotion largely due to Ballance.

was a brilliant man in many ways. He was well educated, a big man physically, had been good-looking, but was now rather going to seed. He had been through the CID, the Chief Constable's Office, and uniform branches. He was obviously destined for even higher rank if he behaved. But he was vain, and had an almost pathological suspicion of being superseded. He directed this strange behaviour for years towards the Deputy Town Clerk, a Mr Barr, who was also a Deputy Controller. It was most unreasonable; Barr was no threat to Ballance, they were in different fields, yet we had to listen constantly to his diatribes against Barr. Later, as Jack Crofts was nearing retirement, he directed some of this spleen against him, as though this might hasten the retirement, and assure Mr Ballance of his next move up the ladder.

When Ballance was ill, I had to take the work each day to the Chief Constable for approval of action taken, of orders to be given, and so on. I then called on Ballance to tell him what was happening. Although

An increase in the Report Centre, standing PC Dineley, sitting from left to right, Quinn, O'Leary and Morgan Jones.
Quinn jumped me for a time in promotion stakes but left once he returned to ordinary duty. O'Leary became coroners officer. Morgan-Jones was called up, he achieved rank of Lieut. Col. and never returned to police force.

we had been on excellent terms for years, he did not like me as an understudy or he feared I was trying to oust him. I had more sense than that and knew he was the next superintendent. I was hardly in the position as a sergeant to endanger that. However, this for me was a most unhappy time. The Chief Constable was treating me badly whenever I had to attend upon him, for what reason I could not then guess, so I was being attacked by both men. I would not have minded had I not been working about twelve hours a day, instructing, organizing, out most nights, carrying a pretty heavy load, while they, from what I gathered, were out at night enjoying themselves.

The Divisional Warden for Penn was a Councillor Marlow, a chemist. As the organization grew, businessmen joined it. They wanted to reorganize it on more businesslike lines, but poor old Marlow was not that kind of go-ahead man. The result was a groundswell of opinion in Penn that he should step down and let a more forceful type take over, but he did not see it that way. Now, I was a friend of Mr Marlow and often visited him at his home. The Penn wardens brought things to a head when they called a meeting to propose a vote of 'No Confidence' in Marlow. Neither Tilley nor Ballance would attend the meeting because Marlow was a councillor, and they funked it. I had to go to the meeting and chair this delicate matter. With an audience of 150 wardens, Marlow was voted out. I was as fair and uncommitted as a chairman should be, but I should not have been placed in that position. When Jack Crofts retired, Ballance was made Superintendent. I was the 'Crown Prince' in the department, and should have taken over as Inspector, everyone expected this to happen, but instead Quinn was promoted Inspector. He had been a sergeant for only two years, and that time had been spent enforcing fire guard regulations. To say I was dumbfounded is an understatement, I was shattered! Five years of hard, devoted, self-sacrificing work, with all I had achieved in building up the service, counted for nought, and the plum was given to an inexperienced man who had been my subordinate two years before. I don't know how I survived the next few weeks. I had nothing against Quinn, I had always got on well with him – he was lucky and I couldn't blame him. But for Ballance and Tilley, whatever revenge they were seeking, they got it. It was interesting to note the reaction of people one knew – some remained staunch friends, others switched to the new luminary.

Ballance never spoke to me about it, he came often to brief Quinn who had to learn a lot very quickly. I pondered on my position at some length. There was not much I could do about it. I could go back to ordinary duty as a protest, but that would achieve nothing. I couldn't leave the service in wartime. I could grit my teeth and continue to do my best for my own satisfaction, for the good of the job, and perhaps make those who had treated me so badly feel a little ashamed, so this is what I finally did. I class it as one of the best things in my life, it did something for my character, and gave me renewed confidence in myself. Some of the best work I ever did, I achieved after that, as I turned my hate and despair into constructive work. I presented a Fire Guard Plan on which even Tilley had to congratulate me! I also presented Mr Barr's intricate Zone Control Scheme as an explanatory playlet to a high-level audience, again to high praise.

Quinn and I got on very well. We had a chat at the beginning of his reign, and got our relative positions sorted out, after that we worked well together.

The End of Tilley

He had been living it up and power seemed to have gone to his head. Being Controller gave him great power and authority, which in the subsequent Home Office Enquiry he was alleged to have abused.

Dinely and Whetton, both PCs, brought the charges to the notice of the Watch Committee. I was away from the scene, so I do not know all the details. A Home Office Enquiry was instituted into misuse of police manpower and motor vehicles by him. After a lengthy investigation by an Inspector of Constabulary, he was acquitted of the charges. The Watch Committee would not accept this, and resigned 'en bloc'. There was great to-and-froing from London. A threat of withholding the grant was made, but the Watch Committee were adamant, they would not have this man any longer as Chief Constable. Eventually he was allowed to resign and retire on pension, with a small gratuity. He had a job for a short time with a firm in the town and later took over a pub. He died not long after, of cancer, I believe.

After he had gone, my wife Rose told me that a few years before, after a demonstration at Penn to encourage volunteers, he had taken her for a drink while I took the parade back to town. She went, thinking it a friendly gesture on his part. At the pub he made it clear that if she was to be 'friendly', he would guarantee my quick promotion. She replied that she had sufficient confidence in me to achieve promotion without any so-called 'help' from herself. He obviously later tried to prove her wrong. It was as well I did not know of this during his bad treatment of me. Anyway, he lived long enough to see me patrolling the streets of Wolverhampton wearing the insignia he had withheld from me. I think sometimes that he might have felt a little remorse before he left. He was kinder when I had to see him, and even praised my work, for example, the Fire Guard Plan. He also recommended me for a post with the Army. They were recruiting fire and police officers to join the 'Allied Military Government of Occupied Territories' of A.M.G.O.T. Successful candidates all obtained commissions and went into Europe to act as town marshals etc. I attended an Army Selection Board in Hampstead, did all the tests and exams, and according to a Divisional Fire Officer I had palled up with, I was a 'cert'. Some days later I received a notification that 'After *Final* Consideration, your services are not required'. Tilley could not understand this and was quite puzzled.

As events turned out, it was a good thing for me that I was turned down. Whilst on this matter, Tom Marsh, who joined the force with me, and was now an Inspector, volunteered later and was accepted. He went to Italy and became a major. He told me he was going to volunteer as he felt that sooner or later we would be called up, and he felt it better to go when you could pick your job.

Press Reports

Before I move on to the next phase of my career, I would like to quote a few press reports of the time. I had a number of friends on the two local papers, the *Express and Star*, published in Wolverhampton, and the *Birmingham Post*. For the *Express and Star*, Leslie Duckworth and 'Daddy' Ayers had often published my exploits, and 'Paddy' Larmer, the photographer, had supplied a great deal of photographic copy over the years.

Whenever we needed publicity to interest the public in training schemes, they were always more than helpful. We also had good co-operation from Harold Small and Bert Jeffcock of the Birmingham paper. Leslie Duckworth eventually became Editor of the *Birmingham Post*; he was one of our wardens and always a good friend. These will I think give an outside opinion of the scope of my work during this period.

POLICE OFFICERS ENTERTAIN WOLVERHAMPTON A.R.P. WARDENS

> Three members of Wolverhampton Police Force were loudly applauded when they entertained the A.R.P. Wardens of N Division, of St. Philips Ward, at a dinner given at the Molineux Hotel, by Councillor W. H. Farmer last night. They were Sgt. Stonier (dramatic monologue), P.C. O'Leary (songs), P.C. Howard (pianoforte).
>
> The dinner was in appreciation of work done by A.R.P. members of the ward during the crisis. Mr F. R. Hook proposed the loyal toast, and Mr. A. Rollaston, that of the A.R.P., to which Sgt. Stonier replied. He said that he was pleased to see the Wardens spending their leisure hours together, and hoped they would retain their interest in A.R.P.

TRAINING CLASSES FOR WOLVERHAMPTON FIRE WATCHERS NEXT WEEK

> A big effort to train Wolverhampton people who have offered their services as fire watchers is to be made next week. Next Sunday,

January 19th, 1941, at the Civic Hall, three lectures on the theory of incendiary bomb control, will be given at 11 a.m., 2.30 p.m., and 4.30 p.m. Two of these will be given by Sgt. Stonier, Chief A.R.P. Instructor, and the third by Mr. A. J. May, L.A.R.P.

Then three times a day next week, demonstrations of how to deal with fire bombs will be staged at the demonstration yard, Darlington Arms Passage at 11 a.m., 2.30 p.m., and 4.30 p.m. Admission to the lectures will be by ticket only.

NEW WOLVERHAMPTON CIVIL DEFENCE OFFICIALS

New appointments of Three Wolverhampton Civil Defence Officials have been made by the Civil Defence Committee on the recommendation of the new Controller, Mr. J. Brock Allen. Mr. R. K. Stevens becomes Fire Guard Officer, Inspector J. Quinn A.R.P. Officer, and Sgt. F. Stonier Deputy A.R.P. Officer.

GAS BOMB IN WOLVERHAMPTON TEST IMMUNISED BY NEW METHOD

With army and police officers, and civil defence representatives from various parts of the West Midland Region, I walked yesterday through a concentration of mustard gas, and suffered no harm. (*Express & Star* report). Our respirators gave complete protection.

It was during the first of four demonstrations to be given in Wolverhampton, of a new method of road decontamination. On a road running across a piece of waste ground on the outskirts of the town, two walls had been built to represent houses, and between them a 50 kilo. mustard gas bomb was exploded. After a demonstration of detection, reporting, and identifying the gas had been given the spectators were allowed to walk down-wind of the drenched area, putting on their respirators after first catching a whiff of the gas. Then the decontamination squad got to work. Instead of hosing and brushing, the method used hitherto, they spread undiluted bleach powder on the contaminated area. The effect of this was to neutralise the gas and the heat generated by the chemical reaction, drew the gas from the surface, and caused it to burn in flares. Commentaries were given through a loudspeaker from a police car by Sgt. F. Stonier, Staff Officer and W. Joyce, Chief Instructor of the regional training school at Whitmore Reans, Wolverhampton.

GOSSIP COLUMN   EXPRESS AND STAR

I looked in at the Wulfrun Hall last night for the last demonstration of the week of the new Fireguard plan. The hall was packed, as it has been all the week – 200 people could not get in on Thursday night, and although it is true that fireguards have been directed to attend, as part of their duties, I have known nothing in this service which has aroused so much interest as these demonstrations. It may also be taken as a compliment to those who have arranged and presented it, Inspector J. Quinn, and Sergeant F. Stonier. It was indeed one of the best staged and presented affairs of its kind I have seen.

There are 25,000 fireguards in Wolverhampton, and 1,000 are on duty every night. The fireguards are now as Sgt. Stonier appropriately called them, 'The little brothers of the National Fire Service'.

FOR THE FIRE FIGHTERS

On Wednesday, there will be opened at Beatties, (Ground Floor), a special display provided by the Ministry of Information called 'Fire Guard'. The Wolverhampton Civil Defence are co-operating, and lending some types of bombs which fell on the town some weeks ago. Sgt. Stonier, known to us all for his zeal in this department, is making the arrangements.

WOLVERHAMPTON ADEQUATELY PROTECTED, SAYS LORD DUDLEY

'I don't think Wolverhampton has much to fear about adequate protection from anything with which the Luftwaffe can threaten you,' said Lord Dudley, West Midland Regional Commissioner, in a tribute to the town's civil defence services, at their sports association's dance at the Civic Hall last night.

Lord Dudley presented the many sports trophies won during the year. Sgt. F. Stonier (Chairman of the Sports Association), thanked all those concerns which had provided playing facilities, the donors of trophies, and those who had run the competitions. Attending were 1,100 civil defence workers and their friends.

500 FIRE GUARDS DEALT WITH 3,500 INCENDIARY BOMBS

Wolverhampton Fire Guards last night faced their biggest test, and came through with flying colours. Five hundred of them from Heath Town, and St. Mary's ward are (station ground I. R.) took part in the first full scale exercise held in Wolverhampton, to test the working of the new plan. Although primarily a Fireguard and N.F.S. exercise, other civil defence services co-operated. Industrial, business premises, and street party fire-fighters all worked together enthusiastically. Afterwards, at the fireguard headquarters, the producer – umpires gave brief preliminary reports on the exercise, all of which showed it had been a great success. Mr. P. G. Baddely, regional Fireguard Training Officer, expressed congratulations to all concerned, particularly to Sgt. F. Stonier, director of the exercise. Watched by representatives from Birmingham, Coventry, Worcester, Stoke, and Dudley.

600 IN WOLVERHAMPTON TRAINED FOR PHOSPHOROUS

Nearly 600 fire guard officers, wardens, N.F.S., and Home Guard Officers in Wolverhampton have now been trained in precautions against phosphorous bombs. The training which began last April, (although some elementary training has been given since 1942), has been carried out by Sgt. F. Stonier, C.D. and F.G. training officer, and Lieut. H. J. Reynolds, 20th Battalion Staffordshire Home Guard, who is chief chemist of the Wolverhampton Gas Company.

WOLVERHAMPTON TEAM 100% IN CIVIL DEFENCE QUIZ

100% marks were scored by teams competing in the Council Chamber, Wolverhampton last night, in the Wolverhampton semi-final of the Midland Region quiz for women civil defence personnel. Each team consisted of representatives of N.F.S., Wardens, fire-guards and W.V.S. services. Sgt. F. Stonier, Deputy A.R.P. and Training Officer presided.

CIVIL DEFENCE SPORTS ASSOCIATION REPORT

The cricket knock out competition between Y division and Volunteer Transport, will be played twice, on Saturday and Sunday this week, to settle the problem to both parties' satisfaction, and the team with the largest aggregate of runs will be the winner.

It was reported that the bowls competition was a great success, and Mr. Joe Baker, the chairman of that sub-committee was thanked.

It was announced that the N.F.S. had given a cup for a snooker competition, and a sub-committee was appointed to organise competitions in snooker and billiards. It was decided to run a darts competition in which women can compete. There will be a team, and individual competitions – a cup has been given for the team competition. Three women's teams have entered for hockey, a sub-committee has been formed.

Sgt. F. Stonier, chairman, welcomed two new members to the

committee, Councillor T. Phillipson, Chairman of the newly elected football sub-committee, and Inspector Marsh in place of P.C. Cooper, who has joined the forces, will represent the Police.

Later in December, 1943, I earned a commendation from the Chief Constable:

'The Chief Constable highly commends Police Sergeant 14 Stonier for his excellent work in connection with a fire at Messrs. Rudler Bros, Bell Street, Snow Hill, on Monday, December 13th, 1943. When going off duty, he noticed a glow on the roof of Rudlers shop, and upon investigation found that the chimney was on fire, and that this ignited the premises on the ground floor.

Sgt. Stonier gained access to the premises, and attacked the fire, first with buckets of water, and later stirrup pumps, in which he was assisted by personnel of the town pool. He continued his efforts until the arrival of the Fire Brigade, and was slightly injured by falling plaster and brickwork.

Sgt. Stonier's prompt action undoubtedly was the means of preventing a serious fire, and this commendation has been entered on his personal record.'

This was a bit hair-raising. A roaring, out-of-control fire can be a frightening thing at close range. I was surprised at the response of my fire guards. They had been exercised and had not done very well, in fact they were a bit bloody minded. As soon as I espied the fire and asked for their help, they were splendid. We had to climb a high wall to get to the rear of Rudler's and they kept me well supplied with water, called the Fire Service, and guided them to the scene splendidly – top marks!

Regional Recognition

Because of my fire guard activities and successes, the Regional Staff of Baddeley and Bloomfield often invited me to address meetings and courses of other Regional Fire Guards at Queen's College, Birmingham. Here I again met Reg Reynolds from Worcester City Force, whom I had first met at Falfield. He had the same kind of job as I, but he had got his promotion. He was a giant of a man, fair, a proper 'brummy', rough but jocular in manner, with no finesse, but an honest way with him. We always met at the Training Officers' Conference, held every month in Birmingham, and we assisted each other at exercises – I would visit his, and he mine. We examined each other's candidates for instruction and always seemed to be crossing each other's path. It was to go on for some time to come.

Baddeley liked to have us both on the same programme – Reg was the 'broadsword', I was the 'rapier', was how he put it. I can't say we were close friends as he was a 'bar fly' and avid card player, and sought this sort of company when we met on courses; I didn't go much for that sort of thing.

Incident Control

It was about this time that I obtained another qualification – 'Incident Control Officer' Instructor. First I went for a few days to the Civil Defence Staff College at Stoke D'Abernon, near Chobham in Surrey. This was a beautiful country mansion and I attended with a number of senior officers from various services. We were to witness a floor demonstration of incident control by a Mr Harold Brandis. Brandis had been a tally clerk at London Docks and was trained in ARP. When the raids took place on the docks Brandis had organized the aiding services which came to his area to assist. He did this so well that it established the principle of incident control, and he was the expert. A handbook was published and all training officers had to be able to pass on the gospel.

Brandis did his demonstration very well. We returned to the Midlands, and quickly qualified to pass on the instructions. We had our exam on a real bomb site, using real services in Birmingham. By this time, the pattern of Civil Defence or ARP had changed. (Note: ARP by decree was now called Civil Defence.)

Chapter X

Civil Defence in the Blitz Period

The Fire Service started the war as a few regulars and a large number of volunteers, or AFS. It was quickly realized that fire was the greatest hazard. The National Fire Service was formed incorporating regular firemen and volunteers. The volunteers could opt to join the Fire Service or Rescue Service, instead of the armed forces. The service was based on the regions and broken down to divisions and stations. Columns could quickly be formed and had to be available for immediate deployment whenever needed – within the region, or between regions. In this way, badly attacked parts of the country could be assisted by those more fortunate.

Our Fire Brigade Inspector first became a Divisional Officer, and later a Regional Fire Force Commander. Any police-fireman who elected to go over to the Fire Service did well, much better than those I knew that remained with the Police. From then on, the Fire Service severed its connection with the Police, and became a separate service.

The Rescue Service, too, had cause to change. First it swallowed up the First Aid Service, whose members either joined the Rescue or Ambulance Service. Then, as reinforcement of attacked areas from unattacked ones became policy, rescue columns were formed. Nearly all local authority personnel were taken, formed into large self-contained columns, and stationed outside the large built-up areas. Ours were stationed at Sutton Park, a large area of natural parkland between Birmingham and the Black Country.

This left towns like Wolverhampton practically without Rescue and First Aid personnel. Wardens were trained to do quite a lot of this work. Special Rescue and First Aid courses were organized, and the younger type of warden, men and women, trained in a simplified form of operation. They based it on the street's organisation, and in many cases obtained their own equipment. Rescue in Wolverhampton was the Borough Engineer's responsibility. He was fortunate in finding one of his workers, Bill Joyce, who qualified a little later than I. Joyce did a splendid job in building up the Rescue Service, and at one time ran a School for Rescue. I trained a few of his colleagues as local instructors ARP, then Bill would complete their training in rescue techniques, and they became members of his training team. Eventually, when columns were formed, they all obtained officer rank, and saw service in Belgium after the Allies occupied it.

Police, too, were reinforcing on the same basis, except that we gathered our reinforcement from duty men, and never had men standing by in columns outside the town.

Wolverhampton Police sent aid to Plymouth during the 'blitz' there. Wolverhampton itself was lucky as we had only small, spasmodic attacks, lone bombers usually. There was one rather heavy incendiary attack when large fires were started, but it was not followed by the usual HE attack. We heard later that it was because of the low cloud descending on the German airfields in Northern France.

I went to Coventry the morning after their terrible ordeal. We had sent assistance there and were going to see how our men had fared. I shall never forget the scene as we drove into the town. All was silent; the buildings stood gaunt and grim; there was only the sound of dripping water from the wrecked buildings, rubble everywhere, a scene of terrible desolation. We spoke to many people during the day. Their spirits were good, but they were all badly shocked, and in fact, one of the mortuary attendants was so upset by the overwhelming numbers of dead, we took him back to Wolverhampton for a couple of weeks' recuperation.

We could always see when Birmingham was being attacked, as the red glow in the sky was plainly visible from our house. The enemy bombers very often came over our town en route for the North, or Birmingham and I shall never forget the drone of their engines as they flew overhead. One cowered in bed, or wherever one happened to be. We had an anti-aircraft battery on each side of our house at Penn, about two miles away, and when they let fly from both sides it was almost as alarming as being bombed. It was a common practice to wear part of a motor tyre on the shoulders, in addition to the steel helmet, to give some protection from falling shrapnel and shell fragments.

London

When the enemy attacked London with rockets, Quinn and I went to see the results, and to visit our detachment of wardens who had volunteered to relieve the hard-pressed London wardens. We found them in good heart. We inspected bomb damage inflicted by the V2, the rocket, as opposed to the 'buzz bomb', which you could see and hear. It was eerie to feel that damage such as was inflicted by this rocket could descend without any warning.

We visited the tube at night and saw the people settling down in their bunks on the platform, all quite cheerful. We also went to the tube end where work had ceased on the outbreak of war, and a great underground area had been turned into a communal home for literally hundreds. It was a unique spectacle – canteens at intervals, beds, games, lavatories, all laid out with great efficiency, and everyone seeming to be quite cheerful.

We were invited to visit the London Civil Defence Control Centre. This we did, we were shown around by the staff, and finally met the Regional Commissioner, Admiral Evans or 'Evans of the *Broke*', a title he was given by the press for an heroic action in the First World War, when in command of a destroyer, the *Broke*. He thanked us for sending our relief forces to aid his hard-pressed men. He was, I recall, a small man physically, but he gave an impression of confident authority, speaking decisively and to the point. He had, if memory serves me aright, been given this key post after London's first heavy raids had reduced his predecessor to a nervous wreck. It would probably have reduced most people to the same state. Admiral Evans, from his previous record, was just made for the task.

We spent the night lying on the floor of a garage which served as a rescue depot, and both caught a stinking cold! Before I leave this period I should mention the Ambulance Service which was the responsibility of the Medical Officer of Health, Dr Jolly. He had Sgt. Llewellyn from our department seconded to him. Llewellyn had been a chauffeur, and knew something of cars; he had also been a police-fireman working in the fire station but had declined to transfer to the Fire Service. He made a great success of the Ambulance Service which he built up with some paid personnel and a lot of volunteers. Vehicles had been requisitioned and modified while depots had been chosen and adapted to house both vehicles and personnel. The staff were instructed in ARP by our training staff and by Sgt. Llewellyn and others in their duties. They did a great deal of transport work for our department, and were used after the invasion of Normandy for handling casualties from train to hospital. In 1944 he was awarded the BEM quite deservedly for his services.

Film Producer and Actor

I had an idea that a film of the work of an incident officer was a practical and good idea and sold the notion to my superiors, but more importantly to Wilfred Guy, a keen amateur photographer. Wilf, and his brother, Reg, held the local Ford agency. Reg was the extrovert, was a councillor, and later Mayor, and also ran a volunteer transport pool throughout the War, which proved to be extremely useful. Wilf was the quiet type. We had a slum clearance area in Wolverhampton which lent itself to the project. We worked out a script, filmed it on Sunday mornings as a rule, sought and obtained the co-operation of all services, as it is never difficult to get people to allow themselves to be filmed, I found, including myself! Altogether, we obtained an hour-long film which required a narrator; it had its premiere before the heads of services and was highly praised. After taking it around the services, I showed it all over the Midlands – it now rests, I believe, in Wolverhampton's Town Hall archives.

My Last Months in the Department

After Tilley's departure, Ballance was appointed Chief Constable. He was popular in the town, and generally in the Force. Thus his great ambition was realized, to be Chief Constable in his own force. Fortunately for me, the Home Office saw it differently, and would not approve the appointment. No local man could have control of our force after all the upset there had been with Tilley. There was, of course, a muted outcry, but it quickly died away and a compromise was reached. Ballance was given the job of Chief Constable of Barrow-in-Furness, and the Chief Constable of Barrow-in-Furness, Goodchild, was appointed to Wolverhampton. Barrow was a smaller force. So disappeared my two enemies – Tilley and Ballance.

By this time training was almost at a standstill as the War had progressed to the point where raids on this country had more or less died out. Services were stood down and one could begin to look ahead. I considered my position. My sole preoccupation for the past six years was almost over, so I decided to try to impress myself favourably on the new Chief.

Shortly after his arrival he announced that a promotion examination would be held within a few months. I decided to sit for it although I need not have done so as I had passed my Sergeant to Inspector examination before the War. By sitting again, I could at least prove that I had not forgotten my police work, although it was quite unprecedented! I have never heard of anyone taking the Inspector's examination twice – it was a bit of a gamble, too. I had passed well on the former occasion, could I do so again? Well, I had plenty of time to study and the work in our department had almost stopped, certainly the training side had.

I got out all my books and studied hard. I had a notebook full of copious notes on a CID course that Tom Marsh had attended some years before at Scotland Yard. He had returned, and in a series of classes, passed on his information. I had taken full notes at the time and in the ensuing examination at the end of the course, I topped with 93 per cent. The notes had proved invaluable as I had learned the whole notebook off by heart.

BEM

Whilst I was engaged in this, I was notified, six months after Llewellyn's award, that I too had been awarded the British Empire Medal, in June 1944.

Six months later, Reg Reynolds of Worcester got his BEM, but by then the King had ceased to present them. To Reg's disappointment, he received his from the Lord Lieutenant of his county.

On Tilley's retirement, the Town Clerk, Mr Brock Allen had been appointed Controller, and Mr Barr, his deputy, was, as a result, at Chubbs a great deal.

I had come across the Town Clerk on a few occasions during my ARP career, and he had been very complimentary. I had worked with Mr Barr a great deal, and had sold his beloved Zone Control Scheme. I recall him saying to me, after he had finally completed writing it, that he was relying on me to sell it to the senior officers of the Authority, which is precisely what I did when I staged my demonstration. Whether my change in fortune came from them, I don't know, someone 'up there' was pushing me and I had more friends than I realised. I had dozens of letters of congratulation, for example:

9. 6. 44. (from a schoolmaster)

Dear Mr. Stonier,

May I offer my sincere congratulations on the high honour of the award of the B.E.M., which has been conferred on you. I am confident that I am voicing the thoughts of all the A.R.P. Services in Wolverhampton, when I say that never has an award proved

COPY

Central 2571

Telegrams Emregoom Birmingham

Regional Headquarters
Civic House
Birmingham, 3.

7th June, 1944.

Sir,

        I recently drew the attention of the Minister of Home Security to the excellent manner in which you have carried out your duties as Training Officer for Wolverhampton, since your appointment in 1937. Also to the keenness and enthusiasm which you have maintained in your work, which has acted as an inspiration to all concerned.

        On consideration Mr. Herbert Morrison felt that your devotion to duty and meritorious services were deserving of high praise and he took steps to bring the matter to the notice of His Majesty the King. I now have the pleasure of informing you, at the request of the Minister, that His Majesty has been graciously pleased to award you the British Empire Medal, Civil Division, in recognition of your services to Civil Defence.

        The notice of this award will appear in His Majesty's Birthday Honours List, to be published as a Supplement to the London Gazette on Saturday, 10th June 1944.

        I am,
           Sir,
              Your obedient Servant,

              Signed.

            Regional Commissioner.
            Midland Civil Defence Region.

Police Sergeant Frederick Stonier,
Penn Police Station,
Penn Road,
<u>WOLVERHAMPTON</u>.

so popular or so deservedly well merited. We have only a small idea of the tremendous amount of time which you have given so freely, to make Wolverhampton C.D. Services so efficient, but we do know how easily, and yet so forcefully, you have imparted your knowledge to the innumerable people who have had the privilege and pleasure of attending your lectures and demonstrations.

    You have brought honour to Wolverhampton and to her Civil

Defence Service – you must feel proud of your Wardens, and believe me, Mr. Stonier, your Wardens are mighty proud of you!

Yours very sincerely,
ROBERT HODGSON

Meanwhile, I passed my promotion examination very well, so a little bird whispered.

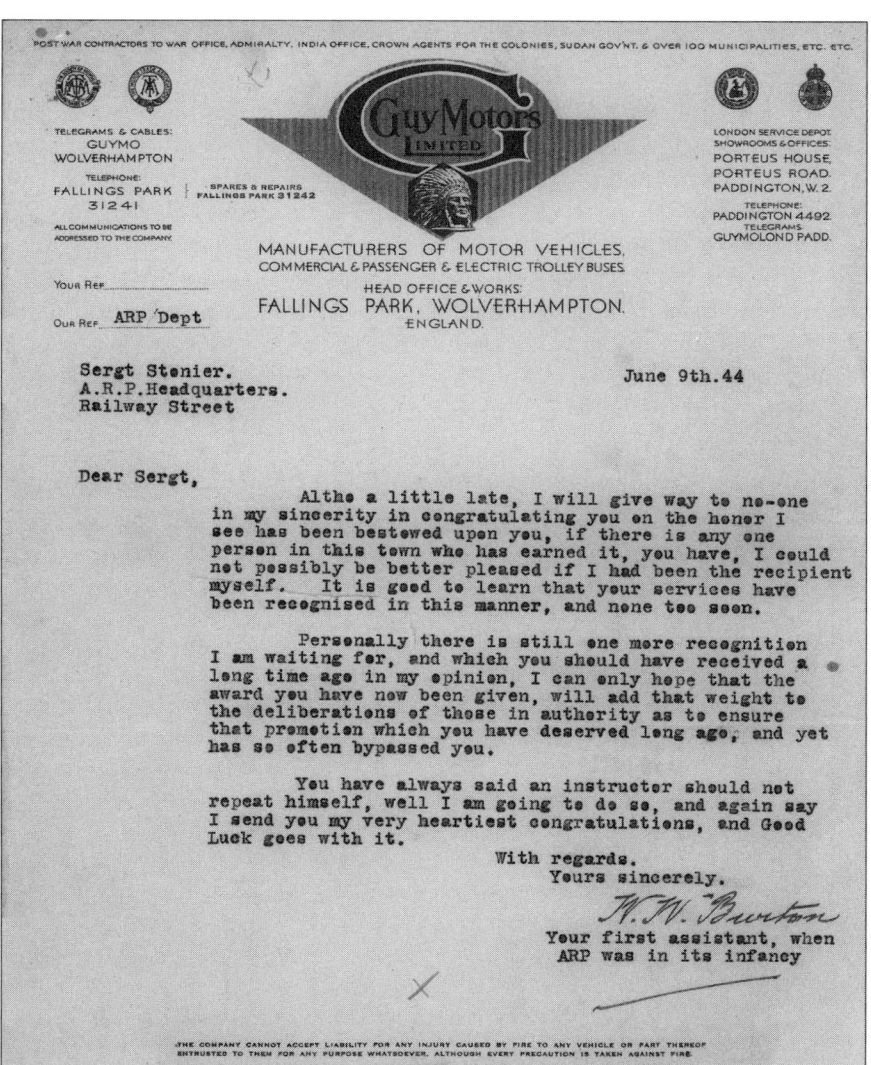

Hutton Advanced Driving Course

In March 1944, Llewellyn, Barnwell and I were sent on an advanced driving course to the Lancashire Police Force's recently re-established school at Hutton, near Preston. Our new Chief Constable was about to establish an information room and someone was to run that and the Motor Patrol Section.

We were all keen to do well and off we went, friendly competitors. It was an enjoyable course although rationing was still very much in being, and as I recall, we had a great many eggs to eat, as these were plentiful in that part of the country. After about ten days we all had skin eruptions from a surfeit of eggs. We slept in dormitories and had a very enjoyable time. The course was a copy of the Hendon Course which had been designed by the famous racing driver, Earl Howe.

We had to forget the old way of driving and relearn how to do it correctly. All the time we were driving, we had to commentate on what we were doing and why. We had speed tests, had to pass a test on the skidpan and had an examination in driving theory. We had the opportunity to drive some beautiful cars that had been under wraps during the War. All three of us qualified. Barnwell came top overall. I was top in theory, but his practical was a bit better than mine, although there was little in it. Llewellyn was well down on both of us. We returned home.

Chapter XI

Promotion

On Friday, 13 April 1944, I was promoted Inspector and went before the Watch Committee with Sgt. Gwilliam from the CID.

Our Chief Constable had not been in office long enough to form much of an appreciation of any of us, so he must have had to rely on advice from some source or sources. Again, I felt that someone high up had given me a helping hand, so my decision to soldier on, and do my best, had at last paid dividends. I again had dozens of letters of congratulation.

I had not told Rose that I was to attend the Watch Committee, but had decided to be sure, and tell her when I had got the promotion. She learned of it at work when her workmates brought the *Express and Star* with a full account and picture of both Gwilliam and myself.

The reason Rose had gone to work was purely economic. Early in the forties, we found it difficult to live on my wages and I was having to sell things like my typewriter, cycle and the child's pram.

As soon as this became obvious, Rose volunteered for a job, twenty hours a week, at the Sunbeamland factory, where parts of Lancaster bombers were being made. She was put on a capstan lathe, and became so good at the job, they tried to persuade her to go on full time. She could not do this, of course, as she had two young children, but had she done so, she would have earned around £20 per week, a great deal then and far more than I got.

Patrol Inspector

After a short celebration, I was told that I would take over the Night Relief. This I did, and for the next nine months I had such a hectic time that even the Chief Constable had to admit that I was having a baptism under fire. I was glad that I had previous experience as a sergeant on patrol work, and reserve or station sergeant. The latter entailed accepting or refusing minor charges, and calling in the Inspector for anything serious. As Inspector, the decision to accept or refuse

> Telegrams THORAM, WOLVERHAMPTON.
> Telephone Nº 23076.
>
> **THORNE, BECKETT & Cº**
> SOLICITORS.
>
> W. A. B. BECKETT.
> COMMISSIONER FOR OATHS.
> G. J. B. THORNE.
>
> B/B.
>
> Old Bank Chambers,
> Lich Gates,
> Wolverhampton.
>
> 14th April 19 45.
>
> Dear Inspector Stonier,
>
> There are two occasions upon which I am impelled by the "Express & Star", to write a letter to somebody. One is consequent upon the announcement of the untimely demise of a friend, a client, or a friend and client. The other occasion is of course, whenever honours or decorations are showered upon you.
>
> The first type of occasion does not lend itself to enthusiasm or humour, but of necessity calls for restraint and sympathy. I am glad that this is not one of those occasions. It was with great pleasure that I read in last nights "Express & Star" the news of your promotion to the rank of Inspector.
>
> Great as was the honour conferred upon you in the form of the B.E.M., it did occur to me that there was possibly a slight catch in this. It seems to me that your present promotion gives you two more tangible things, namely, better status in your profession, and presumably larger deductions under P.A.Y.E. Why you have been obliged to wait ten years for this promotion is something which many of us have been unable to understand.
>
> This will mean I presume that you will now lay down what at one time looked like being your life work and return to normal duties. If the Local Authority should decide to present each member of Civil Defence with a Medal in commemoration of their services during the present war, may I suggest that a suitable design upon one side of such a medal would be a STONIER RAMPANT astraide a Warden and a Fireguard both COUCHANT with the words "OB HAS CAUSAS" below.
>
> Please accept my congratulations.
>
> Yours sincerely,
>
> Inspector F.S. Stonier,
> c/o Civil Defence Head Quarters,
> Railway Street,
> Wolverhampton.

charges was mine. In the daytime, it was comparatively easy as there were plenty of superiors around to consult, the CID was manned and they could take over any serious criminal charge. At night-time, none of this existed, you only called out CID if the matter was vital, and a superior only in case of homicide or something akin.

During my baptism, I almost went through the book with rape, breakings, woundings, even ending up with a murder. It was only a

TWO NEW W'TON POLICE INSPECTORS

—And Two Sergeants

SERGEANT F. STONIER, deputy chief warden and A.R.P. training officer, and Detective-sergeant A. Gwilliam were promoted to the rank of inspector at this afternoon's meeting of Wolverhampton Watch Committee.

Police-constables F. Howard and W. L. White were promoted sergeants.

Inspector Stonier has been responsible for training thousands of Wolverhampton civil defence personnel.

He was awarded the B.E.M. in June of last year.

He joined the police force in 1927, and was promoted sergeant in 1935 after five years service with the police motor patrol.

Since the beginning of the organisation he has been associated with A.R.P. work, and in 1937 attended the Home Office training school at Falfield, qualifying as an instructor with highest certificate award.

He started his original class at Wolverhampton police station in 1937. He comes from a family of policemen, both his uncles having been members of the constabulary in various parts of the country.

Inspector Gwilliam joined Wolverhampton police force in September, 1925, and was promoted sergeant in December, 1939. He entered the Criminal Investigation Department in April, 1932, and has been in that department ever since, having at one time having had charge of the aliens department and the security office.

Police-constable Howard joined the force in November, 1930, and entered the chief constable's office in 1937.

Police-constable White joined in January, 1931, and entered the C.I.D. in November, 1938.

Insp. F. Stonier.   Insp. A. Gwilliam

mercy killing, but still murder. I think I acquitted myself reasonably well.

Day duty was relatively easy in comparison. I now had the task of covering large football matches, race meetings and a host of new and interesting tasks.

VE Day

I was on late turn on this momentous day. Strange to say, I can only recall going into the town centre during the early evening. For some reason people assembled in the town centre as though they must be in a crowd with their fellow men and women to properly express themselves. There was no chance of carrying out normal duties, such as visiting the men, and the streets were packed with happy, singing people. Every policeman was more or less stuck where he was. We did, of course, bring in outside men to assist but there was not much that could, or needed to be done. I don't think I got any further than Queen Square. The place was packed, all traffic stopped, the people dancing and singing. The Prince Consort Statue was draped with folks, and the poor Prince, who had stood there for seventy or eighty years, lost his spurs and reins for the first time. At one point, a young and pretty bus conductress flung her arms round me and kissed me, to roars of approval from the throng who asked for an encore, and got one too! Then, of course, the beer started to flow, and we had drunks galore. It was no use trying to arrest them, they were left alone. So the long, tiring but thrilling evening and night wore on. By about 1 a.m. things had quietened down, and late turn went home at last, leaving the now quiet town to the night relief. I thought to myself, as all this went on: What a time we had all shared together, the phoney war period, the shock of our early defeats, and Dunkirk; the large numbers of strange uniforms that appeared overnight in our town, Czechs, Poles, Free French, Belgian and Dutch, which after about a week suddenly disappeared; the rundown of food in the shops, the rationing of food, clothes, sweets, the almost rationing of beer and tobacco by shortages; the horrible blackout and driving with hooded lights; the threat of invasion and the road blocks guarded by the Home Guard, with a road block outside my house at Penn where I was challenged for a while each time I came home; the bombing raids and the depths of despair when Singapore fell; then the turn of the tide, culminating in the build-up to D-Day; mile after mile of vehicles going past our house at Penn; the happy faces of the young Americans on their way south, seeing the children standing at the gate, waving to them, and throwing to them chocolate bars, chewing gum and Horlick's milk tablets; the invasion, and the way we all held our breath until the beachhead was secured; the drive on to Germany, and now, at last, final victory in Europe. It was a great time to have lived – and survived, and I feel strangely grateful to have played a small part.

Buckingham Palace – the Investiture

I attended as summoned on 28 June 1945, in uniform. My friends rallied round and I was booked into the Cumberland Hotel for two days by some of them, at their expense – I couldn't afford it. Rose and my eldest daughter, Norah, went with me. The Cumberland Hotel was splendid, and of course we enjoyed it, but the food, as everywhere else, was terrible, including powdered egg and a doubtful sausage for breakfast. We travelled by bus from the Cumberland to Buckingham Palace, entered the hallowed precincts, and parted at the door. Rose and Norah went with all the other relatives and friends of the recipients, and watched the proceedings from seats in the room where the awards were

At the Palace to receive BEM, 1945 with Rose and Norah.

to be made, being entertained by a band playing light music. We recipients were taken into an adjoining room, briefed on the correct way to behave on presentation to the Sovereign, and lined up – soldiers, sailors, airmen, Merchant Navy, Police, Fire, and women too. We were all about equivalent awards – MM, MC, BEM, DFM.

As we walked up the ramp on hearing our name called, the speaker gave the words of the citation. At the top of the ramp one turned left, bowed to the King, George VI, who was in naval uniform, and advanced a few paces. He pinned on the medal, and shook hands, asking me when

CENTRAL CHANCERY OF
THE ORDERS OF KNIGHTHOOD,
ST JAMES'S PALACE, S.W.1.

26th April 1945.

CONFIDENTIAL.

Sir,
    The King will hold an Investiture at Buckingham Palace on Tuesday, the 26th June, 1945, at which your attendance is requested.
    It is requested that you should be at the Palace not later than 10.15 o'clock a.m. (Doors open at 9.45 a.m.)
        DRESS:—Service Dress; Morning Dress; Civil Defence
            Uniform or Dark Lounge Suit.
    This letter should be produced by you on entering the Palace, as no further card of admission will be issued.
    I am desired to inform you that you may be accompanied by two relations or friends to witness the Investiture, but I regret that owing to the limited accommodation available for spectators, it is not possible for this number to be increased. The spectators' tickets may be obtained on application to this Office and I have to ask you, therefore, to complete the enclosed form and return it to me immediately.

                I am, Sir,
                Your obedient Servant,

Sergeant Fred Stonier,
        B.E.M.   Secretary.

I had received the award. I replied appropriately, bowed, backed three paces, and passed on.

On leaving the Palace I was approached by a press photographer who told me that the *Express and Star* had requested him to take our photograph. He did this, next night we appeared in the local paper and I was sent three copies of the photograph – altogether a wonderful experience.

During this time we had a visit from the great Winston Churchill, probably a booster for the local Conservative candidate during the run-up to an election. He came to Molineux Ground where he addressed a vast audience, with a temporary erection as his platform. I was supervising the policing and went near the platform to hear his speech. When he left, he rode in an open car, cigar in hand, and I was struck by his small stature, and his baby pink appearance. He stood up to acknowledge the cheers of the crowd, obviously enjoying the hero worship.

It had been a wonderful twelve months but now my career took another turn.

Ryton-on-Dunsmore Police Training Centre

The Home Office had decided to establish training centres for dealing with the influx of men joining the Police Force. Future policy was to standardize procedure all over the country by using schools set up and staffed by Home Office nominees, to train all recruits, and also to provide refresher courses. To do this they decided to open the first training centre at Ryton-on-Dunsmore, near Coventry. The Midland forces were circulated and asked to send possible instructors to a course at Hendon. Sgt. Eric Cameron was sent from our force, and he qualified, being then posted to Ryton. Others were sent from Birmingham, Dudley, Coventry and Staffordshire.

The first Commandant was a Mr G. S. Jackson, Chief Constable of Newcastle-under-Lyme; the Deputy, Chief Inspector Galloway from Birmingham. Once this small team had established the training centre, further instructors were required. Forces were circulated, and Quinn and I went from our force as candidates.

We met about fifteen to twenty other candidates from the Midlands, mainly sergeants and inspectors, including Reg Reynolds. After interview, we came home to await the result. Shortly after, Quinn and I were ordered to attend a week's course at the centre, along with most of the other candidates.

The climax of the course was a half-hour lecture, which was in effect the examination, I suppose. I gave a talk on 'The History of the Police Force' and was in good form. I felt I would like a two-year secondment to this job as it would sharpen up my law and police theory. The lecture was well received, and generally, even among my competitors, considered far and away the best. I was led to believe I was 'past the post'.

On our return to Wolverhampton, Quinn and I were interviewed by the Chief Constable. Quinn told him I was bound to be accepted. Sure enough, a few days later I was informed that I had qualified, and that the Watch Committee had agreed to my secondment for two years to this, the first established Home Office Police Training Centre in the whole country, excluding Hendon, which was really Metropolitan Police. I took up my duties in January 1946.

The training centre was a large complex which had housed industrial workers from the Coventry area. It had plenty of sleeping accommodation, office, messing facilities, and open tarmac space suitable for drill and parades. There was a large assembly room with a stage, altogether ideal for its purpose. It could accommodate several hundred trainees at a time and the country around was pleasant, with a few pubs nearby.

The instructors were housed in one block, where each had a bedroom with all facilities, and a small sitting room on the other side of the passage, simply furnished, but comfortable. The bathrooms were at the end of the corridor. This was my home for the next two years.

Training

Our courses were to be of thirteen weeks duration, during which time over 150 lectures would be given. Some of these had not yet been written so we spent much time drafting suitable lecture notes. Later, before I left, these were consolidated, and formed the basis of the training syllabus at other police training centres, which opened subsequently all over the country. Eventually we were ready to start, and my first course was Number 8.

Staff

We instructors were a mixed bunch, with some experienced policemen among which I numbered myself, some with CID experience, traffic experience, general police duties, and at least a third had come almost straight from the Services. These latter had been policemen before the War, had joined up, received commissions, and had now returned to

The First Instructional Staff at Ryton-on-Dunsmore 1946.
Left to Right: Front Row: *1 Author; 2 Cameron; 4 Galloway; 5 Bond; 6 Tetlow; 8 Conliffe; 9 Hickey. 9 of the last two rows became superintendents.* Second Row: *1 Miller; 2 Shephard; 6 Holland; 8 Higgs; 10 Baggs* Third Row: *1 McCrory; 2 Nicholson; 3 Froggat; 5 Geddes; 4 Hubble; 6 Walker.*

their forces. They quickly learned the ropes from us more experienced men, and most of them subsequently became Superintendents.

The Commandant

Mr Jackson was a very able policeman and administrator, which was just as well as our bunch were not easy to handle. The ex-officer types had a slight superiority complex whereas the experienced policemen were rather contemptuous of them, so there were all the ingredients of trouble. The fact that it never reached serious proportions speaks volumes for the patience and forbearance of all. As time went on, the two sides became more compatible and learned to respect each other.

Mr Galloway

The Deputy was also a very able man, but he had an unfortunate manner of rubbing up his superiors the wrong way, although he was kept in his place by Mr Jackson. Mr Bond, who followed Jackson, and was a more gentle man, had some difficulty with him.

The New Recruits

I enjoyed my first course. I knew now that my vocation was teaching, particularly lecturing – I had found something I did extremely well. We were supposed to be able to teach all subjects and were not allowed to specialize. This, of course, was silly as some of the men had experience in certain aspects of police work that made them practical experts on certain subjects, and they should have been allowed to pass on that knowledge.

Nobody wanted to deal with Trade Disputes Legislation, so I took it on. We had a good archive department where I studied all the relevant case history and law, and drafted out a fair lecture on it. This I gave in my colleagues' classes at their request. Galloway disapproved on principle, but he turned a 'blind eye'.

We lectured for about five hours a day – hard, exacting work. Our students, men and women, had largely come straight from the armed forces, and were a fine lot. Probably the best type of recruits ever taken into the police service were those recruited in 1930 until the War, most of whom were grammar school, and those joining immediately after the War. We had large numbers of commissioned officers among them, including one who had been a lieutenant colonel, rejoining as a police constable.

The standard achieved in their examinations was of a high order and I felt privileged to be training such fine types. Alas, two years later, when they should have returned for a refresher course, a large proportion were missing. Enquiries elicited the fact that they had left the Service because of the low pay, the shift work that was unacceptable, the fact that their wives did not like the unsociable hours, and many could not accept starting as constables after having held officer rank.

This to me seemed to be a turning point in the Police Service. From being a job it was difficult to attain, and which one never left except in the most exceptional circumstances, the new recruits seemed to get in fairly easily, as most forces had an exodus of men eligible for pension when the War ended. They found the job uncongenial in many respects

My first recruit course 1946.

I stage a demonstration for the Home Secretary, Mr Chuter Ede, Ryton 1946. The oriental-looking gentleman behind is Sir Frank Newsome, Permanent Secreary, Home Office.

My class at Ryton 1946–8.

and did not hesitate to leave as there were other jobs available – no 2–3 million unemployed then. Discipline in consequence began to suffer, not very noticeably at first, but by 1950 it was a very different type of service to the one I had joined, but more of that later.

As my first course came to an end, a party was held by my class at a local pub, a spread was laid on, I was the guest of honour, and was presented with a pewter tankard. I was sorry to see them go, as in thirteen weeks I had grown fond of them and it was quite a wrench. I felt this about all my classes. The following courses followed the same pattern. I joined in the swimming lessons, as did the other instructors, which were part of the course, held at Leamington Swimming Baths. We had a fine time, going to Leamington several times a week in a utility truck. There were badminton and table tennis sessions in the evenings and I became quite adept at both, although among these young lions there were always one or two who were too good for the instructors.

It was about this time that we were honoured by a visit from the Home Secretary, Mr Chuter Ede. He came with Frank Newsome (later Sir Frank), the Permanent Secretary, and other officials. We staged various demonstrations, and I was in charge of one, showing the procedure for dealing with a serious traffic accident. The stage was set. I have a large picture of the Home Secretary and Newsome having the scene explained to them by myself. He visited, and saw all there was to see, expressed his satisfaction, and departed. A memorable day at the new Police Training Centre!

Characters

We had, of course, characters among our staff. Jim Weaver, from Staffordshire, was a bluff old sergeant major type, and was the drill instructor, a hangover from the First World War veterans of whom very few were left. After a few months, he retired on pension and his place was taken by Cunliffe, also from Staffordshire. He had been a lieutenant in the Army, and came to us as a Temporary Inspector. He was dark, good-looking, a good drill instructor, a splendid organizer of concerts, a good actor, but an indifferent police lecturer, mainly I think because he knew very little about it. He was a terrible poseur. When off duty he had a habit of trailing around in a flowered dressing gown, and Roman-type sandals. He was married to a plain, adoring wife and went no further in the Police Force on his return to normal duty.

Geddes

A sergeant from Northampton. He was the Physical Training Instructor, rough as they come, no intellectual, but he was good at his job, which was not easy, handling some of these ex-service types. He was, however, quite capable, and willing too, of punching their heads if they got too big for their boots (off duty of course). He was too outspoken for his own good and remained a sergeant throughout his police career.

Froggatt

Ex-RAF pilot, came from Stoke-on-Trent. Long handlebar moustache, his off-beat, flamboyant attitude hid a shrewd, calculating mind. Ended as a Superintendent.

Higgs

Another ex-RAF pilot. Same type, a little more naive than Froggatt. He had a good singing voice. Not terribly strong on his law, but worked hard at it. He too became a Superintendent.

McCrory

Ex-Commando, long moustache, clever comedian, sharp mind, good instructor. He had an unhappy married life, divorced his wife. He eventually became a Deputy Chief Constable.

Nicholson

A sergeant from Northampton. Sturdy, dour, a good policeman, shrewd, good lecturer, no nonsense man. He had the constant task of keeping his pal Geddes out of trouble. After a long delay, eventually promoted to Superintendent. Coming from a small force like my own, he knew what it was like to have to wait for the prizes to reach one.

Baggs and Simons

Two sergeants from Birmingham. It is unusual to find lasting friendships in the police force, the struggle for promotion makes this difficult, but these two were friends all through their service. Very good instructors, but not likeable characters, inclined to be openly contemptuous of anyone they felt was a little inferior. Both good policemen. Baggs became a Superintendent; I think Simons died whilst still serving.

These were the chief characters when I joined the staff at Ryton.

2,000th Recruit Parade, Sept. 1947. Myself, 7th from left.

There were several other instructors, but they left within a few months. There was a growing feeling that secondment was not necessarily good for one's career. Three left in my first few months because they felt they were losing ground in their own force – 'out of sight, out of mind', as it was succinctly put. It was felt that it was a good posting for a young ambitious sergeant, not necessarily for an inspector.

As these men left, others joined, among them Reg Reynolds. It now became apparent that when we attended the training course, we had been graded first choice, second choice, and so on. I felt pleased at having been in the first category. Reg stayed for a few months, and took a course through from start to finish, but he was not happy. This work was more exacting then Civil Defence, there is only one interpretation of law – the correct one – not a subject that can be loosely dealt with. He may have had pressures from home, I don't know, but he quickly departed back to his force.

Eric Cameron was the next to go. He returned to Wolverhampton and was fairly quickly promoted to Inspector. This now left me as the sole force representative.

Concert Party

Under Cunliffe's guidance we staged a concert for the outgoing course, McCrory, Higgs, Froggatt and myself being the main characters. I took part in a sketch, a quartette and worked the lights. There was one amusing scene when a telephone bell was supposed to ring. On the night, the bell failed, nothing would make it ring, so in desperation I spoke out plainly from behind the curtain, 'Ting-a-ling, Ting-a-ling'. Roars of laughter, but at least the cue was given, and the play proceeded. It took a bit of living down; it was a good job the course was on its way out.

Cunliffe's behaviour during our rehearsals was in the highest theatrical tradition. He raved and ranted, was full of praise one minute, sarcastic the next – he was having a ball. Anyhow, the show was a great success, so much so that we were invited to give it at a Leicester City Police gathering. We went to Leicester and to a full house gave a very good performance; this time the bell worked! I enjoyed this, having given monologues on many occasions during my Civil Defence days; like all lecturers and instructors, I loved being on-stage with an audience. After all, the art of lecturing and acting have much in common.

Visitors

While I was at Ryton, Rose and the two children often came and stayed with me. This was allowed and they always enjoyed the trip. My cousins, Florence and Ethel Crofts came too with their families to visit me, and I, in turn, visited them at their homes. I also called on my cousin Sam Crofts. That was the last time I saw any of them.

Change of Command and Professor Webster

Mr Jackson left after a few months and was appointed Chief Constable of Hull, which was a much larger force than Newcastle-under-Lyme. He later went to a still larger force, Newcastle-on-Tyne, where he finished his career. Mr Bond, the Chief Constable of Rutland, was the next Commandant. A nice quiet man, he remained during the remainder of my stay. His force was very small, about twenty-eight men, no larger really than a relief in a larger force. He ran the centre quietly and efficiently.

Birmingham held a course of their own, using the centre's facilities, but providing their own staff. One of their frequent lecturers was Professor Webster, a forensic pathologist of great repute, particularly as a pathologist. His lectures were always worth attending. He had a unique style, breaking all the rules of lecturing. He would pace up and down the stage, hands behind his back, calling us all 'laddies'. He had the most gruesome slides as exhibits, all authentic cases, that he had been called upon to deal with as the Regional Home Office Pathologist. He was, of course, called out to all murder cases in No. 4 Police District. After showing a slide of violent death, he would turn to the audience and ask, 'Well, was it suicide or murder?' Very fascinating. We were taken to his laboratory in Birmingham to inspect the exhibits. I can only recall one thing, that there were several large jars of uteri that had been lacerated by illegal abortions. Some of the wounds were terrible. I thought of the despair that had forced those females to adopt such a course and the agony of their deaths – another of those experiences which left one low and subdued.

Messing

The food throughout my stay was pretty terrible. Rationing was still in force, and remained so for years to come. The catering staff were not very expert – at one time the chef was an Austrian refugee professor.

If we had peas at lunch, it was a safe bet that the leftovers would appear at supper as soup. It was difficult to remain satisfied for long as the food lacked body. We all scrounged bread and butter, or most likely margarine, took it to our rooms, and toasted it on our electric fire as a snack at night. Almost everyone had indigestion, and 'Rennies' antacid tablets were the best selling line in our centre shop! Meals were formal affairs. The duty officer for the day would wait until all the students and instructors were in the dining room, and then lead in the Commandant and Deputy. Everyone would stand on the order, and resume their seats when the two were seated. The duty officer sat by the side of the Commandant, and had a large bell which he rang before making any announcements, which he did after the meal was over. The Commandant and Deputy then rose, and left, while everyone stood to attention. The instructors always sat at the top table. This was the drill for lunch and dinner; breakfast was quite informal.

Passing Out Parades

At the end of the courses, a parade was held. A Chief Constable from one of the larger forces would attend, inspect the recruits and take the salute, all done very professionally. He would then address the students and that was the end of it. On such occasions the instructors would line up separately but take no part in the drill, which was Cunliffe's big moment!

The Last Few Months at Ryton

After about twenty months, I wanted to return to my force as I had nothing to gain by remaining at Ryton. It had been a useful experience, but I already felt that I had perhaps been away too long. I heard that Llewellyn had been put in charge of the Information Room (now set up in what had been the wartime Report and Control Centre) and the Motor Patrol, and had been promoted Inspector. To his credit, he carried out his new duties quite well, backed as he was by an experienced staff which included old Bill Churchward (ex-Inspector), who returned and worked in the Information Room as a civilian clerk. His knowledge and experience must have been of great value. Eventually it was agreed that I could return, which I did in January, 1948. Before leaving I was presented with a wall barometer by my colleagues. When I left, there was talk of a new Police College being established at Ryton for the training of potential senior officers. The training centre was to move to a similar type of accommodation in Staffordshire.

Other recruit training centres were also being established in different parts of the country to serve the various police districts.

A few months later the College was established, and potential instructors invited to apply as members of the staff. I applied, but my Chief Constable turned down my application on the grounds that only chief inspectors and above were permitted to apply. This may have been so, but it was strange that one member of the Ryton staff was appointed, Inspector Holland, from the Surrey Constabulary. However, the Chief could have been forgiven for feeling that after so much secondment, I ought to do a little more for the Wolverhampton Force – I don't know.

Chapter XII

Return to Duty

I went back to the old routine of early, late, and night turns, races, football matches, preparing the duty book, making up the parade state, and so on.

The parade state was always prepared by the Night Inspector. One had to show where everyone on the Force was that day, whether sick, on leave, on annual leave, on a course, which department, which relief – OK, if everyone else had made their returns correctly, a headache if not. It could be done in an hour if all went well, or it could take all night, if not. It was every inspector's nightmare. If one was in charge alone, and there was a spate of difficult charges brought in, there simply was not time to do justice to both. In my opinion, it was a clerical job, and should have been undertaken by the Chief Constable's Office staff, who had no such distractions, and had available in the daytime all the various departments who could supply necessary information. However, it went on until I left. So my life went on in a routine manner for the next two years.

Medals

In 1949, I, with several other officers, was presented with my Police Long Service and Good Conduct Medal for twenty-two years' service. We lined up in the Mayor's Parlour in the Town Hall, the Chief Constable and Chairman of the Watch Committee were present. The mayor gave a short address and gave each of us our medal. I had received the Defence Medal after the end of the War, as did nearly everyone else, so now I had three medals to display. I don't think from that day on, I ever had an opportunity to wear them again.

Changes

The Superintendent was now George Pendered, a tough 'brummy', shortish, thickly built, who never altered his rough Birmingham accent until the day he left. Many men as they rise in rank try to improve their speech, but not so George, so that eventually he was accepted, rough speech and all, as a character. He was shrewd and quite ruthless. If he took a dislike to a man, he would make that man's life quite difficult. I know at least three men, good policemen too, who left because of his attitude towards them. On the other hand, he was hardworking, completely dedicated to police work, and had been a brilliant detective, knew his law, and had been quite an athlete. He was a fine walker, and always won the mile walk at our Police Sports, which were held every August Bank Holiday until the Second World War. He had been a pretty formidable footballer too, when younger. He was a First World War veteran, ex-Coldstream Guards.

Tom Marsh had returned from war service, and was now Chief Inspector, CID.

During the next two years, Inspectors Chance and Dawson, the ex-traffic point duty experts of yesteryear retired, as did Aston, the brother of Jimmy, the ex-CID Chief. This enabled Barnwell, Rivers (who joined with me) and a new character to these notes, Frank Howard, to be promoted from the Chief Constable's Office, from which more promotions came than any other department. He was a keen Police Federationist, and had been Secretary of the Constables' and Sergeants' Branch Boards.

Note. The Police Federation includes all ranks up to, and including Chief Inspector. Membership is automatic, and it is really the policemen's union. The superintendents have their Association, as do the Chief Constables.

Police Federation

I had never taken much interest in this – like many ambitious people, I felt it was detrimental to my career. When I became an inspector, I was voted in to the office of Secretary to the Inspectors' Branch Board. It did not entail much work – occasionally a meeting, but not often, an annual visit to the conference in London, and a report on one's return. I held the office until the promotion of Frank Howard, when I voluntarily relinquished the job to him, as he had been associated with it as Secretary to the Constables' and Sergeants' Branch Boards.

I enjoyed my three trips to London. On the first occasion I accompanied Rivers, the sergeants' representative, and Phillips, the constables'. We had all joined together in 1927 and now held different ranks, but we largely forgot this during our two nights' stay in London. We stayed at the Russell Hotel in Russell Square. I remember the place had, at the end of the War, a very shabby appearance. The food, as everywhere else, was pretty poor, but we enjoyed ourselves. We attended conference during the day and the evenings were spent looking at the sights and having a drink.

I was very impressed with the standard of debate at the conference; those chaps who took Federation work seriously could marshal their facts, and speak very well. The election to officers of the Central Committee which negotiated for us with the Home Office and Local Government, was by general concensus at the latter end of the conference. By then the hopeful candidates had by their speeches either impressed the rest of us, or not, and were voted in on that basis. Of course, some of the existing officers were re-elected because of their sterling work during the year, and ability to express our views.

The last day was always watched by the Home Secretary as an occasion when he could, as the responsible minister, address the rank and file. It also gave our newly elected Chairman a chance to impress us, and the Home Secretary with his ability. All very interesting! Many men had won national recognition, and almost another career by their performances at conference, and their appointment to the Central Committee. It was, of course, normal Trade Union procedure, but we were not allowed to be called a union, and could not withdraw our labour.

On my two subsequent visits to Conference I accompanied Gwilliam, who had been promoted with me and we became quite friendly for a time. We visited the shows *Bless the Bride* and *Oklahoma*. I tried my first Chinese meal on one trip – one mouthful was enough for me and Gwilliam finished mine as well as his own. There was one strange event that went on every year – it was the fascination that talking to the prostitutes of Piccadilly and its environs had for some of our delegates. Nowhere, at that time, was prostitution flaunted as it was in London. We had it in our provincial towns, of course, but it was under cover and very furtive. There was nothing sinister in all this as the girls knew we came each year at the same time; we just chatted to them, our chaps eager to hear about the kind of life they led, and they, able to speak to a policeman without fear of being arrested – a kind of truce. I don't think there were many occasions when our chaps succumbed, they knew a bit too much of the business for that risk to be taken. I was particularly struck by the hatred and contempt of these girls for the numerous homosexuals who were importuning on their patch – it had to be seen to be believed! One final point. I was never tempted to have a go at conference, to make a speech and perhaps an impression, with a view to seeking office. Despite my undoubted ability to speak in public as a lecturer, I was never much good at after-dinner speaking, and would have been frightened to death to address conference – funny when I think of it!

We had a uniformed Chief Inspector – Jordan. He was more or less office-bound, and acted between the inspectors and the Superintendent. Pendered and Jordan hated each other and had done for years. They shared the prosecuting duties in the courts and Jordan had to submit all reports from us to Pendered. The bad feeling between the two was never allowed to interfere with their work. Jordan was a quick-tempered Scot, ex-navy, First World War veteran, and had been a rather heavy drinker in the 'bad old days'. He had been a close friend of Sid Holland, whom I succeeded on motor patrol. When he retired his job and rank were 'up for grabs', as the saying goes.

It was during this same period that Jim Quinn resigned. He had not been very happy on his return to ordinary duty. Also, he seemed to have upset Pendered and that could always be bad. This was rather strange, because Jim was a smoothy with his superiors, and it was out of character for him to fall out with his boss. Anyway, he resigned at about eighteen years service, which meant no pension, just reimbursement of superannuation contributions. He bought a Post Office/newsagent shop at Stechford, Birmingham, and seemed to prosper.

I always felt that his lack of experience as a patrol and station sergeant had ill equipped him for the responsibilities of inspector. As only two years had elapsed between his promotion from PC to inspector, he had no opportunity of gaining this experience and knowledge. Running the Civil Defence Department with a highly trained and experienced staff was very different from the exposed position of a patrol inspector, particularly on nights.

Pendered rather liked me, much to my surprise. I had worked with him on gambling school raids when he was a sergeant, and I was on motor patrol, when we had been very successful. Many people in our force felt very strongly that I had been treated abominably over Quinn's promotion in the Civil Defence Department and it could be that Pendered's attitude to Quinn was coloured by this. I shall never know. I was rather sorry to see Jim go for we had been quite friendly in spite of everything.

It was decided to let the senior inspectors have a spell of acting Chief Inspector for a month each. Cameron was the first, out to create a good impression, naturally. He sent back reports for correction, with the most trivial and pettifogging errors so that he became intensely disliked by his colleagues. Williams followed and he tried to outdo Cameron — altogether a traumatic period. I was last and during my spell I had to make the disposition for the Annual Flower Show. This was a tremendous task, covering three days' police cover of this event, using every member of the force at some time or other, meal reliefs, traffic problems, and so on, but I got it done alright in the end.

We had hoped the Flower Show had died with the War, but no, it was resurrected again, fortunately continuing to lose money, and so this was the last to be held. During these acting Chief Inspector duty spells, the incumbent had to take the Court prosecutions, if the Superintendent was not available — an interesting and useful experience.

Promotions — a Season of Discontent

Eric Cameron was favourite for the vacant post but spoiled his chances by his involvement with a woman, the daughter of a prominent townsman. As a married man with children, Cameron could not hope to get away with it. He was quietly warned, to no avail — he continued his escapades. Eventually, Pendered and others caught him flagrant deliciti, as it were, and that was the end of his career as a policeman. Shortly after, Bill Williams and Barber, who was an inspector in the Chief Constable's Office, were made Grade 2 Superintendents, the rank of Chief Inspector, except in the CID, was discarded, the old B Division was restored, and Bob was put in charge of it.

Williams had earned a chance as he had run the Special Constables during the War, and had considerable experience in the Chief Constable's Office and on the streets. He also ran our hostel for the single men of the Force, which in itself was quite a job.

Barber had served nearly all his time in the Chief Constable's Office and had little or no practical police experience. The dice was always loaded in favour of the Chief Constable's Office staff, and was terribly discouraging to the uniformed patrol branch. I realized that my further progress was now over. The rank and file thought I was a cert for promotion, so for the second time they were proved wrong.

It was during this period, that I had a most successful run of raiding betting houses and pubs allowing betting on their premises. Persons sent letters, usually anonymous, giving us bare information. Pendered passed these on to me for action. I worked my plans most carefully, picked my team, arranged the timings, and after obtaining the warrant, conducted the raid. Those involved were arrested, charged and bailed.

They appeared in court the following day. I conducted about eight of these raids, of which seven were successful. One sergeant I regularly used was Douglas Petersen. He had joined just before the War, gone into the Services, and had been commissioned. On his return, he, like several others in our force, found it difficult to accustom himself to being a PC again. These chaps were a bit of a headache for a time as they resented being corrected for any mistakes they made, and still had a complex about having been officers. They had only to be patient and keep out of trouble, and their subsequent advancement was certain. I spoke to some of them, including Petersen along these lines, and he obviously appreciated this, as I shall show later.

Meanwhile I had about five years to go for full pension for thirty years' service. I thought I might try for a Civil Defence Officer's job. Wolverhampton was filled, so I applied for a post at the Amblecote, Brierley Hill and Sedgley sub-division of the Civil Defence Corps. The post only paid about the same salary as I was receiving as an inspector, about £750-£800 per annum. I considered that if successful, I might move to a better job later. The Chief Constable approved my application and gave me the following testimonial. I also obtained testimonials from the Town Clerk and Fire Chief.

<u>Testimonial from the Chief Constable. 24. 12. 53</u>

The Chairman and Members of the Urban District Council, Moor Street, Brierley Hill.

Ladies and Gentlemen,

Inspector F. Stonier of this Force has my approval in his application to you for appointment as Civil Defence officer, and I am pleased to give him this testimonial in support of his candidature.

The fact that he has achieved his present rank in the Police Service is testimony in itself to his ability, character, and personal qualities for it must be remembered, eight years of his service were spent in Civil Defence work prior to and during World War II. Even upon his return to normal duties he was still so abreast of Police Work to be seconded to No. 4 District Recruit Training School. Upon his return he received the promotion he had earned.

Although, as you will be aware, Police Officers may not normally be seconded for Civil Defence work – Inspector Stonier has been my right hand man in Civil Defence matters since 1948, and has assisted substantially in the Civil Defence Plan for this County Borough, so far as it affects Police, Special Constables and Wardens.

This plan, indeed, is largely built up upon the scheme formulated for 'Exercise Wulfruna' which some of you may have witnessed; and in the preparation of which Inspector Stonier played a leading part.

In order to meet the responsibilities I have placed upon him, Inspector Stonier has kept himself thoroughly well versed in all matters pertaining to post-war Civil Defence organisation. I have no hesitation in saying that his extensive knowledge, long and wide experience, and excellent qualities of leadership fit him thoroughly for such a post as he seeks. Personally I should be sorry to lose his services, but I feel with him that he has a material contribution which he can make to Civil Defence, which is very much needed, and I would not therefore, stand in his light. He is heart and soul in Civil Defence work, which is why he is prepared to leave the Police Service before he has reached the maximum service for full pension, even though this has material disadvantages for him.

Yours faithfully,
NORMAN GOODCHILD
Chief Constable.

I attended for an interview having reached the short list in December 1953. I was not very enthusiastic, I must admit. Whilst waiting for the decision of the committee, I had more or less decided to refuse the job, belatedly reasoning that I was giving up a job of prestige for another one of no prestige – for the same pay. I was also losing the chance of adding a fair amount to my pension, as the last five years of police service add considerably to the final pension – the difference between retiring at twenty-five years on half pay, and two thirds of pay at thirty years.

In the event, I did not get the job, thank goodness.

Old Civil Defence Staff

When Civil Defence was finally closed, Quinn, as I have said, returned to duty. PC De La Cour had been in charge of the civilian respirator depot at Chubbs for several years. He was a good instructor, with a pleasant disarming manner, who returned to duty as a sergeant, as did PC Wykes, who always described himself as the 'working man's' instructor. He was rough spoken, quite sharp, but a little eccentric. Gribben got nothing, which was a bit unfair and he was rather unlucky, as was Taffy Watkins, whom I have mentioned before. PC O'Leary, our resident comedian, became Coroner's Officer, a quite lucrative if morbid post.

The FA Cup, 1949

This was the year Wolverhampton Wanderers won the coveted trophy. I had been to Wembley just before the War and seen Stan Cullis, the skipper, and his men lose to Portsmouth. Now they were in the Final again, with Stan Cullis as manager. As the Wolves won their matches up to the semi-final, the crowds grew bigger and bigger. People queued all night for tickets for the Final, some ten to fifteen thousand. For weeks the town was football mad, which meant police problems. Men had to be brought in from outside beats, shifts had to be changed to allow more men to cover the vital periods, e.g. after closing time at night, and when the ticket office opened at nine o'clock next morning. People lit small fires, brought oil stoves, sang, tried to go to sleep, and so the nights dragged on. But it was all quite orderly. I think we had this performance three times, as we led up to the Final.

Wembley

I managed to get two precious tickets from my old friend Jack Howley, the Secretary. I gave one to an antique dealer I knew, Jim Morris, a sergeant in our specials and quite a wealthy man. We went to Wembley by train, saw the match, had a meal, and came home. Wembley is always a great thrill, it has an atmosphere on Cup Final Day which is unique, particularly if you are a supporter of one of the teams.

The next day the team came home with the Cup. Such scenes! I was the duty inspector that day. We had sought reinforcements from Staffordshire and Birmingham Forces mainly of mounted men, who were worth their weight in gold. With a good-humoured crowd, mounted men can control better than any foot men, who tend to get overwhelmed. Cars are quite useless under such conditions. The team were met at the railway station, and put into an open-topped coach. They then made their triumphal way along Lichfield street to the Town Hall. There were thousands of people lining the pavements and every vantage point along the route. I had seen nothing like it since VE night. With a struggle we reached the Town Hall. I had escorted the coach, walking in front with a few men along the route. The mounted men patrolled along the flanks in front of us to keep the way clear. The crowds were

Wolves coming home with the FA Cup. I was just in front of the coach, off picture, in charge of officers.

in raptures of delight; it was a memorable occasion at which to be present and take part. There was the usual VIP appearance on the Town Hall balcony, speeches, much display of the cup, players waving to the crowds. Finally, all withdrew, and the crowds gradually broke up and departed for home. I have an *Express and Star* photograph of the procession passing through Queen Square.

The Family

During the war years and afterwards, things had changed quite a lot on the Home Front. Uncle Phil Holland died, and I attended his funeral, the last time I was with the entire Holland clan.

Herbert, too, had passed on, having had a stroke whilst living at Four Oaks. Sister Edith called her parents from next door, but he was dead. He had prospered during his last years, although his firm were poor payers and he had been with them since leaving school, however, he did some private work which paid well. Despite his years of service, Edith could get no form of pension or gratuity from his employers. She and her daughter managed by taking a series of teaching jobs, specializing in speech training and drama instruction. Florence, whom I had not seen for many years, also lost her husband who died from a heart attack. She was left with four children. After her two youngest children were born, she became a Roman Catholic. Her life for the next few years was a mystery to me. Somehow or other she managed to get the four children well educated, and they became teachers in due course. Florence and Edith in their different ways faced the calamity of losing their husbands prematurely very well indeed. They were born survivors and their children owe much to them.

Walter, after living at home for a few years, went to live in South Wales. He married a second time but his wife soon left him for a doctor. He divorced her and married a third time. This marriage lasted until he died, leaving a son Graham who also became a teacher. Walter had a number of jobs but always had this obsession to be his own boss. He achieved it in the end, but it really came too late in life.

Mother and Father often stayed with us at Penn for weeks at a time which put something of a strain on our slender finances, and was a bit of a problem while rationing lasted.

Goodbye, Penn

Shortly after my return from Ryton, our landlord, John Fox decided to sell our house. The police authority did not wish to purchase, so we had to leave. We were found a new police house on a council estate on the opposite side of town, at Bushbury. It was a better house in many respects, but we didn't like leaving Penn. We stayed at Northwood Park Road for five years before leaving. I had noticed a house for sale on the Stafford Road. It was a pre-war £675 type of house, and was now, in 1950, £2,100. Rose and I, and the girls liked the house very much, but decided we could only afford to buy it if we shared with someone. Mother and Father wanted to live with us, so we decided on that. They lived with us for twelve months but it did not work out. Mother became more or less bedridden, Father was crippled with rheumatism, and the girls resented the work they imposed on their mother who seemed to spend every minute of her spare time looking after them – with no thanks. I was working shifts which imposed restrictions on the family when I was sleeping in the daytime.

By mutual agreement Mother and Father went back to Olton and lived again with Edith, sharing expenses, and living rent free in the house which was owned by Walter. This was an agreement Walter had made with Father years before, when Father had lent him money to start a building firm. Edith and Margaret continued to work at their teaching jobs, employing a daily woman to clean the house and look after the old folks. It was a struggle meeting all the expenses of the house, but we managed. Rose got occasional temporary jobs, and with my special duty pay, we managed.

An Irish Holiday

Rose, the two girls and I took a holiday in Eire about 1947. We went over by boat and landed at Dun Laoghaire, where we were to be met by car and taken to a small hotel in Wicklow, in the Vale of Aughrim. As we had some time to wait, we went shopping. Rationing was still in force at home but we found in Eire there was no such thing, except by price. A tin of Libby's peaches was 5/- old money; today that would be £1, if not more. We were hungry for a change in our miserable diet so I bought a tin of peaches, a tin of salmon and some bananas, we found a quiet spot and ate the lot in a glorious feast! The children, for the first time, could buy sweets without the eternal coupons. Quite an experience, and hang the cost we thought!

Our car arrived and we set off for Aughrim. On arrival, we saw it was a one-street village in beautiful countryside. The hotel was 'scruffy', there was no other word for it, and not very clean. Had we been able, we would have straightaway gone back home! Well, it might have looked 'scruffy', but my word, we were fed like 'fighting cocks'. Homemade bread, fresh butter, plenty of bacon, eggs, sausages, steak, liver, and chocolate biscuits, it was marvellous! And to crown it, fresh trout from the river behind the hotel.

There were two other English couples staying with us, an elderly pair, and a couple a bit younger than Rose and I. We had a pleasant time together.

At about 10 p.m. each evening, the electric lights dipped for a moment, which was the signal from the local garage that he was about to stop his generator – our sole supply of electric current. We had our candles ready, and that was our source of illumination thereafter. The taps in the rather splendid bathroom functioned peculiarly – the hot tap sent out cold water, the cold tap nothing at all.

The meal times were terribly irregular so we took a morning walk before breakfast around 10–10.30 a.m. Lunch was sometimes at 1 p.m., sometimes nearer 3 p.m. Time seemed of no consequence to these people. We fumed a bit at first, but by the end of a fortnight we had slowed down to their pace, and didn't mind at all. Everyone was very polite and wished one the time of day. If I went into the pub, a place was made for me at the bar with the remark, 'Make room for the gentleman.' One Sunday afternoon, there was a Gaelic football match against a neighbouring village. The players assembled on the village pitch, wearing football strip and cloth caps. They played with some kind of a stick which they wielded with ferocious efficiency. I could not understand the game, but it was great fun. Meanwhile, the pubs in the village had removed the tops off dozens of bottles of Guinness, and the barrels of porter were at the ready. When the match finished, everyone flocked to the pubs and promptly set about the task of getting drunk! After a suitable period to allow this to take place, a band appeared – a strange band with pipes, drums, fiddles and flutes, which made a weird but rhythmic noise. They marched up and down, looking very smart in gold and green tartan. The pubs emptied as men and women, arms linked, faced each other across the main street and began to dance. They moved towards each other, then back again. The Guarda Siochan looked on, smoking. Occasionally he would move in and pull out one of the dancers, if he or she appeared to be getting quarrelsome. Other members of the dancing teams would disentangle themselves at intervals, men and women, and go into a shop doorway to relieve themselves, elemental stuff this! It seemed to go on for hours. Eventually, the coach arrived to take the visitors home, and the party broke up quite peacefully. A day to remember!

One day we witnessed a funeral procession in the village. The coffin was carried on a small flat cart, drawn by a number of men. People fastened on to the procession which continued to swell until nearly every able-bodied member of the village joined. So they moved on, slowly, silently, but strangely dignified to the cemetery.

Market day was a great event too. Farmers brought in their stock to sell and buyers came from other parts with all types of vehicles, to take home their purchases. The shop next door to the hotel sold ironmongery, lamp oil, and miscellaneous goods during the week, including herrings in an open-topped barrel. On Market Day the shop changed over to the sale of meat only. Health and hygiene were not, I'm afraid, very high on the list of priorities in Aughrim, sets of livers hanging on hooks outside the shop in the sun, covered with flies!

The farmer and buyers all took their lunch in our hotel, the dining room of which was packed, but all they seemed to be eating were huge slices of bread and jam, with great quantities of tea to drink. No meat, eggs or vegetables seemed to be served.

Then there was the night of the ceilidh. This was the local dance held in some vaguely described place out on the bog. We were not invited as this was purely for the natives only. I shall never forget them leaving the hotel as they seemed to pack a dozen people into one taxi. As they went in one side, they fell out of the other. Hampers of food had to be stowed in too – all very amusing.

The gymkhana was held in the beautiful Vale of Avoca – splendid horses, good riding and jumping, set amidst gorgeous scenery. There was a ride for us in a jaunting car, with a probably very humorous discourse by the driver, which was utterly incomprehensible to us, a pity really. I think what he was saying was very funny – he obviously thought so, as he was laughing most of the time.

The teacher at the school often took meals at our hotel where she questioned Rose about children's education in England, and was very surprised at the variety of subjects taught.

The most amusing event was when we were out walking one day in the village and approaching us was a child about eight years of age, dressed in a long cassock-type garment. He, or she, took one look at Rose, who was wearing a red dress, made the sign of the cross, turned tail, and ran, as if the very devil himself was chasing him (or her).

One dark blot on the holiday – well, two really. In a pub I saw a 1lb. box of Cadbury's Milk Tray Chocolates and bought it as such things were unobtainable at home. I also bought a bottle of Irish whisky from another pub to take home. When we opened the chocolates, we found the top layer was Cadbury's Milk Tray, while the bottom layer was plain, inferior, and almost inedible chocolates. The whisky, too, had been heavily watered – a poor way to attract tourists! I remember these two dishonesties much longer than the many kindnesses and hospitality I was offered.

Coming home, we smuggled some butter, bacon and tinned fruit about our persons. It was not really allowed, and I saw one woman in the customs queue have a piece of bacon seized and forfeited. What did they expect of people after eight or nine years of subsistence rationing? So ended a quite eventful holiday.

Civil Defence

Since 1946, there had been two Civil Defence officers appointed to Wolverhampton. The first was a retired brigadier, whose name eludes me, but he didn't stay long, anyway. The second was a Lieutenant Colonel Hughes BEM, an ex-Birkenhead inspector who had been appointed at 'AMGOT', and served for several years in Germany. He was a tall, prepossessing man, who now had the task of trying to resurrect the corpse of Civil Defence. The Chief Constable was responsible for wardens, as well as police and Special Police. This tended to bring us back into the game, but interest was negligible. It was too near the last war to expect a reawakening of interest in the next one. We had a visit from a serving soldier and his small team of experts. Brigadier Hulton Harrap was visiting all the local authorities responsible for making Civil Defence arrangements in our region and he set each authority a problem.

If an atomic bomb of the size dropped on Hiroshima and Nagasaki – a 20 KT – dropped on their territory, and here he produced a map of their area showing (i) the damage rings, and (ii) the fallout problem, how would the various heads of services deal with the consequent problems? This was the basis of 'Exercise Wulfruna', a military co-operation effort.

The heads of services met – the Town Clerk, the Borough Engineer, the Medical Officer of Health, the Chief Constable, and all others likely to be involved. I went along as the Chief Constable's side.

I won't bore the reader with all the details. The exercise was worked out, I sorted out what I thought wardens and police would have to do and how I thought they might respond. The Chief Constable kept closely in touch throughout, and all services did the same.

The exercise was finally wound up with Hulton Harrap listening to every service's response to the demands made upon it – we came out of it quite well I think.

The object from the Government's point of view had been achieved, whether we were enthusiastic or not: here was a weapon that existed, and which could be used against us in time. We had to have some defence against its consequences, which would be on a scale far beyond anything experienced in the last war.

A year or two later, the Ministry of Food held an emergency feeding exercise in Wolverhampton, again involving the police and wardens. I took part with the Chief Constable in this. Early in December I had asked the Chief Constable to allow me to attend a Civil Defence course at one of the schools. There were now three technical training schools run by the Home Office for this purpose: Falfield, where I had twice attended, Easingwold in Yorkshire, and Taymouth Castle in Scotland. I eventually obtained a vacancy at Easingwold, attending the fortnight's course in January 1954. I had been to Easingwold once before, in 1944. I did not mention it before, as it was called a Post Graduate

Course, and had obviously been held to provide the School with work during a slack period at the War's end. I again met Reg Reynolds, who also attended. We looked upon it as a part vacation and quite enjoyed ourselves although we learned nothing new. I had obtained my third 'Special Certificate', but since then there was the advent of the atom bomb, and its impact on civil defence training, so I was keen to obtain a new qualification in the light of my decision to apply for Civil Defence posts. Whilst on the course I had a letter from Doug Petersen who enclosed a Home Office circular advertising a vacancy at the Civil Defence Staff College, Sunningdale, Berkshire. It was for a Police Staff Officer Instructor, starting salary £1,010, rising to £1,060, for a two-year secondment. I immediately made application to the Chief Constable to ask permission to apply, which he granted without delay. I drafted out my application and record, and asked Rose to get it typed professionally in Wolverhampton, and post it to the Home Office, which she did. I then settled down to complete the course I was attending, the climax of which was a night exercise in the grounds with all the necessary effects. It was at Post Warden level, and the key was Post Controller, who had to organize his wardens, receive services, ambulances and rescue, and put them to work to the best advantage.

There was another inspector on the course named McAlpine, a decent sort of man, I suppose, but for some unaccountable reason we disliked each other on sight. It was, I feel on reflection, that we were both unconsciously competing for the leadership of the course – he had his followers, and I mine. In the event, the school staff chose me for the job of Controller. I had an unfair advantage, I suppose, as I had been to Easingwold before; I was an 'old boy', and one of the staff, a Mr Jackson, had been Assistant Regional Fire Guard Training Officer in the Midlands, and had often attended my exercises with Baddely, the Regional Fire Guard Training Officer. Anyway, friend McAlpine did his best to sabotage my efforts on the night of the exercise by the simple process of disappearing at a crucial stage when I needed his presence. However, it all ended well in the end, I suppose, and the critics at the inquest were quite kind. Jackson asked me to give the first lecturette in the examination at the course end. He said he wanted to get the course off to a good start, and I could do that for him. I gave a talk on the weapon effects of the atom bomb – I subsequently got my fourth Special Certificate.

Retirement of old Colleagues

Before I go on to the next stage of the Staff College saga, let me mention what had befallen a few of the characters in the force whom I have previously mentioned.

Dineley

He left on some kind of ill-health pension, shortly after the Tilley resignation. He started a taxi business, and took over a large house as a boarding house, catering largely for theatrical people. He prospered and then for some unknown reason left to go to live in Margate. He became, I believe, Deputy Mayor, but never Mayor. He came to Wolverhampton from time to time, and brought sweets for our annual Christmas Police Children's Party, which was a kindly thought. The last time I saw him was on the occasion of the valedictory dance, when Wolverhampton Force ceased to exist, and was merged with the West Midland Force, but that is a later episode.

As a post-mortem on his police career – he had the ability to make a first-class detective, and would have gone far had he been able to gain the confidence, or perhaps the word is trust of his superiors, and the courts, but this is only my opinion. He was better at business where his talents had more scope. I learned a lot from Joe.

Wetton

He was the other arm of the Dinely-Wetton team against Chief constable Tilley. After Tilley had gone, a reasonable time elapsed, and he was promoted sergeant. He was the type of man who was good at representing his comrades, and would have made an excellent shop steward, or union negotiator. He was quite a good policeman, too, although his abrasive manner was not appreciated by his superiors who always resented the 'barrack room lawyer'. There is, or was, a strange code of loyalty in the police service, no matter how badly a superior officer behaves – it was not playing the game for his men to shop him. Wetton felt this, I am sure, and was uneasy in his new rank, or so I thought. As soon as he reached twenty-five years service, and was entitled to retire on half pay, he resigned and became the licensee of a pub. On his last morning on duty, we walked out of the police station together to make our rounds. He said to me, 'Well, gaffer, this is my last day, and now I can say what I like.' I thought, Oh dear, here it comes. He continued, 'I've told the chaps that you are strict but fair, if they put up with your bad temper before ten o'clock, they will be alright with you.' I thanked him, wished him good luck, and we parted. I then reflected on what he had said. I knew I was testy on early turn till about 10 a.m., but I didn't realize it showed so obviously; I was pleased about being described as 'fair'.

Llewellyn

He retired too at about twenty-five years service. He obtained the post of head of a driving school. This had been established by Councillor Reg Guy, the Ford Agent in Wolverhampton, and did quite well.

Arthur Burge

He had been on motor patrol with me in those early days, retired as a constable, and joined Llewellyn as a driving instructor.

The Turn of the Tide

Shortly after my return to Wolverhampton from Easingwold, I received a notification from the Home Office that I was on the short list for the post at the Civil Defence Staff College, and was to attend for interview at the Home Office, Whitehall, at 2.15 p.m. on Friday, 19 February 1954. The Chief Constable wished me luck, but I felt that he did not fancy my chance very much. I travelled by train to London, made my way to the hallowed precincts of Whitehall and found my way through the labyrinth of corridors to the interview room. There were others waiting and I discovered later that I was the most junior in rank applying.

At 2.15 p.m. I was ushered into the interview room, where I was courteously received and told to be seated by the Chairman – a Mr Bunker, an Establishments Officer. Present were the Staff College Commandant, Major General Bruce, HM Inspector of Constabulary, Mr Tarry, and an Assistant Secretary from the Home Office, Mr Richard Wood. I was questioned for some forty minutes, and it was quite searching. They were impressed by the fact that I had published a pamphlet. It was, in fact, a training aide of thirty pages, in the form of questions and answers on gas, incendiary bombs and high explosives, with the steps required for self-protection. I had sold about 6,000 copies. I came away from the interview feeling that I had done justice to myself

COUNTY BOROUGH OF WOLVERHAMPTON

AIR RAID PRECAUTIONS

THIS COPY OF CLASS QUESTIONS AND ANSWERS HAS BEEN COMPILED BY THE WOLVERHAMPTON AIR RAID PRECAUTIONS DEPARTMENT.

Issued by kind permission of
EDWIN TILLEY, O.B.E.,
Chief Constable, and
A.R.P. Co-Ordinating Officer.

Reprinted July, 1941.

William Cox & Sons, Cleveland Street, Wolverhampton.

Tel. Address: Monebis Parl, London
Tel. No.: WHitehall 8100
Ext. ..

Any communication on the subject of this letter should be addressed to:

THE UNDER SECRETARY OF STATE

and the following number quoted—
WEM 2/1/15

Your Ref..........

HOME OFFICE,
WHITEHALL,
LONDON, S.W.1

3rd March, 1954.

Sir,

    I am directed by the Secretary of State to say that he has appointed you to the post of Police Staff Officer (Lecturer) at the Civil Defence Staff College with effect from 2nd March. The appointment, which has been made with the concurrence of the Wolverhampton Police Authority, will, subject to confirmation after six months, be for a period of two years.

    In addition to your pay as an Inspector, you will receive a non-pensionable allowance which will bring your pay to the scale of £1065 x £25 to £1115. Arrangements will be made to safeguard your pension rights. Since you will normally be expected to wear plain clothes, you will be entitled to plain clothes allowance. On occasions when

/you

Superintendent F. Stonier, B.E.M.,
  Civil Defence Staff College,
    Sunningdale,
      Berkshire.

[Other side of page.]

you wear uniform you will be entitled to wear the badges of Superintendent. Your pay and allowances will continue to be issued by the Wolverhampton Police Authority.

    I am, Sir,
      Your obedient Servant,

– I wanted this job, and this must have manifested itself in my manner. I really did not think I should get it reasoning that if I could not get Amblecote at £750 per annum, I was hardly likely to land this plum job at £1,050!

The following Wednesday I was on early turn. On getting home at 2.20 p.m., I had a snack, then went to bed for a few hours. The telephone rang, I was called, 'The Chief Constable's Office wants you.' I came downstairs to answer the call, and after a bit of leg pull, was told I had got the job, and was to report to Mr Lee at the Home Office on 2 March at 2.30 p.m.

Rose, the girls and I were, of course, overjoyed at the news. My next few days were extremely pleasant. Plenty of congratulations came from obvious sources – the Chief Constable was, I think, genuinely pleased as it did, after all, reflect credit on the Force. What particularly pleased me was the reaction of the men, who seemed to feel that I had put one across the authorities who had passed me over. One of them, a chap named Appleby, with whom I had very little contact, met Rose one day in town and told her how pleased the lads were, saying, 'He showed 'em, didn't he.'

My last official duty was at the Wolves-Newcastle match at Molineux Ground when I was in charge there for the last time. I was standing at the main entrance when who should come to speak to me but Ballance. He was often in town and had come to see the match among other things. He congratulated me in a perfunctory way, and then said, 'Try not to tell your boss how to do his job.' I thought to myself, Yes, and I could give you some good, but unwanted advice, too. I saw him once more at Sunningdale when he attended a course. There he saw me in 'full flower', as it were, at my best. He retired in the middle sixties, but lived only twelve months longer. He had got to the top, but not where he wanted, as Barrow was a bit of a backwater.

Chapter XIII

To Sunningdale

I left home on 2 March 1954, travelled to London by train and after lunch presented myself at the Home Office at 2.30 p.m. I was seen by Mr Lee, a Principal in the Home Office. He outlined the job to me, but warned that I should be 'out on a limb' as the police representative at the Staff College. This sounded rather sinister, but I saw what he meant later. He wished me well, I was often to see him in the future.

I left London for Sunningdale where I was met at the station by a

With my grandson, Sunningdale in background.

*Police Staff Officer, Lecturer for UK 1954–57, 3½ years.
Grade 1 Superintendent at Sunningdale Staff College.*

driver and car, and transported to the College. I was impressed at what I saw – a long drive along a rhododendron-lined road to the mansion, which was a very imposing building, set in beautiful grounds.

I was taken to see the Commandant, General Bruce, who warmly welcomed me. He introduced me to some of the staff who were to be my colleagues. I was then taken to my room in a sleeping block, very similar to those I had occupied at Ryton. Having unpacked, I moved over to the Lethbridge Mess for dinner at 7.30 p.m. In the bar there I again met Commander Edwards, to whom I had previously been introduced. We had a drink together, but were rather constrained. Edwards was about fifty, quite good-looking, perfectly mannered, with a very upper-class accent; he had the OBE. When I knew him better, I learned that he was a 'heart case', and had to take things quietly. He was a fine lecturer, with a rather sardonic humour, a terrible snob, but very kindly, and always charming to ladies.

The next day I took over my desk in an office in the mansion, sharing the beautifully commodious room with the WVS representative, a Mrs Hamilton. She was short and stocky, by no means handsome, but very efficient, and obviously brimming with energy and good health. She was the widow of a doctor, I later learned, comfortably off, and had before her marriage been a teacher of physical training. She was an excellent golfer of county standard, devoted to WVS work, and an excellent lecturer. She had a dog called 'Brucy' to whom she was greatly attached, also a small car which she drove very badly. She held the MBE. For a few days she was rather off-hand with me – she too had an upper-class accent – and was also an unmitigated snob. Gradually I was accepted by her and we became quite friendly, although I always suspected she resented my later successes. All our offices were in the mansion, a Georgian type of building. The ground floor consisted of an entrance hall, reception desk, secretary's office, and offices of the Commandant, his PA, the typing pool, the Course Paper Clerk, and the illustrators' workroom. Off the reception hall was a larger main hall, leading to the dining room, the lounge, and the stairs leading to our offices, the library, a small television room for Directing Staff, and an odd bedroom or two for important visitors.

All was beautifully kept. Large valuable pictures on loan from art galleries hung on the walls. In the main hall and lounge were Adam fireplaces. On the mantelplace in the lounge was a Louis XIV ornamental clock, a present from the BBC. Courses always left a presentation gift to the College – usually silver for the mess.

The lounge was equipped with comfortable chairs and writing desks

Main Hall, Sunningdale.

along one wall. The tall windows looked out over the grounds, leading down to the lake.

Our offices were splendid with Wedgewood designs on the cornice, blue in our DS room, and green in the other; again valuable pictures hung on the walls. About five DS were accommodated in each room, each with a desk and filing cabinet. Between the two DS rooms was the office of the Chief Instructor and Deputy Commandant.

The office windows also overlooked the gardens and lake, so different from the grubby accommodation I had always used in our old Town Hall police buildings, and the even grubbier offices at Chubbs in Wolverhampton. As attached DS, Mrs Hamilton, or 'Emma' as she was always called, and I, had a separate office in a large room overlooking the drive, but on the same floor as the College DS. The students, or course members, as we had to call them, were accommodated in sleeping blocks away from the mansion. There were two blocks, each capable of sleeping approximately sixty people, on similar lines to Ryton, both in layout and furnishings.

Between the two blocks was the Hodsall Hall, the main lecture theatre which had a large floor space for map demonstrations. The seating surrounding this on three sides was raised so that onlookers could obtain a good view of any movements shown on the floor map. There was a large stage opposite the entrance doors with facilities for projection, slides, hanging drops of maps, information, facts and figures. Two small green rooms led off each side of the stage for actors to await their entrance cues. Outside the main theatre were syndicate rooms which could accommodate sixty course members.

On the other side of the sleeping block was a repeat of this, except that the Lethbridge theatre was smaller, and had no facility for displaying floor maps; it was an intimate theatre, with the lecturer nearer his audience. The main building of the Lethbridge complex was very utilitarian, being modern, efficient, but with no style. It had the same facilities as the other side — a bar, a mess, an efficient kitchen — but it did lack the atmosphere of the main building. People who came frequently always felt second-class citizens if allocated to the Lethbridge Mess.

The Grounds

I must say something about these. These were superb! Well wooded, the ground sloped away steeply from the mansion on the south and east sides. The south side descended through rockeries to the lake which was small, with an abundance of water lilies and rare shrubs around its edge. After the lake, open lawn stretched to a cypress hedge with a field beyond, further on still, woodland until the estate boundary was reached. On the east side was a long, steep, grassy slope, used as a chip and putting course, with a long line of sequoias, tall and dignified,

Above and following page: *Sunningdale, house and grounds.*

forming a boundary to screen the kitchen garden – now sub-let to the gardener's brother as a market garden. At the bottom of the grassy slope was a summer house abutting the estate road, which went all around the grounds. On the north side was a swimming pool which had been a static water supply, but had been converted into a splendid pool, with diving board and stand. It was a very popular feature during the summer. Beyond that were a car park, more trees, and the estate boundary. The other side of the grounds were largely taken up with the buildings used for courses, and beyond those, further woodland as far as the estate boundary.

This had been the home of a millionaire, Cunliffe-Owen, a late chairman of the British American Tobacco Company. The Government, on his death, had taken Sunningdale Park in lieu of death duties, we were told.

Anyhow, it was a beautiful place in a lovely part of the country. I often thought of this as time went on – strange living there as I did for many years, getting just as much pleasure from it as ever did its millionaire owner.

When Rose came to join me there, rarely a day passed without her taking her daily walk around the grounds, studying the flowers and trees in all seasons: the daffodils and crocuses growing on the grassy slopes in spring; rhododendrons and azaleas, lilacs and laburnums in early summer, with one magnificent red camellia tree which had to be gazed on every day; in high summer, the flower beds were filled with multicoloured dahlias, and there was the herbaceous border, interspersed with apple trees. A gardener's paradise!

But to return to the stern present.

Introduction to Work

The day after my arrival I tried to find some trace of what my predecessor had left behind. What line had he taken? I didn't want to copy it, but it would have given me some sort of a lead. All he left was a map of Sheffield, the part of the country used by our Tactical Wing who worked mainly from the Lethbridge block, for their exercises. It looked as though he might have departed nursing a grievance – it seemed strange, no handover, no papers, just a map. Everyone was rather reticent when I raised the matter. I was advised to start from scratch and put over my own work, so I didn't have much option. I had been advised at the Home Office to read a book on the Police, by a Mrs Hart. I found a copy in our library. In general she seemed to be advocating acceptance of a much higher degree of centralization of the Police, whilst not going quite so far as a national police force.

The first day at work I received the following instruction from the Commandant:

Supt. Stonier.

I should be glad if you would attend the whole of No. 72 Senior Officers Course on the Staff College side, beginning on the morning of the 8th of March. This will give you the background against which all instruction here is carried out.

I suggest that you spend the following week 15–20 March in assimilating the instruction put over during the previous week, studying the notes that have been left for you by Superintendent Arnold, and in general liaison with other members of the Directing Staff.

I would then like you to go through No. 21 Tactical Instructors Course with the Tactical Wing as an observer. By this method you will get the complete build up of the tactical doctrine from the first day. For this reason I suggest that you should not attend any of the sessions on the previous tactical Course No. 20.

I would like you to undertake the two small commitments planned for the police representative of the Directing Staff on the Staff College side for the G.P.O. courses which are being run in the week commencing March 29th. Chief Instructor Staff College will tell you what his requirements are for that. Police lectures on the Staff College side will be given to Senior Officers Courses by the panel of Chief Constables arranged by the Home Office. This system will continue until the summer break, when we will reconsider the matter. I should like you, however, to give the lecture on the Role of the Police in Civil Defence to No. 77 Civil Defence Officers Course which assembles here on May 13th.

G.C.B. Major General
Commandant.

Well now, at least my programme was mapped out! I started to think meanwhile what line I would take in my future lecture on 'The Role of the Police in Civil Defence'. There was no policy other than the old Mutual Aid reinforcement scheme which had been in operation almost from the foundation of the Service, and entailed forces helping each other in emergency, such as strikes, and the aid sent to attacked areas in the last war – Wolverhampton had sent aid to Plymouth. It had only required ad-hoc planning, with the aided force area reimbursing financially the aiding force area. An atomic war envisaged something on a much larger scale.

Meanwhile we had a 'Restoration Study', which lasted for two days, at the latter end of my first week. It was a study on what would be required to restore an attacked area, and its survivors to at least a subsistence level, after atomic attack. A lot of top brass were present, including John Hodsall, Inspector General of Civil Defence, and Darlow, an ex-Wolverhampton Deputy Town Clerk, now Town Clerk of Reading, and a leading light in the problem of restoration. I sat in and saw my future colleagues in action in a demonstration-playlet on the floor map. Taking part was the Chief Instructor, Staff College – George Moran. He was a thick-set, heavy-featured man, with a slightly Eurasian appearance, highly competent, a splendid lecturer, he emanated confidence as he spoke. He was, I found, the best brain in the College on the wide ramifications of Civil Defence and its impact on other local authority functions. He had, prior to his appointment, been in local government. I, too, found later on how my experience as a local authority servant gave me the edge over my purely military or service background colleagues.

All I saw during those two days left an impression with me that I was to work with extremely competent people. The atmosphere was more rarefied than any I had so far worked in. The speech and delivery of the various lecturers, many from the ministries, made me wonder at my nerve and presumption in coming to this place at all. I had grave self doubts. Of course, I was looking at the ultimate in Staff College work, the 'exploratory study', so perhaps I should have felt better had my first 'looking-on' sessions been with the Tactical Wing.

The following week I sat in on the Senior Officers' Course. This was usually restricted to the heads of services, departments, businesses, service officers of the rank of major and above, or its equivalent, town or county clerks and deputies, Chief Constables, or superintendents, managers and upwards; these were the type of people sent to us for these courses. The police lecture was to be given by one of the panel of Chief Constables set up to give the talk, until the police staff officer was properly installed, and, I suppose, competent enough.

I listened with particular interest to this talk, but apart from giving me some idea of what chief officers were thinking, I got very little from it, as obviously there was no cut and dried plan for the Police in a future war as yet. I kept quiet throughout this first week, absorbing the atmosphere, and making notes of anything which I felt might impinge on my future work.

Tactical Wing

The second week I went over to this wing of the College. The Chief Instructor was Harold Brandis, whom I had last seen giving the Incident Officers talk and demonstration during the War at the old Staff College at Cobham. I told him of this, and how impressed I had been with his performance. I sincerely meant this, and it didn't do me any harm either as Brandis and I got on extremely well thereafter. He, like Moran, had five DS allotted to him. The Tactical Wing dealt with the NCOs of the Civil Defence Corps, the sector and post wardens level, the Civil Defence officer. The work was on similar lines to the Staff College side, with regard to lectures, demonstrations and syndicate work, but they also ran exercises, usually a telephone battle at the end of each course, appropriate to the level under instruction. On these occasions Staff College had to send their DS across to help stage the exercise.

Brandis quickly got me into action, and on the Wednesday I did a small piece of demonstrating police action on the floor map. I had only a few minutes notice of what was required, but I managed my small part quite well. I sat in on all the many demonstrations, and was often called upon to answer any queries which involved police action. I had to be careful because on all these courses there were always a few policemen present. I enjoyed the Tactical Wing work as it was at a level with which I was familiar, and the DS seemed more friendly. I again haunted the syndicate rooms, as I had during my week with the Staff College. I wanted to watch the way DS handled their occasional difficult clients, as this side of the work was new to me.

I Show my Teeth

Towards the end of this first fortnight, Moran stopped me one day in the drive, and rather petulantly told me that he would appreciate some kind of comment from me on what I thought of things, DS presentation etc. – he would appreciate some contribution. I felt a little nonplussed, I thought my withdrawn demeanour was what was required in a 'new boy'. At the next DS meeting at which course programmes were discussed, I had my chance to let off steam. Colonel Boyle, one of the Staff College DS was querying the value of a talk by Major General Irwin, an Assistant Secretary at the Home Office, and a power in Civil Defence planning. I had heard him lecture in Wolverhampton, and had seen how highly regarded he was. Boyle was, or could be, quite abrasive when he liked. He was a very bright boy, had been on the British Army Staff in Washington for a period during the War, and was quite good as a critic. I made a mental note of his criticism of Irwin. A little later he queried the value of giving the Police three-quarters of an hour for talk, and three-quarters of an hour for questions in the programme.

This was the last straw, I really blew off steam! First, they were criticizing General Irwin, one of the finest of lecturers – they should get out on the ground and see what the public thought of General Irwin as a speaker. Secondly, I had watched Boyle's demonstration on debris clearance, which left a lot to be desired, I thought. I gave my reasons for this from notes I had made at the time. Then this cutting down of police time, before they had even heard me speak! I pointed out that they had lost the army representative at the College because he had not enough to do; they might well lose the police representative if he was underemployed, and that must lower the prestige of the place in the long run. (I had learned about the army rep from 'Emma'. Later the Army Representative was reinstated, and the RAF also sent one). My small audience looked at me dumbfounded, they had not expected such passionate rhetoric from this quiet, diffident fellow. The meeting ended, and as we sat at lunch, George Moran, with a twinkle in his eye, leaned across the table and said, 'You'll do.'

My First Lecture – 19 March 1954

My first real commitment was a half-hour's talk to the GPO on the role of the Police. These GPO course members were to be their higher executives and engineers. The rehearsal was for content and timing. There were six GPO representatives present, all high officials, and George Moran. I can't remember if the script I was using was my own, or one provided for me. In any case it was pretty boring stuff. As I ploughed on, I felt it was all wrong, I lost my nerve, my mouth went completely dry, and I could not articulate. I almost left the stage, it took quite an effort on my part to stay at the rostrum and carry on. I finished the talk and left the stage to a pregnant silence. I apologised to George Moran for the effort, and left.

I don't know what went on afterwards, but anyhow the session was left in the programme. I went home that weekend in the lowest of spirits. What was wrong with me? I asked myself. I had been speaking in public for years. What was I afraid of? I couldn't have been much fun when I arrived home as I was still full of self-recrimination. I had ten days in which to do something about it. No-one mentioned the matter to me, so it was up to me alone; if I fell down again, I could not really expect to stay. Before the test came, there was a presentation ceremony from the BBC. They had attended a short course in which their communications were the main feature. We had the usual cocktails, and then the beautiful clock, Louis XIV, I think, was presented to the College by Air Chief Marshal Sir Norman Bottomley, Director of Administration, BBC.

Monday, 29 March 1954

This was the day of my first lecture at the Staff College. I had worked hard on the script, and as I waited to be called into the Lethbridge Theatre, I still felt the anger at myself for my pathetic rehearsal. I was really in a bad temper. Caswell, a Staff College DS, was waiting with me; he had a short ten- or fifteen-minute talk before mine. He was, as usual, a bundle of nerves, walking up and down, talking his notes to himself. He was really a good lecturer, and gave an impression of complete composure on the stage, but this was behind the scenes. I was not nervous, just still very angry.

When my turn came, I went in and noticed that the Commandant was sitting with Caswell, out in front. I was introduced and began – I gave a blinder! I was forceful, which is my style, occasionally sardonically humorous, altogether in great form. I noticed out of the corner of my eye, General Bruce nodding approval and speaking animatedly to Caswell, who was nodding his head in agreement. I finished on a high note, and to my pleasant surprise, the audience broke into frantic applause. Courses were always told at the start not to applaud Staff College DS, and this was usually observed, so it could be said that a performance was beyond the norm when it was spontaneously applauded, particularly by a technical course which is often the most difficult to please. I left feeling much better!

The Commandant said nothing to me, but he must have spoken to Moran. George was away, whether by accident or design, I don't know. I often felt he thought I might make a hash of it, and stayed away to avoid embarrassment, but perhaps I do him an injustice. Anyway, next day he called me in to the office and said, 'They tell me you mowed 'em down, Fred. Well done.'

I repeated the talk on the following Thursday with much the same result.

Whilst playing golf with the Secretary on the chipping putting course a few days later, he said, 'I think you can say you are in, Fred.' This rather indicated that up until my successful performance, it may have been in doubt.

General Instruction Duties

After that I was gradually absorbed into the training cycle, doing the small police parts on the floor map, and in playlets in both wings of the College.

The next big event was an invitation from Croydon Corps Authority for the DS of the College to act as syndicate members in a large-scale exercise that they had planned for 22–23 April 1954. We attended and had quite an interesting time. To show the attitude of some DS at this time, I asked one of them, a man called Robinson, who lived in as I did, for some advice on what was expected of us on visits such as Croydon. He replied to the effect that a chap with all my qualifications ought to have no difficulty. Strange how later on we became quite friendly. Mr Lee at the Home Office was right when he said I should be 'out on a limb' and my first few weeks at the College were not happy ones. There was the strange uniqueness of the place which to someone like me, with no experience of Staff College life, was daunting. There was the fear that I would not be able to measure up to the very high standard. The obvious difference in my education, upbringing, and life to that of my colleagues acted as a barrier to friendly intercourse until they got to know me better, and decided to accept me on more or less equal terms. Then at home, Rose was having troubles. Norah had fallen and damaged her wrist, which had gone tubercular, she was in bed and under treatment with expensive injections, which fortunately were met by National Health. Carole, too, had developed a strange illness, which eventually turned out to be poliomyelitis, but in the early stages seemed like a severe 'flu attack.

I thought what would I do if I gave up the job. The prospects were not very rosy. I could not go back as a failure, and what could I go back to? No, I had to work it out here at the Staff College.

Meanwhile, I was thinking hard how to present the 'Role of the Police in War', which, whilst I was seconded to the Staff College, would be my major contribution, in particular to senior officers' courses. It was of the utmost importance that it should be a success. I tried many approaches, and it was by a stroke of fortune that I found my answer. Attending a course in the Tactical Wing was a police sergeant named Piggott from the Lincolnshire Constabulary. He showed me a report by his Chief Constable, Sir Raymond Fooks CBE, of the Lincolnshire floods of 1952. It seemed to be the answer I was looking for. I wrote to Sir Raymond asking his permission to use extracts from the report in my lecture. I quote from my letter to him: 'I have in mind, particularly the analogy between peace and wartime functions of the service viz: mutual aid, incident control, first service in action aspect, enquiries from the public, cordons, passes to admit to damaged areas, signposting, evacuation, and prevention of crime. In dealing with the possibilities resulting from air attack these points are covered, but it does add point to one's exposition if recent examples of how this is achieved can be quoted.'

Sir Raymond answered courteously in the affirmative and sent me a copy of the report to use. This was just what I needed for the body of my lecture. I added a little of my own experiences as the resident of a police house for ten years, a few of the strange jobs the public expected a policeman to perform, but principally making the point that when in trouble it was to the Police the people turned. This was my underlying theme, and I always got a good laugh with the true story of the woman who came and asked me to give a 'good talking' to her children. She felt they would be more likely to take notice of me as a policeman. 'If they did, I said, it's more than my own two children do.' Loud laughter from similarly placed parents in the audience. I built the lecture to last three-quarters of an hour, leaving a further three-quarters of an hour for questions. I rehearsed it time and time again, polished it, redrafted it until I was satisfied.

Meanwhile on 12 May the College made a presentation to Sir John Hodsall on his retirement as Inspector General of Civil Defence, and his appointment to a post as CD Adviser to NATO.

I met several chief constables who came on courses, and settled them in, saw that they were not lonely in the bar in the evening, and generally nursed them.

Then came a long CDO's course, my first. It lasted three weeks, and was for newly appointed Civil Defence officers to equip them for their job. I was to give my police lecture for the first time. On Thursday, 13 May I gave it. The reception was very good indeed. I made a few adjustments, but was generally very satisfied with the way it had turned out.

Meanwhile, the panel of chief constables gave the police lecture on the senior officers' courses. I listened to some six altogether. I made a few notes, but really did not get anything of much value to my own forthcoming lecture. It did, however, give me the police line on many matters of policy, and I saw how the question period was dealt with, and the kind of answers given. All this proved of value to me later on.

Royal Review

On 14 July 1954 there was a Royal Review of the Police in Hyde Park and I was given permission to attend. It was a splendid sight, every

Lt Col Baxter; Major Andrews; Mr Coulson; Mr Brandis and Major Gen. Bruce.

force was represented, and they made a fine spectacle. They were arranged in thirty-seven blocks, the Wolverhampton contingent in Block thirteen, under the command of Superintendent Marsh. I visited our small contingent, exchanged pleasantries, and then watched the proceedings. The Queen and Duke arrived at 3 p.m., received by the Secretary of State for the Home Department and Scotland. Her Majesty was conducted to the dais where she received a Royal Salute, after which she drove down the three lines of the parade and returned to the dais. The parade then marched past in columns of eight, a repeat really of the parade I attended in Hyde Park in 1938, except that then I was a participant, and it was ARP, not Police. It was an interesting and pleasurable day, and I called at the Home Office to have a chat with my contact there, Mr Lee.

Home Force Changes

There had been a few changes in Wolverhampton. Pendered had retired and was replaced by Marsh. Gwilliam took over the CID as Chief Inspector. Llewellyn retired and was replaced by Petersen.

Meanwhile, the courses churned through at Sunningdale, both sides being fully committed. One weekend I went to Bognor for the day with a Pakistani named Durrene. He was staying at the College for the weekend, as I was. We joined forces, went by coach to Bognor, and had a pleasant day. He was the Civil Defence Officer for Pakistan, and told me that he was the grandson of a King of Afghanistan.

On 24 July, a Saturday, we had our annual garden party. This event was paid for from funds established with a small levy on each course member which paid for newspapers, books for the library, notepaper, sports equipment, and the garden party. It was a fine affair. A splendid cold buffet was laid on by our catering staff. The grounds were open to the guests, and we had the Metropolitan Police Band, a few side shows, but generally it was a pleasant walkabout to meet old aquaintances. All the dignitaries from the Home Office, the ministries, the armed forces, local government, particularly those nearby, and friends of the College Staff were included, and usually turned up. The show went on till quite late, the bar was open, and a good time was had by all.

Sport and Recreation

Emma, who was an enthusiastic golfer, soon had me playing golf.

Usually we went to a small nine-hole course in the middle of Ascot racecourse where she was a member, and sponsored me. The fee was quite reasonable. I bought an old golf bag and clubs, and took a few lessons from the club professional. I played quite regularly for the next twelve to thirteen years, never a good player, but I enjoyed it, and it was healthy relaxation. I later joined Sunningdale Ladies' Club, an eighteen-hole course of great beauty, but much shorter than the more famous Sunningdale and Wentworth courses. It had a nice clubhouse, and was used quite a lot by the Civil Defence Staff College staff in later years. In our grounds we had an excellent hard tennis court. I used this in the first six or seven years, until the advancing years put a stop to it, and I found my wrist became arthritic if I played much.

The swimming pool at the back of the mansion was very popular in the warm weather and the water was always cold, but it was bearable when the sun was shining. I used this a great deal.

At odd times I went with course members to play the difficult Sunningdale Old and New courses. I never managed to get round in much under ninety, but it is such a beautiful course, a pleasure to even walk around.

We had no table tennis or badminton, which was rather a pity, unlike

Royal Procession, Windsor 1957–68.
Our courses at the Staff College always wanted to see this so we always arranged to let them see it from good vantage points.

Ryton where it was a cult, but then there was a great difference in the age of the clients! There was bar billiards in both messes, and of course, cards, darts, and chess.

Our local cinema was in the adjoining village of Sunninghill, a very small 'flea pit' type of place, but I often went there, either alone, or with 'Andy', Major Andrews, the DS Co-ord, who lived in. Andy had obviously risen from the ranks, was an Engineer, and had been recruited as an instructor on the Tactical Wing. He was one of the several ex-Indian Army members of the staff. He lost his job as instructor, when during a dissertation on debris clearance, his lecture overran the slides he was supposed to be describing. That was the penalty of being tied to a script – we were not supposed to read from our script, but of course everyone did to a greater or lesser extent. There was a certain amount of hilarity as the Commandant was present and he was very strict on accuracy and presentation. Andy never lectured again. His job as DS Co-ord was nevertheless very important as it tied up the use of the two halls to avoid clashes between the two wings. The demonstrators, of whom there were three, were allocated to their tasks by him. Obtaining slides, films, or any presentation material was his task, while programmes had to be agreed between the senior instructors and DS Co-ord. The show could not have gone on without him. It was a service idea which I had never seen before, but then I had never worked at a staff college before. Andy was very much a lone hand, separated from his wife, and he spent much time alone in his room. He was sociable enough, but very reticent about personal matters. Apart from the cinema, he and I often went to spend an evening with Frank Coulson, his wife and young daughter at their home. Frank had a television set and this was a great attraction. We often stayed until midnight. Coulson was an instructor on the Tactical Wing, one of the few civilians on the staff. He had been a Local Government Officer in Lincolnshire, had gone on to Civil Defence in the War, and in time, a post at the Staff College. He was very efficient and had a pleasant manner. I well remember the excitement when, with Andy, Robinson, the Coulsons and myself, we watched those exciting games when Wolves played Spartac, Honved, and other famous foreign soccer teams in the fifties. Robinson swore he was black and blue where, in my excitement, I had dug my elbows into his ribs.

'Robbie', as we called him, went with me on my first trip to Ascot Races. The College always took a half day off on Hunt Cup day and we took our course members to a good vantage point where they could view the Royal Procession, as it came from Windsor Park towards the racecourse. We then made our way to the course and enjoyed a good day's racing. I say 'enjoyed', but racing never appealed to me as I had spent too many hours, when I ought to have been in bed, on duty at race meetings. But I liked the crowds, the Royal Procession, and the company.

Robbie was another loner – his wife was, I understood, in an institution, and one never spoke about it. He had been at one time in the Navy, but before joining the Staff College had served in some capacity in 'Amgot' in Germany. He was a pedantic type, very precise in speech and manner, a snob, good at his job, but not a man one could warm to.

We all went to the Victoria Palace one night – Andy, Robbie, Emma and I – where the Crazy Gang were performing. It was pleasant, but I thought the show rather vulgar, however the others seemed to enjoy it.

The chipping and putting course at the side of the mansion was great fun, and very popular.

During my first year, the European Horse Trials were held in Windsor Park. The Commandant, with his wife and two daughters, took me in their car each day for the three days it lasted. It was very kind and considerate of him, and a new experience for me, which I enjoyed very much. After the day's events, we would repair to his house in the grounds and have tea.

Major General Bruce was a spare man, ex-Ghurka Regiment. He had been a member of the ill-fated Everest climb in the early twenties, when Mallory and Irvine lost their lives. The General had a collection of slides and film of the expedition, and he gave an excellent talk on the facts of the climb, and how near it came to success. He gave this talk to courses occasionally, if asked, as an extra. I went several times, and always found it fascinating. His father had been a Regional Commissioner for Wales during the War, and had left him a considerable fortune. He was always very kind and helpful to me once I had proved myself. If he met me in the drive after my lecture, his greeting was always the same, 'Taken them by storm again, Fred?' he would ask. He was a keen birdwatcher, getting up at impossible times, and hiding in the rhododendrons to view particular species.

He was a keep fit fanatic, and terrified to go near anyone with a cold. He was also strangely mean about some things. He did not have a television set, just a decrepit radio. The College under his command was run very tightly; he dropped in on syndicate discussions, and always attended lectures by visiting lecturers. He would know if ever a DS strayed from laid-down policy. Altogether a very efficient Commandant.

The College closed during the second half of August. No-one wished to attend courses either immediately before or after the August break. We used this period to bring scripts up to date, write new ones, rehearse new or changed presentations, hold DS and mess committee meetings, and were quite busy.

The courses restarted on the Tactical side on 30 August – the establishment was never allowed to remain empty for long. Training Division of the Home Office kept us well supplied with customers. The cost of running the Staff College was of necessity very high which had to be justified to the paymaster by sending as many people as possible through the turnstiles, as it were, thus reducing the cost per student.

With the commencement of the new season, I was ordered to give the police lecture to senior officers, and any special courses held, if appropriate. I now felt an accepted member of the Directing Staff. The lecture was a great success. Every lecture given had another DS acting as Chairman – to introduce the speaker, and take, and pass on the questions at the end. Herewith is an extract from the DS reports on my first efforts.

1.9.54. An excellent lecture. Far better than any earlier Police lecture I have heard either from Staff or Chief Constables. Questions took up the whole of the time available. – Lt. Col. Bassett.

9.9.54. Realistic down to earth lecture which was well received. Questions few and not good. – Caswell.

24.9.54. A first class talk, well put over, and packed with human interest. Audience were very appreciative. Excellent question period – Robinson.

24.10.54. A burst of applause at the end told its own tale, but the course still refused to ask many questions. Supt. Stonier altered the beginning of his lecture by stressing one of the peace time roles of the police, that of meeting peace time disasters by quoting their activities during the east coast floods. – Caswell.

Note this lecture was given to the instructors and assistant instructors of the three Home Office Schools, Falfield, Easingwold, and Taymouth; and as they were professionals, it was particularly rewarding, and appreciated by me.

11.11.54 Excellent lecture, exactly 45 minutes. The question period was poor, only two of importance were asked, one on Martial Law, and one on the legal aspects of trials in regions. – Caswell.

22.11.54. An excellent talk which was well received. – Edwards.

2.12.54. A most interesting and entertaining talk, which held the close attention of the audience. The questions lasted the full period – Robinson.

16.12.54. A first class talk received by the course with applause; there was much comment and congratulations after the clear exposition and method of dealing with the subject. The subject was fully covered and there were few questions, and those of little importance. – Caswell.

The book stopped here, the practice was discontinued from thereon.

The End of the Tactical Wing

This came as a bolt from the blue. It was decided by T Division, our masters at the College. This division was largely, so far as we were concerned, under the command of J.B. Patterson CBE, Assistant Secretary. Next was the Chief Training Officer, Brigadier G. Pennycook CBE. Both were frequent visitors to the College, and always attended the frequent high-powered studies that were held from time to time.

Brandis, and one of the Tactical Wing instructors, Jack Holliday, were moved to Falfield. The two wings at the College were merged, and George Moran was now Chief Instructor of the whole.

Poor Brandis, he was very sad at leaving in such a manner. It was rumoured that he had serious differences with Patterson, and this had led to the change. He was a kind man, good at his job, but perhaps better at a technical school than a staff college. A staff college does, of course, demand a different approach and attitude as I had found out. The detail so beloved of a school is a hindrance at a staff college, where the outlook must be of altogether wider horizons – the larger picture. Tactical training still went on, while the DS were divided into A and B teams under senior instructors, and took it in turns to work both sides of the College. I floated between both.

The Dorchester Hotel

During my short time at the College we had several studies devoted to looking at the problems of different services, industries or ministries.

The Steel Company of Wales were one such. We liked these studies, they made a change and enlarged our knowledge. A member of the Directing Staff was always appointed as Staff Officer to the course, helping to prepare the papers and presentations with experts from the industry and the ministry concerned. There were rehearsals, criticisms, rewrites and finally the show itself. The course members were then set problems affecting their own industry, and put into syndicates to work out their solutions. Then in general discussion a concensus was reached, and this was often the first step towards a ministry decision on policy for the future – big stuff really.

But to return to the Steel Company of Wales. Their Chairman at that time was a Mr Spencer, a Wolverhampton man, having started with a small steel works there. He knew my uncle, Jack Crofts, and they had been fairly close friends in earlier years. Once he knew who I was, he was very friendly, and this raised my standing just a little with my snobby, but now quite friendly colleagues. After a successful study, the Steel Company decided to make a presentation to the College of a piece of silver. They would do this in style at the Dorchester Hotel in London, and we were sent six invitations to attend. Lots were drawn, and I was one of the lucky six. On 11 November, we set off in the college utility truck to London. On arrival at the Dorchester we were shown to the Mountbatten Suite, high up in the building, where we were ushered in to partake of drinks in a sumptuous lounge. Obsequious waiters attended our every wish – you no sooner put a cigarette in your mouth than a waiter was to hand with a light. Mr Spencer and four of his colleagues were our hosts. After drinking and chatting for a while, we went into a private room for dinner where we sat at a circular table. In came a chef with cooked pheasants on a tray – they looked beautiful, if that is the right expression – which he showed to the Chairman for approval. As he did so, one of his colleagues exclaimed in a frightfully loud voice, 'What, pheasant again! I suppose I can toy with a little!' How splendid, I thought, to be so familiar with this luxury that you could behave like that. We other poor mortals probably tasted pheasant a dozen times in a lifetime!

We had a splendid dinner, the liquor bottles passed round the table, cigars were offered and accepted, and stories were told, everyone making a contribution. Finally, the presentation of a silver cigarette box was made which the Chairman did very charmingly. A few more drinks, we parted, and set off for Sunningdale. Quite an experience – dinner in the Mountbatten Suite at the Dorchester. I had come a long way in twelve months. As a result of this, Robbie and I were invited to visit the Ebbw

Vale Steelworks. We were booked into a hotel in Abergavenny, and shown round the works next day. The strip mill, I well remember – the speed at which the red-hot strip tore over the rollers was quite startling. We were well treated and quite enjoyed the outing, though what it had to do with our work I could not imagine. Yet I often referred in syndicate for years afterwards to this trip, how the locality was dependent on the works, and how the works relied on its local labour force – how this communal mutual reliance might be turned to advantage in a survival period. Recent events and the closure of the Ebbw Vale works has somewhat changed that view, but it was valid at the time.

Camberley

Every November we went to the Army Staff College at Camberley to study military aid to the civil power in future war. Our DS looked forward immensely to this. To mix and work in syndicate with these up-and-coming senior army and other service officers was stimulating; in addition, it recalled for many of our chaps their own younger days.

I was a bit apprehensive as things were happening so swiftly. How would I fare with these razor-sharp young intellects? I need not have worried and had a great time. I was called very early on in the first syndicate I visited to explain a traffic plan on the blackboard. This was bread and butter stuff to me, I revelled in it, and the result was I was passed from syndicate to syndicate to expound. I took part in a floor demonstration and a playlet.

Camberley was quite an experience. Set in beautiful grounds next door to the junior establishment of Sandhurst, it was an impressive building inside and out. The entrance hall and lounge were lined with pictures of the great generals of the past who had passed through its portals; it was like a history lesson to go around them and read the names. There were stands of arms of the past, and a splendid library.

The mess was large, of course, although only the top table had waiters, the rest was self-service – even our greatest establishments had to come to terms with economics; at our College, at least we had waitress service.

The lecture theatre was an immense place – the stage faced a forum-type of auditorium, a half circle of seats going back in tiers overlooking the floor and stage. All the visual aids imaginable were to hand, though I must confess they had no better equipment than we at Sunningdale. We had sufficient leisure time to look around the grounds, and visit Sandhurst Chapel and Museum, both of which are worth a visit. The Chapel is full of memorials of the past, particularly of India, and there is also a beautiful gift on the altar from America. The Museum, too, is full of Indian mementoes including the uniforms of some of the famous regiments – 'Hodson's Horse', and similar strange-sounding titles – a fine example, I felt, to the young officer cadets of Sandhurst, something for them, if not to emulate, at least to inspire.

The syndicate discussions were quite a revelation and it was surprising how quickly a trained, alert mind can grasp the fundamentals of a new doctrine – civil defence, in this case. There was no sign here of the vacuous, rather stupid, upper-class accent type of officer so beloved of humourists, and many among them had unmistakeable regional accents – the Army was becoming democratic. Their own Directing Staff were carefully selected officers who carried lieutenant colonel rank whilst on this duty. It was pleasant in later years to note how many of them achieved General Officer rank. I enjoyed my annual trips to Camberley.

Our last course in 1954 ended on 3 December. After then until Christmas we had training conferences, and other necessary chores. At Christmas, the Directing Staff gave a party to all the rest of the Sunningdale Staff, the gardeners, handymen, housemaids, cooks, demonstrators, illustrators, and office staff. The DS wives did the cooking, and we, the DS, served the meal. This was apparently the old officers' mess type of Christmas party, and it took place every year I was at Sunningdale. We had a jolly time, enjoyed by all.

Then we all went home for Christmas, and I didn't have to bother about race meetings or football matches now!

Home Affairs

During this exciting if anxious time for me, Rose was battling with the two sick children. They both recovered, but by the nature of Carole's illness, she was left with a leg weakness and had to wear a leg-iron support for quite a time. Showing great resolution, she exercised daily, running regularly to strengthen the leg muscles still intact. It paid off in time, she was able to discard the leg support and gradually her leg became quite strong again. It looked normal, if still a little weak on certain sharp turning movements.

Norah had left the Wolverhampton Girls' High School and joined the Civil Service, being employed first at Cosford Royal Air Force Station, then transferring to the RAF Recruiting Centre in Broad Street, Wolverhampton. Carole had won a scholarship from her elementary

My parents 'Diamond Wedding' Anniversary, 1954.
From Left to Right: *Niece – Margaret Lincoln; part picture of Phoebe Holland; Daughter – Norah Stonier; Willowby Crofts; Father; Mother; Jack Crofts; Author.*

school in Penn, and had been admitted to the Girls' High School. Rose, too, had attended this fine school, and had matriculated as it was then called. Many of the same teachers taught her and the children, and during the War I had given a short course on Civil Defence to the teaching staff. So, I presume, we knew the Girls' High School, Wolverhampton pretty well!

Rose collected my pay monthly from the Chief Constable's Office. The sum was quite large now by our standards. The Chief Constable very kindly advised her to open a bank account, and gave her an introduction to Lloyds Bank Manager. Until then she had been keeping it between the bed and mattress! I was now the second highest paid man in the Force, receiving more than Tom Marsh who was Deputy Chief Constable – very gratifying! I'm afraid I was leaving rather a lot to Rose, I was so engrossed in my new career. There was so much I had to do to consolidate my good if slightly delayed start, that I concentrated on this completely. This is my way I'm afraid. Rose shouldered the burden in her usual efficient way, and the children and her own relatives were very helpful.

To Sunningdale
1955

The courses recommenced. On 11 January, I received a letter from the Chief Constable:

Dear Stonier,

I enclose a letter which is an entirely unsolicited testimonial to yourself from Mr. Browne, the Chief Constable of Nottinghamshire, who has recently been with you at Sunningdale. As you probably know, I am due to come to the Staff College on the 17th of next month, and I should be grateful whether what my colleagues are now putting over to the students is in any way advanced to what I told them when I came last summer?

I am very delighted to receive Mr. Browne's letter, which shows how highly your work is appreciated.

Yours etc.
NORMAN GOODCHILD

Mr Browne's letter:

My dear Goodchild,

Recently I returned from Sunningdale, where I spent a week on the Senior Officers' Course, which I found both interesting, and rather frightening!

Your Supt. Stonier is down there on the Staff, and I want to say how very impressed I was with him. His paper on 'The Role of the Police in Civil Defence' was excellent, but his address surpassed any of the others heard down there, and this opinion was shared by many other representatives who attended. The substance of his address was constructive and his approach to the many problems was realistic, and put over in splendid fashion with just the right amount of light heartedness introduced.

I gather that the Police Services have hitherto been somewhat 'out in the cold', believe me, Stonier has certainly altered that, and has put us well on the map.

I thought you would like to know this.

Yours sincerely,
J. E. S. BROWNE.

This was what I had been awaiting, recognition from my own service! It is alright to impress the general public, but for my own peace of mind I had to know what the top policemen felt about my material, and now I knew. I wrote to my Chief and told him what had been said by his colleagues, which was nothing very much that he could use, I'm afraid. When he did come, his material was rather boring, and the audience lukewarm, but he was sufficiently experienced as a speaker to sense this, and on the way back to his car, he asked me what I thought had been wrong. Difficult! I put him off with, 'It was fine, Sir, these people are rather difficult, you know.' What else could I say, I had learned enough with Ballance to know how vain top men become, and how fatal it is to criticize them, but I should be less than human if I had not felt that here on my own ground I was better than he.

No chief constable gave the Police Lecture after that, as it was realized that it was better given by me.

February, 1955

We had a 'Special Army Course' – such an audience! The Queen's uncle, Lt. Col. Bowes Lyon MC, Commandant Guards Depot, Caterham, Officers Commanding Grenadier Guards, Scots Guards, Welsh Guards, Brigadier Sir John Hunt, and a host of the commanding officers from lesser-known regiments and units, about sixty in all.

I gave my police talk, and in addition I had worked up a second lecture demonstration on 'Transport and Traffic Problems'. This was not such a blockbuster as my police talk – it's difficult to get emotive over such a mundane subject, but it always went down well. I had sought out my background information from Birmingham City Police who kindly gave me maps etc. on their own complicated traffic scheme. I remember chatting over the ideas with the Deputy Chief Constable, who asked me why, if I was a Birmingham man, had I not joined their force. I told him that in my joining days, you were not allowed to join your home force.

I had a lot of help from the Birmingham Force, and Mr Dodd, the Chief, was always helpful. When he sat in on some later courses, he always laughed loudly when I had a crack at Birmingham's complicated one-way traffic system.

The Fallout Study

This was the next major study to be held at the Staff College.

Our new Inspector General was General Sir Sidney Kirkman who had commanded the artillery at Cassino, and gave a very interesting talk on the whole battle for this bitterly contested monastery. He was tall, grey, finely featured, a little arthritic in the hands. His manner was decisive, no nonsense – shrewd, all you would expect from a top commander. I got on very well with him, except on one occasion when he was climbing down the short, steep ladder from the stage in the Hodsall Hall. With the best of intentions, as I was on the ground, and he up in the air, I offered my hand as he negotiated the ladder; he brusquely waved me aside as if to say, 'I'm not that old yet'. Actually, he said nothing, the gesture was enough. Otherwise he was always very kindly with me – but back to the Study.

General Kirkman was the Director, his Chairman, Major General Irwin, and the Scientific Adviser, Dr Purcell.

This study was to examine how to deal with the massive radioactive fallout from a hydrogen bomb ground-burst explosion. The scientists had been working on this for some time and had come up with certain facts and figures. These were to be presented to the officers of all government departments, including Admiralty, War Office and Air Ministry. It was big stuff and required large floor maps, drops and rehearsals.

I had a small part on police operations in these circumstances, the fire part was given by a Mr Middleton, HQ Fire Service Inspectorate, and the Civil Defence by a Mr Devy, a principal in the Home Office. Otherwise the whole thing was the scientists' presentation.

It went on for three days, and ended in syndicate considerations of the problems raised, and a general discussion from which a concensus was obtained. On this basis the planners could draft out the future policy of the various departments responsible for Home Defence.

It was interesting to all us DS, because we could now see the drift, and how it would affect our future instruction. It was also an opportunity to hear the scientists and ministry spokesmen deliver their talks. The standard was usually very high. The debates, too, were always interesting, the young principals and assistant secretaries attached to the various departments were able debaters, and I quite enjoyed listening to the cut and thrust of their exchanges.

Family

In April of that year Father died. He was buried, as he wished, at Chasetown. The service was attended by a few relatives, including brother Walter who came with his third wife and young son Graham. This was the last time I was to see Walter alive.

Mother took on a new lease of life, left her bed, and managed to get about without too much difficulty for more than ten years. Edith, Margaret and mother eventually left Olton, and went to live at Folkestone, where Florence had also finally landed with two of her children – now, of course, grown up, both being teachers.

Father's estate required little clearing up and he left just enough for the funeral expenses. I helped to support Mother for the rest of her life.

The Police Study

Meanwhile at the College things were moving. The Police Division of the Home Office decided it was time to hold a study to determine how the police would cope with nuclear war. The Assistant Secretary was Graham Harrison, rather weedy physically, but very intelligent, a nice enough man. He prospered in his highly competitive world, and the last I heard of him was on his promotion to Deputy Secretary of State. It was with him that I had to work preparing this study. The result was a floor map of the Midland Region with a ten-megaton bomb on Birmingham, with its resultant fall-out pattern and damage rings indicated. I had to draft out a lecture/demonstration covering reinforcement, traffic control, aid to other services – and a great deal of imagination. The idea was for me to sell certain ideas to the invited course. Problems would then be set for them to consider, and in a later general discussion, some indication might be forthcoming to aid the planners in their future deliberations on how policy for the police was to evolve. It was the general pattern of all studies and I took part in a great many over the years. This one was, however, particular for me as I had to present the 'Pièce de Résistance', and to sell it to the top men of my profession. The invited audience were: Home Office officials, including the permanent Secretary of State, Sir Frank Newsome; the four Her Majesty's Inspectors of Constabulary; the ten Regional Police Commanders who were the Chief Constables of the largest forces in their regions; and the Commissioners of the Metropolitan Police and City of London. Goodchild, my own Chief, was invited as the Secretary of the Chief Constables' Association. Training Division were there, of course, in strength – Patterson, Pennycook, and lesser lights.

After the opening talks, and when the study was off to a good start, I had to present my piece. I had worked hard to make it interesting, informative, and forward looking. I had learnt it by heart, went out with my pointer onto the floor map, and talked for nearly an hour to dead silence. Towards the end, the city of London Commissioner, Sir Arthur Young, got up and quietly left. I had a momentary feeling of panic — was it that boring? — but I knew deep down I was getting it across. I ended and returned to my rostrum. I was amazed at the result — loud applause, the four H.M.I.'s arose as one man and came to congratulate me. My Chief could hardly contain himself — this was one of the proudest moments of my life! I had worked hard on this presentation, took risks with my suggestions, but it had come off. I never gave that presentation again — it was a once only — but how rewarding!

At lunchtime I was taking a drink with my admiring seniors when Colonel Eric St Johnstone, the Chief Constable of Lancashire, came to me, and told me that Sir Arthur Young apologized for having to leave before I finished, but had given St Johnstone a note: 'A splendid talk by a very fine officer'. My cup almost ran over! The study went on for two days, and that was that!

Meanwhile, we had a few staff changes. Robin Boyle, the colonel who never used his rank title, left us. He had secured a nice post with the Steel Company of Wales whilst their course was running at the College. He was a real go-getter and just before he left, I remember, we had a staff meeting to discuss programme changes. There was the usual problem of finding something after the lunchbreak which was not easy, as the course members were always likely to doze off after a hearty lunch and a drink or two. Boyle said, 'Put Fred on, he's a spellbinder.' I declined the honour whilst acknowledging the compliment. His place was taken by Air Commodore Charles Luce DSO, a very tall, gingery, rangy man, of excellent family; his father had been a doctor of note, and a knight. His cousin was a Lord of the Admiralty and the family was very well connected. I had quite a close relationship with Charles. Until he was settled in with his family, we used to go to the cinema together in Windsor, played golf a lot, quarrelled quite often, but generally got on well together. When both our families came to Sunningdale, we visited them for musical evenings. Charles had been trained as a gunner at 'The Shop' as Woolwich Academy was called. He admitted he had been idle, or he might have gone very high indeed. He had been to Cambridge (College), had a keen brain, was a good speaker, but he had a devil of a temper. He had received his rank of Air Commodore on his transfer to the RAF Regiment. I mentioned earlier how the Army had withdrawn their representative from the Staff College before my arrival — now, for some reason, they replaced him and we had a Lieutenant Colonel seconded for two years with us, thereafter. Their job was on the same lines as mine, but to represent the armed forces in Civil Defence.

I had by this time been roped in to take syndicates which was a new departure for attached DS. I was the only one up till then so privileged, which was a good omen.

Penny Tries It On

Brigadier Pennycook, the Chief Training Officer, was a very frequent visitor to the Staff College. He attended all studies, and was an influential voice at rehearsals. The only time he kept quiet was when he was outranked by the presence of his bosses – Patterson, Irwin, and Kirkman. He had a rather ingratiating manner at times, but on the whole was a likable and quite shrewd member of our larger team. Once, when staying overnight, he took me for a walk. The DS at the time were complaining, as a body, on the council house type of accommodation which was offered to those who wished to live close to the College with their families. There had once been a suggestion that they would have nice houses built in the grounds, but this had fallen through. All there was, now, was a row of six council houses on the estate which adjoined the college grounds. Penny had heard of the undercurrent of dissatisfaction and he wanted me to act as his informer as to 'who' was saying 'what'. I was quite taken aback – it was policemen who used informers, they were not informers themselves. I told Penny I could not countenance such a proposition, these men were my colleagues, I had to work with them, we had to trust each other. This was the second time in my career that this had happened. Years before, Jack Crofts had tried to persuade me, on my promotion to sergeant, to spy on Joe Dineley, whom he suspected of having a paid job outside the Police Force. I had declined to do this, although I often wondered whether Dineley in my shoes would have done the same.

Penny took it quite well, and probably thought better of me for my refusal, although he never said so.

Regional Directors

When General Kirkham was firmly in the saddle, he set about the appointment of regional directors in the ten Civil Defence regions. Until that time, the Home Office merely maintained a small staff of about three civil servants in every region. The directors were with one exception retired service officers of general rank. The exception was a retired judge from the Sudan.

A course was held for these men at the Staff College. They were addressed by all the ministry representatives, and generally put in the picture. The police side was given by Graham Harrison, who grumbled, saying that I was better equipped than he to give it. However, it had to be from the 'horse's mouth', as it were, the ministry men could not put it over so well, but they could answer the searching questions with authority. After this brief instruction, the directors were posted to their regions. We DS were allocated to them as liaison officers. I was given Midland Region with Air Marshal Sir Lawrence Pendred as my director and we got on famously from the beginning. I worked hard for him, and he in turn was appreciative.

Outside Commitments

I was often asked to give my police talk outside the College. General Bruce did not agree with my doing so, saying I had enough to do at the College; if people wanted to hear me, that was the place to come. I was, however, allowed to give a talk to the Assistant Prison Governors' Annual Conference which was to be held at Worcester College, Oxford. They had attended a Civil Defence course at the College, heard me, and thought I should speak to their conference. When I asked 'on what subject', they replied, 'Anything but Civil Defence'. I thought about the matter and decided to give a 'History of the Police Service'. I had given a short version of this years before at Ryton as my test piece – this one needed to be fuller as it had to last forty-five minutes. I had heard from my Chief, Mr Goodchild, that he gave a talk on this, so I wrote and begged a copy of his script, which he kindly sent and I used it with some changes. I went to Oxford and gave it to a large audience before lunch. It was well received, and I was thanked by the senior official present – Sir Lionel Fox.

Lunch in the hallowed halls was a great disappointment, very poor fare, I recall. Anyway, I can say I lectured at Oxford University, for what value it has.

Eastern Command

Early in 1956, the College was asked by Lieutenant General Sir Francis Festing, to provide lecturers for Police, Welfare and Weapon Effects to the officers of Eastern Command, of which he was General Officer

Commanding-in-Chief at Hounslow Barracks. Emma and I went from the College, and John Batchelor, the Assistant Training Officer from the Home Office Civil Defence Department, filled the other place. We went to Hounslow on a Sunday morning in the College utility van. The barracks at Hounslow are quite large, so was the lecture theatre which followed the usual form – stage, floor, with a semi-circle of seats going back in tiers from floor level to about dress circle height.

We were introduced, I went on last with my usual 'Police Role in War' talk. The hall was filled – there must have been 250–300 officers,

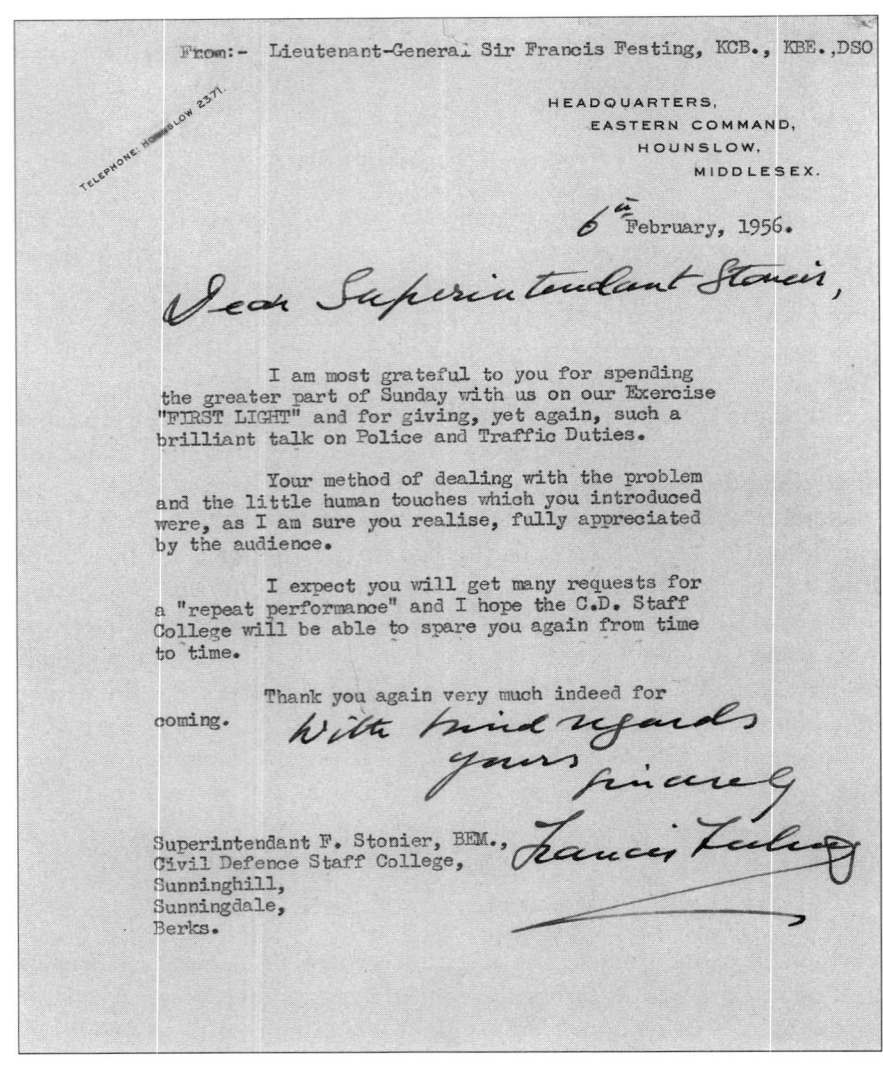

regulars and territorials, in uniform present. All our talks were well received and we adjourned to the officers mess for pre-lunch drinks, which seemed to go on for ages, and we were all tiddly. We had lunch, and left in the van for Sunningdale. Altogether, a worthwhile, interesting morning. A letter of thanks was sent to the Commandant, and I received the following from General Sir Francis Festing, K.C.B., C.B., K.B.E., D.S.O.:

Not bad, I felt, from a future Field Marshal, and Chief of the Imperial General Staff.

Regional Studies

After the appointment of the regional directors, the next stage towards their war readiness was for a study to be held at the Staff College for every region in turn. This was quite a task, and took a few years to finally accomplish. Large floor maps of every region with appropriate drops, slides, scripts, playlets, demonstrations, syndicate problems, all had to be prepared separately. As time went on, a common thread became established, and this helped considerably, after the first two or three had been finished. The Liaison Officer from the College was always the Staff Officer, responsible with two members of the Regional Staff, who supplied much of the factual material and came to the College with the Director to check progress and generally assist from time to time. I always prepared the police part, and as often as not, the Ministry of Transport contribution. They gave me the material, and I knocked it into shape for presentation. Because of my involvement in this way, I was told to assist every liaison officer as his turn came round. It was urgent, interesting work. I was able to note how my colleagues attacked their task, and pleased that they came to rely on me more and more, as the studies went on; and I became more experienced.

Every director had his own little fads which had to be catered for. The rehearsals were long and drawn out, the slightest error pounced upon, the amount of rewriting was formidable – not because of mistakes, but because when spoken to an audience what had seemed good on paper was found to be wanting on the day. An example – North Eastern Region was rehearsing, General Lamplugh was Director. I gave the Transport Ministry paper as usual – 'It won't do,' said the General. 'But this is the Approved Ministry version,' I replied. 'I don't want the Ministry version, I want Fred Stonier's version,' said the General in a tone of finality. I was flattered, of course, although it meant another rewrite, and another rehearsal. Still, General Lamplugh was a great

Taymouth Castle 1993. The site of 'Western Zone' Study 1956–7, one of my successes.

friend of mine, later on I often went into his region lecturing to WVS, Police and Observer Corps.

The first presentation began before a high-level audience, representing all walks of life in the region concerned. The ministries were strongly represented, and of course, all the top brass from Training Division of the Home Office. The high spot of all the studies was the demonstration, on the huge floor map, of the deployment of forces by Army, Police, Fire, Civil Defence, and Welfare Services. As each service went into action the representative would go onto the floor map, and move his forces as appropriate, giving a running commentary as he or she did so. After a time, some of us became regular performers: I always did the Police; Middleton, a Home Office Fire Inspector always did the Fire; the scientific picture was always given by Stansbury, Black, or Leader Williams of the Home Office Scientific Branch. The Army and Welfare varied from study to study. The cue to move came from the stage, where a playlet representing Region, and staffed by our DS, with George Moran as Regional Commissioner were going through the various stages of life-saving operational control.

At the first study, a police move was made, and I spoke the agreed lines that a particular series of incidents 'would be reported'. A clever young principal from one of the ministries asked, 'never mind reporting it, what are you going to do about it?' In the interval, quick as a flash George Moran said, 'We must have an answer to this in the next period, any suggestions?' I gave him one, and he said, 'Right, let us try it.' Came the moment, I said, 'I shall report the matter.' George Moran, as Commissioner, said, 'Never mind reporting it, are you going to do something about it?' I said, 'With great respect, Sir, when the Police report something, they always do something about it.' Loud applause and great guffaws from any police in the audience.

I think it loses a little of its impact in retelling, but given the electric atmosphere of a large, complicated series of manoeuvres, before an interested audience, a keen series of cross-chat between stage and floor, suddenly broken by the injured dignity of a service representative, ostensibly being slated by a superior, and coming back swiftly with a courteous but devastating rejoinder, and the situation appears differently. It was hugely enjoyed by everyone present, and was always used thereafter in all future regional studies. As a result of our constant working together, Middleton, Stansbury, Black and myself became friends.

As a continuation of the trend towards regional studies, we had to do two for the Scottish, Western, and Eastern Zones. I went to Taymouth Castle, one of the Home Office schools, in beautiful Perthshire, for the Western Zone Study. All the top Scots were present and the study was highly successful. I spent a great deal of the spare time available playing golf on the lovely course adjoining Taymouth Castle with Bill Griffiths, our seconded soldier. Bill was a Lieutenant Colonel, highly decorated, had risen from the ranks, and served in Glubb's force in Arabia. We had some excellent fun together on the golf course. Taymouth Castle is a grim-looking series of buildings. Inside, the furnishings are rather heavy and depressing to my mind, but its setting is superb, alongside the River Tay, a golf course adjoining, hills all around, a tiny village nearby – perfect. We stayed there for nearly a week on the study. I remember Mr Robertson, the Deputy Chief of Glasgow, later Chief Constable, saying something rather significant to Brigadier Pennycook, as we were chatting together one day, 'You don't want to lose this chap, Brigadier, he is good.' Pennycook said, 'It's alright, it is taken care of.' I didn't quite follow, but it sounded interesting.

I forgot to mention that in my first year at the Staff College, once I had settled in and established myself, I asked my contact at the Home Office if I could have a week with the Scottish Police. If I was to represent the police of the UK, I ought to know a little of how the others ran things. To my surprise, they agreed, and fixed through the Scottish Office a week spent between Glasgow, Edinburgh and Lothians. I duly went, saw everything of interest, met all three Chief Constables, and completed a massive report of my experiences on my return. This was where I had first met Mr Robertson. I had been very courteously treated by all the forces.

Clearance of Z Zone

Back at the College the trend was towards the clearing of people trapped in endangered areas of radioactive contamination, which I sensed was a new and profitable field to cultivate. Charles Luce had the same idea, and we clashed for a time on use of facilities, but it ended amicably enough. In time I became the expert Clearance of Z Zone presenter. There was a playlet and floor demonstration devoted to the principles and I was made responsible for keeping scripts up to date. I gave it on all courses, and on occasions took it out to the regions. It needed a great deal of back-up material to properly present as it covered such great areas of country, which limited its presentation to those places able to provide the same.

Major General Bruce Leaves

In 1956–7 certain dramatic changes took place. Firstly, we were told to prepare scripts for a new study to be mounted by Training Division at the Staff College. It was considered important enough for George Moran to be Staff Officer. As he had to prepare the scripts, this meant much 'burning of midnight oil'. He appointed me as his assistant and we worked until after midnight for over a week. The script would be written, typed out next morning, then I hurried to London to a meeting of the Joint Civil Defence planning Staff at Horseferry House, off Whitehall. Here, the collective brains of the Scientific Advisers Branch, and the Planners – Paterson, Pennycook, Irwin and others – tore the script metaphorically speaking to pieces, gave me details of the changes required, and back to Sunningdale I went, more or less in a haze. George Moran and I would work on it until the early hours, and then off to London next day. We developed a technique after a time. George would throw out the requirement, and I would pace the office, dictating what I felt was a suitable piece of script to cover it, and he would write it down; it seemed to work well. About midnight, George would uncork a bottle of whisky to sustain us. So the week went on until we had written the last line, and had it approved. As we drew near to the end of our task, George said to me, 'When your police secondment is over, would you like a job on the staff here?' I was surprised but very pleased ... I had felt for some time that I had established a niche for myself here, I got on well with my by no means easy colleagues, and I had an appreciative public within the Civil Defence field. Of course, I said I would – which answered all my future problems. My police career was nearing its close, I had my thirty years service for full pension completed, or nearly so. What to do next? I was only fifty, at the height of my professional ability – this was just the job for me. The pay was good also, almost the equivalent of my Grade 1 Superintendent's pay. Apparently General Bruce liked the idea, and a canvas of the other staff was favourable. I could see now what Pennycook's remarks at Taymouth Castle had meant. It eventually transpired that I could get a further extension of my police secondment for the six months before a vacancy fell due. The original secondment had been for two years, and I had already been given one twelve-month extension. Hardly had this got under way when General Bruce left the College. He had some disagreement with someone high up in Training Division, and promptly gave up the job. It was a shock to all of us. I should miss him, as he had been a good friend to me, and what would happen now to my offer of a post?

General Bruce quickly departed and went to live in Dorset. He was succeeded by the Regional Director for Wales, Major General Mark Matthews, a tall, slender, grey-haired, handsome man, a great horseman. He had been in the Korean War, his regiment was a Welsh one – I forget exactly which, Borderers, I think.

I did not know him except by sight. He took the post, occupied the Commandant's house, and installed his wife and younger son, Peter. He was quite different to General Bruce, but just as keen on running an efficient establishment. He could ooze charm when he liked, but also had a rather sardonic wit. Fortunately, I was accepted by him, and we got on very well all the time I knew him. He thought out and put on a splendid lecture on the 'World Situation', which was given to all courses as an opener. It needed constant revision to keep up to date with the changing situation, but it became a regular feature as long as the College existed, and was given by General Matthews' two successors. He was a great believer in innovation, and always encouraged new ideas, which was all to the good as far as I was concerned, as I myself was a great 'ideas' man, as I shall hope to show.

He agreed to my application for the forthcoming vacancy. I had to apply in response to the advertisements in *The Times* and *Telegraph*. Eventually, there were two vacancies to be filled as 'Established Civil Servants' – this meant that service counted towards a pension, provided a minimum of ten years service was completed. In the Civil Service one becomes vulnerable at sixty, which means guaranteed employment until that age, service thereafter is with the approval of the ministry concerned, and the department or college in my case. As I should be a few months over fifty if appointed on the date the vacancy was to be filled, I should have to hope for one extension, ten years hence, to be sure of obtaining the minimum pension. Meanwhile, there was a lucrative post and congenial work for ten years ahead, and this was all I asked. In the advertisement, as well as two established vacancies, there were two vacancies for temporary appointments. These carried no pension rights, but could, as vacancies fell due, be upgraded to established rank. Luce applied, as did Commander Edwards, who was a temporary, and Bill Griffiths, who wanted to leave the Army for a post as instructor at the Staff College. So there were four of us applying for two established, and two temporary jobs. Later on, before our interview, General Matthews asked me if I would be prepared to accept a temporary post for a short time, with a promise that it would be made established as soon as possible. He pointed out that Edwards had been there longer than I, and was eligible for the established post. I felt strongly enough entrenched by then to say, 'It is the established job I want. I do not want to have to keep looking back over my shoulder.' In any case, I pointed out, Edwards had heart trouble, so I was a better risk. This sounds a bit hard, I know, but we were all fighting for our livelihood.

A short time had elapsed since the submission of our applications, and we were sent the usual sheaf of papers to complete. I pondered this at some length. The only part which presented difficulty was that asking in *details* for particulars of education. I could imagine my competition – prep school, Sandhurst, Dartmouth, and/or university, plus in some cases, Staff College at Camberley or Quetta. I knew there would be plenty of applicants from the armed services. In my case – Sladefield School, leaving at barely fourteen. Why? Because I had not liked school – oh dear, the 'chickens were coming home to roost' alright. I made as much as I could of my constant education since joining the Police Force – twenty-three courses and examinations of one kind or another, a founder member of the first Home Office Police Training Centre at Ryton and so on, but it seemed a trifle feeble to me compared to those other seats of learning. I posted the forms, feeling less confident now. In due course I was requested to attend a Civil Service Commission, sitting in Trenchard House, 30 Old Burlington Street, London, W.1. I went there and was ushered in for the interview.

Present were the Commandant, Brigadier Pennycook, the Civil Service Commissioner, Mr Hayes, the Establishment Officer, Mr Bunker, and a few other officials I could not place. I really wanted this job and under such circumstances I gave a good interview. To my surprise, the questions were largely on police work: 'What do you think is the cause of serious road accidents?' for example. I went through very well, I felt.

A few days later at the Staff College, I was in my office, when Bill Griffiths breezed in and showed me a piece of paper briefly stating that Luce and Stonier had been successful in obtaining the two established posts. Bill, who must have felt a bit deflated at being pipped by me, gave his congratulations. He and Edwards were given the temporary posts – both were later established, so nothing was lost by them except, perhaps, a little pride.

Back Home

Things kept moving. Norah left Wolverhampton to go to Headquarters, No. 90 Group, RAF, Medmenham, Nr Marlow, Bucks., where she worked as a Civil Service Clerk. Carole had been proclaimed 'Girl of the Year' at the Wolverhampton Girls' High School, and had obtained an entrance to London University. There she read History, and eventually obtained an Upper Second Class Honours degree which was presented along with many others at the Albert Hall by the Queen Mother. Lieutenant Colonel Hughes, the Wolverhampton Civil Defence Officer, had left for a more remunerative post as CDO of Staffordshire and was replaced by a man named Evans. At the time of the changeover about 1955, I heard from Wolverhampton that my application might be favourably received if I put in for the job. I thought it over, and asked Frank Coulson for his advice, but he was no help. I had no great wish to go back. What I had experienced after I returned from Ryton, in trying to obtain and train new recruits, had been very discouraging indeed. The pay, too, was nothing like as good as I was receiving. I also wanted to prove to myself that I could 'make it' at the Staff College level, so I did not bother to apply.

The Town Clerk of Wolverhampton, Mr Brock Allen, had retired, and Mr Barr, his wartime deputy, was now Town Clerk of Ipswich. Brock Allen's eventual successor was a Mr Meddings, whom I knew when he occupied a more junior post in Wolverhampton. I often had a chat with him on his way home from courting his future wife, when I was on nights. I was to meet him quite often at Sunningdale where he was highly thought of as a course and study member. Certain local authority experts were asked to attend studies where their help was of value, and he was one of those invited from time to time. Like so many good men I knew, he killed himself with hard work, succumbing to a heart attack whilst still at his peak in the mid-sixties.

On my visits home, I nearly always called in at the Police Canteen in Red Lion Street. It was pleasant to meet old comrades again, particularly as I now had status!

Chapter XIV

End of Police Service – A New Life Begins

Before the Civil Service Commission approved my appointment, I had to undergo a strict medical. After frequent delays and postponements, I was eventually examined by a consultant in Wimpole Street. More delay whilst the machine ground on; it was obviously not easy to get into the Civil Service. Character references were carefully checked, my referees being Mr Goodchild, Mr Meddings, Mr Jackson, Chief Constable of Newcastle-on-Tyne, Major General Sir Cecil Smith, whom I knew as a representative of the National Coal Board and a frequent Staff College visitor. After being interviewed on 11 July, it took until 31 October for the receipt of the final letter of approval, which read that I was admitted on probation from September 1957. So now I submitted my resignation from the Force after thirty years and nine months service. It was with mixed feelings I did so, as I had a strange feeling that a guardian angel who had covered me with his protective wings for so many years had flown away, and I was left bare and exposed to the hard world. The mood soon passed in the pleasure of my new appointment, but old habits die hard. I shall always be part policeman – there's the tendency to take charge of any accident that I see, or am near, the authoritative tone to the voice that comes instinctively, and, strangely, the way people often obey without quite knowing why; the difficulty in minding my own business; the erect carriage; and a tendency to bristle if I hear my old service criticised.

I had a number of congratulatory letters on my appointment from Mr Goodchild, Mr Meddings, Wolverhampton Watch Committee who placed on record their appreciation of my past services, Mr Patterson, and Brigadier Pennycook from Training Division. One letter worth quoting was from my Assistant Secretary contact at the Home Office at that time, Mr R.A. James:

MDH

Tel. No.: WHITEHALL 8100
Ext.................
Our Ref. ESP. 35230
Your Ref..................

HOME OFFICE
ESTABLISHMENT AND ORGANISATION DIVISION
WHITEHALL,
LONDON, S.W.1.

14 October, 1957.

Sir,

    I am directed by the Secretary of State to inform you that a Certificate of Qualification in your favour having been received from the Civil Service Commissioners, he has been pleased to appoint you to a post of Instructor (Civil Defence) in the Home Office with effect from 27th September, 1957, subject to one year's probation.

    Your salary is £1,105 per annum, on the scale £1,105 x £35 - £1,140 x £30 - £1,200 x £35 - £1,270 x £45 - £1,360 x £40 - £1,425. Your incremental date is 27th September.

    Your annual leave allowance is 22 days rising to 25 days after ten years service.

    A copy of the Handbook for the New Civil Servant and a copy of the Handbook for the Guidance of New Entrants to the Home Department are enclosed for your information and retention. When you have read these documents you should sign and return the form of acknowledgment enclosed.

    The following are also enclosed for your immediate attention:-

    (1) Two copies of a form of declaration relating to the provisions of the Official Secrets Acts. These forms should be signed, one should be retained and the other returned.

    (2) A form of undertaking regarding the payment of unabated sick pay (see paragraph 39 of the Handbook for the Guidance of New Entrants) which should be completed and returned.

/(3)

E. Stonier, Esq.,
    Civil Defence Staff College,
        Sunningdale Park, SUNNINGHILL,
            Nr. Ascot.

[Other side of page.]

    (3) An explanatory booklet regarding the Widows' and Children's and Dependants' Pension Schemes and a form W.P.S.12 which should also be completed and returned.

    (4) A form Est.46 which should be completed and returned.

    If there is anything in this letter or its enclosures which you do not understand, please consult the undersigned.

                I am, Sir,
                    Your obedient Servant,

End of Police Service – A New Life Begins

Dear Stonier,

I should not like the time to pass when you take off the heavy mantle of Police Lecturer at the Staff College, without writing to thank you for all the help and advice which you have given me over the last two years, since I first came to Police War Planning. I am immensely grateful for all you have done, and particularly for the careful and reasoned thinking which you have given to the many problems before us. I should particularly remember Study Zeta as your own special triumph, and I continue to hear praise of the way in which you put on that study on behalf of the College. It was certainly a lively discussion.

It is good to know that I shall continue to see you at the Staff College and no doubt we shall meet again very soon.

Thank you again.

Yours sincerely,
R.A. JAMES.

ES

Tel. No.: WHitehall 8100

Ext. ....

Our Ref. ESP.35230

Your Ref. ....

HOME OFFICE
ESTABLISHMENT AND
ORGANISATION DIVISION
WHITEHALL,
LONDON, S.W.1

Mr. Stonier,
Civil Defence Staff College,
Sunningdale.

I have pleasure in informing you that your appointment as an established Instructor (Civil Defence), to which post you were admitted on probation on 27th September, 1957 has been confirmed.

for Establishment Officer

31st October, 1958

> 7th November, 1957.
>
> Dear General,
>
> I have now learned that I have been successful in obtaining an established civil service post as an Instructor at the Staff College.
>
> Might I take this opportunity of thanking you for kindly allowing your name to go forward on my behalf as a referee.
>
> I have now moved here to Sunningdale : it is rather like starting a new life.
>
> This is wishing you all the best. Don't bother to acknowledge.
>
> Yours sincerely,
>
> Major-General Sir Cecil Smith,
>   K.B.E., C.B., M.C., A.M.I.Mech.E.,
> National Coal Board,
> Hobart House,
> London, S.W.1.

I replied, and also thanked my referees for their kindness and help — so my new life began.

The Study Zeta referred to was my first study, apart from the police one, as the Staff Officer — a bomb of 10 megaton power ground burst on Manchester, and a fallout plume of radioactivity stretching from there to Hull. I gave a session off my own bat, giving 'The Story of the Plume'. I obtained aerial photographs of the territory from Manchester to Hull, read up the industries, towns, and country generally between these two places, and recounted how the population might be affected. I had got it through the awful 'nit-picking' by the Ministry chaps. It had gone down very well as nothing quite like it had been done before. One important course member said to me, 'A splendid show, Stonier, though you did take our eye off the ball a little.' Which only goes to prove you can't satisfy everyone!

Family Move to Sunningdale

There was no longer any need to keep my house in Wolverhampton. Three and a half years separation from my family was now over. I wrote to a firm whose premises backed on to my garden, and offered the house to one of their executives for about £200 more than I had paid. It was quickly snapped up at my price, so I avoided the cost of paying a house agent to sell it for me.

I had been offered Brandis's council house which he was vacating on retirement, just outside the estate fence, very nicely situated. The accommodation was small, but the property was fairly new — there would only be Rose and I, with the girls coming home at weekends. I handed in my uniform and we left for our new home where I bought quite a few of Brandis's fitments, and we quickly settled in.

Visitors to the Staff College

Interesting people came from time to time. Rab Butler, when Home Secretary, visited the College, we were all introduced, and I recall how limp was his handshake; he did not give any formal address. Hughes, the Staffordshire CDO came on a course, and I was shocked at his appearance — he was obviously a dying man, and had the unmistakeable look of death on his face. He had lost a lot of weight and looked a heart-attack case. I was not surprised when shortly after I learned of his death; he was, I suppose, about my age.

Several old Ryton chaps attended in various capacities — McCrory, now an Assistant Chief Constable, Ted Higgs was a Superintendent, Dusty Miller now an Assistant CDO, Reg Jasper too; Mr Bond also turned up. On his tiny force being merged with Leicestershire, he obtained an appointment as the District Clerk for Rutland — as a Bachelor of Law, he was suitably equipped for the job and he seemed very content.

Emma Hamilton had left our staff and was replaced by Esme Cox. She had been a handsome woman, tall, slender, sharp, humorous, and very good company. She was more nervous than Emma, but nevertheless she gave a good show on her Welfare and Homeless subject. It was never easy for the WVS representative, as there was a deal of male chauvinism about our staff, and the feeling was that they could give welfare without the aid of WVS. The difficulty was that Lady Reading, the Chairwoman of the WVS was too powerful a person to cross. It was believed that she had almost immediate access to any cabinet minister, and even the Prime Minister himself. She was a very able person, of that there is no doubt. I had first encountered her in 1938 when she came and spoke in Wolverhampton's Council Chamber to publicize some ARP venture or WVS, I cannot remember. She was then a handsome, striking looking lady, although twenty years later she was heavier, but still a fine-looking woman; and she still spoke dynamically for she was formidable! I shall write of her again.

Esme and I got on together very well. She was divorced – it was strange how many of our staff had broken marriages behind them. Her husband had been a Group Captain in the RAF, and they had a son and daughter. She was closely related to the Sandeman family, the sherry and port people. Coulson obtained the job of CDO for Bristol, a good, well-paid post. He had been replaced by Lieutenant Commander John Alldridge. Alldridge was quite a character, of proportionate build, good looking, with all his hair, a good lecturer, and ultimately the best drafter of an exercise of the entire staff – brilliant but erratic would describe him. He, too, was separated or divorced – he was so secretive, it was difficult to say which. He had a fatal fascination for many women, and could be very charming, or a complete pain in the neck, depending on how he felt. The Chief Instructor and senior instructors had a deal of trouble from him and so did his colleagues.

I was replaced by Superintendent Peter Leplar, from the Nottinghamshire County Police – Mr Browne's force. He was a stiffly built, fair man, thinning hair, a little garrulous at times, a good lecturer, factual rather than emotional. He did a good job at Sunningdale, but it was of no advantage to his career as he had an enemy back in his force who stopped any further progress. He ended up as Chief Inspector, but did, however, enjoy his stay at Sunningdale.

By the time Leplar was appointed, George Moran had left. He became Assistant Regional Director of Southern Region, a promotion. He was replaced by Lieutenant Colonel John Butcher, the Secretary of the Civil Defence Joint Planning Staff, which post he now vacated. 'Butch' was a very forthright character, plain spoken, ex-Indian Army. He had seen and heard many of my police lecture performances, and apparently had seen and heard enough to tell Leplar on his appointment that he would like him to come out and 'punch it home to the audience like Fred Stonier did'. Peter told me this himself.

I was very sorry to have to give up my police talk as I loved giving it, and my audiences loved hearing it apparently, still, it had to go. I heard my successor give his talk with mixed feelings. It was true that Police Planning had progressed a little, and Peter had some factual

End of Police Service – A New Life Begins 257

progress on war plans to include that had been unavailable to me; he was no fool, and made a very good talk of his scanty material.

Visit by HRH the Duke of Gloucester

This was in March 1958, and marked the occasion of the opening of a new lecture theatre, to be called the Gloucester Hall. It had been converted from the stable block for this purpose, and proved very useful, particularly to me as I was able to rehearse my new material there with no disturbance, as it was well away from the other buildings. HRH arrived at 10.40 a.m. to be met by the Commandant, Deputy, Secretary and Colonel Barton, our attached soldier. After coffee, he was taken to the Lethbridge Theatre, where the Commandant gave a fifteen-minute Background to Courses talk. George Stanbury, the Home Office scientist gave a 'fall-out' talk for fifteen minutes, and the Deputy Commandant gave thirty minutes on Civil Defence organization generally.

At 12.15 p.m. he was at the Hodsall Hall where he listened to the latter part of a verbal exercise at sector controller level, then back to the mansion at 12.55 p.m. where we were all introduced. Drinks followed, and I remember what a high-pitched laugh the Duke had – quite unusual.

After lunch the ceremony of opening the new lecture theatre was performed. At 14.15 p.m. he was brought to the Hodsall Hall to witness my demonstration of 'Clearing the Z Zone'. I was now the acknowledged expert on this, and felt greatly honoured and very surprised at being selected to present the biggest item of all – forty-five minutes of it. The floor was all laid ready, I walked up to HRH, clicked my heels, and asked permission to begin. He nodded, and off I went – by Royal Appointment as it were. Well, there was nothing to get excited about in this demonstration, it was hard factual stuff, fortunately with plenty of movement – just the thing to keep awake a lunch-heavy audience. It ended quite normally, with questions from the audience, and at 15.15 p.m., His Royal Highness left.

So ended our first and only Royal visit – I was thrilled to have played a part in it.

Investments and a New Car

After my appointment to the Staff, and my change of home from Wolverhampton to Sunningdale, I began to study my financial position. I had at last some spare cash from savings and the sale of my house.

I had been particularly intrigued with my colleagues' interest in the stock market. We naturally had all the daily and weekly papers delivered to the College, and we were all avid readers as part of our need to be completely up to date on current affairs. I listened to their comments on stocks and shares as many of them were experienced investors. After a careful study of the market and my funds, I invested in Courtaulds, Serck Radiator, Symonds Brewery and Cow and Gate as a modest start. Since then I have been a keen student of form, and a modest investor. I made my first purchases quite fortuitously when the market was rock bottom, and over the years, particularly before 1964 when 'capital gains' began to bite, I made quite a fair profit. It was nice to have some money to spare for the first time since my early milk-round days. I also bought an Austin A35 saloon car from one of our staff, Lieutenant Colonel Fred Bassett. As well as being an instructor of DS, he also owned a garage at Wellington, Somerset, and was always keen to make a sale. Bassett was a tall, fair, good-looking but balding man of about 40–45 years. He was also a very good instructor, having, like many of the others, Army Staff College training. He could easily have been Chief Instructor had he chosen to stay, but he had itchy feet and left whilst a senior instructor. He wanted to devote more time to his business. He had a charming wife, who was so different from some of the 'memsahibs' that others of my colleagues had married. I went with them one Sunday afternoon to a Civil Service motor gathering. They took a picnic basket which I shared. The food was beautifully prepared, but to my surprise there was no bread. Now, I had been reared in the typical working-class tradition of eating plenty of bread with everything, I cannot eat any other way now, so I found it strange for lettuce to take the place of bread. However, we had a lovely day, and Freddy urged me to be his navigator in any rally that he entered, but I got out of that – it had NO appeal for me.

I enjoyed my little car and kept it for a couple of years. I took the family at weekends to Brighton for a change of scene, varying this with shopping trips to Kensington, London, Guildford, and many other towns within easy reach. Mother came from Folkestone for a visit and we took her to Brighton one Saturday. She didn't think much of our pie and chips lunch, eaten in the car – Mother *did not* do things like that. On our way home she salvaged her pride by insisting we stop at a tearoom and have a rather expensive tea!

While Rose went to the village one day, Mother went exploring around the bedrooms, then fell down the stairs, so when Rose returned, she found her in a fine old state. A doctor was called, and Mother spent the next week or two in Windsor Hospital with a broken wrist and shock. However, despite her advanced years, she survived.

Spain

Our first trip to the continent was in 1959. We flew from Lydd to Le Touquet, then boarded a coach en route for San Sebastian via Tours and Carcassone, staying one night in the cognac country at a place called Bergessau. Our hotel was a low, largely wooden structure, very old, and full of cognac. There was a distillery in the small town which we visited, becoming slightly inebriated from trying the samples. We retired that night to bed, only to be awakened long after midnight with the cry 'Fire' or 'Feu', I'm not certain which. We hurriedly left our rooms, grabbing our holdalls, and whatever we could quickly find. Fortunately, on overnight stops, the main luggage was still in the coach and we only carried overnight bags. I shall never forget the sights on the landing – people sans teeth, hair in curlers, or all dishevelled, no make-up, some ladies had overnight packs on their faces, most people were in night attire. No panic, just a hurried retreat outside. There was a fire alright. One couple had been in bed gazing at the ceiling, when to their surprise, smoke and then fire came through above their heads, so they raised the alarm. The hotel was a tinderbox with so much old wood and cognac. The local fire brigade, pulling a hand-cart affair, came on the scene, and were taken over by our coach driver, a sturdy chap from Lyons, who happened to be a part-time fireman there. He quickly removed the coach out of danger, then tackled the fire, while we tourists watched with interest. The fire was fairly quickly put out, and we all went back inside. The 'Madame' in charge of the hotel had laid on coffee and cognac which we gratefully drank up and retired for the second time. It was dawn. Next day, when we were about to leave, madame came to wish us 'bon voyage', and presented a large bottle of cognac to the couple who had raised the alarm.

San Sebastian was a nice resort. I enjoyed the cheap liquor and Havana cigars at 1/9 each (old money). Rose and I drank Cherry Brandy, whilst I smoked my Havana cigar, as we sat on our balcony overlooking the town. 'C'est la vie', alright.

There is one memorable incident worth recording. We went one afternoon to a bullfight, our first and only visit. General Franco had his yacht in the harbour, and on this day he attended the bullfight as its 'presidente'. We did not see him arrive at the stadium, but we did notice how the streets were packed with police and soldiers lining the route. Police were even brought in from the surrounding countryside, as there were green uniforms as well as grey. Both police and soldiers were armed.

Of the bullfight, I enjoyed the spectacle, the ceremony and the Pasa Doble music. The splendidly dressed matadors and toreadors walked ceremoniously to the Presidente's box, saluted him, and were acknowledged, they then moved to their positions. The bull entered the ring, and the crowd watched his angry bewilderment, his search for something on which to focus; he saw the toreador waving his cape and charged. All that I like, it is a fair match. What I, and apparently nearly all other opponents of this spectacle dislike, is the use of the picador, and the deliberate incapacitating of the bull's shoulder muscles by the use of the lance.

The cape work, the passes, the 'Olés' of the crowd, the final coup de grace by the matador is thrilling. No matter how unethical it may be, it does something which stirs the primitive in us. The final dragging off of the dead bull by drag chains is deplorable – a noble death deserves better. There were six corridas, after which we left, with strangely mixed and subdued feelings.

In the streets the crowds were gathered all along the route to the harbour, waiting for Franco's procession to pass. As I said before, the streets were lined with police and military as the cavalcade approached from the stadium, open jeeps or small personnel carriers in front, filled with alert soldiers, fingers on triggers as their weapons pointed outwards. The General's car, with him plainly visible, passed slowly, followed by vehicles filled with armed men.

The crowds were completely silent, even the low talking stopped; it was most eerie. On went the cavalcade slowly and silently. This, of course, was Basque country where there was no love here for El Caudillo. After he had gone, the crowds quietly drifted away. It had been for us an emotion-filled afternoon.

No subsequent holiday in Spain quite lived up to that first one. For one thing, prices kept creeping up until today they are as high and often higher than here at home. The attitude of the Spaniards too has changed, spoiled as always by the influx of tourists splashing their money around. A shame – the sun is so wonderful, and so is the country and its history.

Morale

Now came my biggest break at the Staff College. There were two Civil Defence Officers' organisations: the local authority CDOs, who held their annual conference at the Staff College, and the industrial CDOs who were nearly all from large industrial concerns and ministries like the National Coal Board, Electricity Generating Board, Gas Industry, Steel and Oil Industries, ICI, and so on. I received a letter from the Secretary of the Northern Area of Civil Defence in Industry, asking me to give a talk on 'Morale' to a conference, to be held by them at Stone, Staffordshire in November 1958. I had never thought of this as a subject before. General Matthews encouraged me to accept, and 'have a go'. I searched our library for suitable material and found a paper on the subject by a Professor Treadgold, a psychiatrist of note. I read his paper and drafted one of my own from it.

Shortly after I had completed it, I received a letter from my hosts-to-be, enclosing the programme. Not only was Professor Treadgold one of the speakers, but the Army Director of Psychiatry, Brigadier Phillipson, was also a speaker on the same subject. This meant a complete rethink. I scrapped my paper and thought hard, not helped by Charles Luce who could be bitchy at times, saying to me, 'What do you know about Morale?' to which I replied, 'What does anyone?'

Now I had remembered from my early days at the College that George Moran had used charts for an opening address that gave the figures of bombs dropped on the United Kingdom during the War, and the tonnage dropped on Germany and Japan, the casualties inflicted and houses rendered uninhabitable. He then produced a chart showing the figures for the atom bomb explosions on Hiroshima and Nagasaki. He had quoted figures from the United States Strategic Bombing Survey reports – or Uzz-Buzz. We had these reports in our library, volumes of them standing three or four feet from the ground. They covered all aspects of bomb damage – people, utilities and indirectly, morale. I waded through these and extracted what was valid, in rough form. I could not help but admire the expertise and gigantic labour that had gone into the compilation of these reports.

I examined what people like Napoleon and others had to say about morale. From it all I gave first a general description of the effects of strategic bombing in Germany, and its effects of this on morale; measures by authorities to maintain morale; police force control, the overall dominant factor; propaganda, lawlessness, post-raid labour and evacuation. Then I dealt briefly with the air attacks on Japan and the great movement of population from town to country; of atomic bombing, and reaction of population – after painting this horrific picture of how the populations of these two countries stood up to the massive air bombardment. Leadership – going back in history for examples, and concluding with Churchill. Food – Water – Casualties and their treatment. Work – no idleness, religion, concluding on a high note recalling our great past.

I polished it and rehearsed it until I was word perfect and was reasonably satisfied.

On my journey to Stone I had to fill a long-standing engagement to speak to the WVS ladies of Leamington. I arranged to call on them the day before I was due in Stone, and as I had carte blanche on what I said at Leamington, I gave 'Morale' its first airing. It seemed to go reasonably well, the ladies, bless them, seemed a bit horrified, but they gave me a good reception.

I continued my journey to Stone. By this time thick fog had descended on the Midlands. I was using my little Austin A.35, and had a dreadful journey. When I reached Stonebridge on the Birmingham-Coventry Road, I tagged on behind a heavy lorry whose address on the cab door was Liverpool. I gambled he was homeward bound, and in those days he had to go at least to Lichfield on my way north. My guess worked out and I left him at Lichfield. The rest of the journey was not quite so bad and I arrived safely if rather late. I went to my hotel, and there met one of my fellow speakers, Brigadier Phillipson. He seemed a very suave, self-possessed person I thought. Next day we addressed our audience in turn. There was a large attendance including the Regional Director, Air Marshal Sir Laurence Pendred, and a few important industrialists, including Councillor Owen, chairman of a large engineering firm at Darlaston. There was also a large gathering of both industrial and local authority Civil Defence officers.

I arranged for my large charts to be displayed, and off I went with a talk that I was to give for the next ten years, and with which my name became inextricably associated whenever Civil Defence was the subject. I was in good form, the talk went well and was enthusiastically received. I quote letters:

F. Stonier, Esq., B.E.M.

NORTHERN

W. J. Clarke
Hon. Secretary: E. Philip Scanes.

Newcastle 69299

EPS/LP/C.29 8th December, 1958.

Dear Major General Matthews,

I have much pleasure in enclosing for your information a copy of the Programme of the recent Conference Study held at Stone. No tribute is too high to pay to the contribution made by your Mr. F. Stonier. The Regional Director (Sir Lawrence F. Pendred) aptly expressed our feelings when he said "We expect a high standard from members of our Senior Training Establishment and Mr. Stonier has certainly exceeded our expectations". Many of the members who have had the opportunity of hearing Mr. Stonier before were emphatic that he excelled himself and has never spoken better. You will, therefore, readily realise how much my Committee and I personally wish to thank you for this contribution to what proved to be a very successful Conference Study.

While I appreciate that it is not the normal custom for precis to be issued by your representatives, I wonder if on this occasion, in view of the importance of the subject and the tremendous impact Mr. Stonier made on the members, if you could arrange for him to supply some notes on his talk. I am sure it would be more than appreciated by all concerned.

Again thanking you for your help,

Yours sincerely,

pp. Chairman, Northern Area.

Major General F.R.G. Matthews, C.B., D.S.O.,
Commandant,
Civil Defence Staff College,
Sunningdale Park,
Sunningdale,
ASCOT, Berkshire.

The first time I gave "Morale" it went on for another 10 yrs all over the UK – a winner.

He rather spoilt the effect by asking for notes on the talk. After my herculean efforts in preparing it, I was not going to make a gift of it to anyone, if I could help it.

264 *A Brummie in Search of a Talent*

The Secretary, Phillip Scanes, whom I knew, also wrote to me saying what a great impression my talk had made, and also asking for notes.

But I suppose the greatest compliment was from Brigadier Phillipson, one of the other speakers (see next letter).

> From: Brigadier R. V. Phillipson, O.B.E., D.P.M.,
>
>
>
> THE WAR OFFICE,
> LONDON, S.W.1.
>
> 19 January, 1959.
>
> Dear Mr. Stonier,
>
> I have received the report and notes on the one-day Conference we attended in Stone on November 26th last year but I note that in the transcript there was no mention of the very excellent piece, in your talk, when you referred to the help that religious belief can play in maintaining morale after any large-scale disaster. I was most impressed with the way you put this across and would be very grateful if you could let me have that portion of your talk and permission to use it in some similar talks I give from time to time.
>
> Hoping we may meet soon again and with best wishes for 1959.
>
> Yours sincerely,
>
> R. Phillipson - Brigadier
> Director and
> Consulting Psychiatrist to the Army
>
> Mr. F. Stonier, B.E.M.,
>   Civil Defence Staff College,
>   Sunningdale,
>   Berks.

Praise from an expert! General Matthews was rather keen that I should give Phillipson what he asked. I told the General that Phillipson had some marvellous slides of the aftermath of bombing in Germany – dead in shelters, funeral pyres, and other rather gruesome but authentic and gripping pictorial effects of strategic bombing. He had shown these at Stone and the effect was dramatic. Could we not do a swop? The General agreed, and wrote to the Brigadier accordingly. In fact,

End of Police Service – A New Life Begins

he came to Sunningdale, and we made an amicable exchange. He warned me that they were to be guarded carefully, they were not for general distribution. We met a few times later on when the Brigadier retired, and obtained a post in the Ministry of Health. His slides were just what I needed to give the talk opening impact, and this they certainly did. I used them ever after.

I was pleased about the religious bit as I was a little afraid to put it in – it is a subject that we tend not to discuss openly, being a private matter, and we sheer away from public discussion. It always galvanized an audience. I started by giving the Communist definition from Marx, *Das Kapital*, that it is the 'opium of the people', which shook my audience somewhat – a quotation from Karl Marx, what next? I followed with the simple fact that from the dawn of history, man had felt the need for faith in something bigger than himself. I was non-controversial and sincere in what I said, and its value to morale was what I was leading to. I had many compliments over the years, often from clerks in Holy Orders, who expressed their admiration for my courage in putting such a reference in the talk.

Shortly after my return to the College, we heard that Mr Darlow, the Town Clerk of Reading, was unable to give his talk on Restoration to Senior Officers Courses in future. He had been giving it ever since the Restoration Study in March 1954 had set the scene. Occasionally he was substituted by his friend Mr Schofield, the Town Clerk of Southampton, and once by George Moran. It really needed a town clerk to give the talk, and certainly to answer the questions. In any case, after over four years, the talk was becoming dated.

There was a gap in the programme so I rushed in to fill it. I asked General Matthews to let me give 'Morale', and see how it went. He agreed – he was always ready to take a chance on something new. I tried it out, and it was an instantaneous success, as it had been at Stone. With the slides it went even better. From then on it was a regular feature in our 'bread and butter' courses, the Senior Officers, and later on, all Controllers' Courses, held for town, county and district clerks. I use this term because the new title of Chief Executives was only just beginning to be used about 1966 or thereabouts.

I never took questions, they did not seem applicable to the subject, and I was no Psychiatrist. After a time I ceased to have another DS as chairman, I was just left to it with my demonstrator. My colleagues and others knew when I had finished, they heard the applause, and some of them were, I'm afraid, a bit jealous.

Missed Opportunities

During my time at the Staff College certain opportunities came my way which I will take in chronological order. Firstly, there was the tip-off that if I applied for the CDO's job at Wolverhampton, I had a good chance. I have already mentioned this earlier.

Later on, when Evans, the CDO who replaced Lieutenant Colonel Hughes, was in the post, he was taking me back to Wolverhampton in his car after attending a course. He told me that he had put in for the job of Manager of the Civic Hall, Wolverhampton. If he was successful, he had reason to believe that I would be considered as a successor, if I applied. In the event, he did not get the job, but it sounded as though I was still considered a possible in Wolverhampton.

In my last year as the Police Staff Officer, I was stopped one day by Lieutenant General Sir Ernest Wood, Regional Director of Eastern Region. He had been a very distinguished soldier and was one of the best of a very fine lot of Regional Directors. He told me that the Chief Constable's post for Huntingdonshire was vacant, and that, if I applied, he would be pleased to back me. I don't know what influence he had at Huntingdon, but I don't think a man of his standing would have said what he did without good grounds. I considered: I was forty-nine years old, near the end of my police service, I had no experience of the administration side of the Police Force, or the CID, for that matter, as my service had been spent all in uniform or Civil Defence. I had no great urge to be a Chief Constable. I told Sir Ernest that I was a bit too old now for a post like that, and needed to be five or ten years younger. He seemed disappointed and said, 'Well, please yourself.' Then a strange thing happened. I had been invited by Superintendent Williams, who was Commandant of a Police Training Centre in Northumberland, to address the senior police officers of Northern Region on 'Police Action at a Nuclear Bomb' on their region. He had prepared rough floor map and charts, and I went to his establishment to give a talk-demonstration. On my arrival he was just leaving. He apologized, and left me in his deputy's capable hands, while he went off for an interview for the job at Huntingdon. He was successful. Later he became Chief Constable of Sussex, and on the mergers around 1966, took over the enlarged force. It finally killed him, too, as he died of a heart attack whilst serving, and still fairly young. So many Chief Constables went the same way – Dodd of Birmingham, Simpson of the Metropolitan, White of Kent spring to mind, and Ballance and Goodchild twelve months after retiring. Williams was a university graduate,

End of Police Service – A New Life Begins

and some years younger than I, so had I applied for Huntingdon I would probably have been pipped. I shall never know.

Then one day, during my last twelve months as Staff Officer, I called on Fred Tarry, Her Majesty's Inspector of Constabulary, at the Home Office. I forget what the call was about, but during the course of conversation, he let drop the suggestion that when my secondment was completed, I might obtain a Deputy Commandant's job at a Training Centre. No more than that, although I think that had I pursued the idea, I might have obtained such a post, but it was not very appealing.

One evening I was in the police canteen in Wolverhampton being on leave, now an established civil servant. George Pendered was there, as was his custom. He had a private investigation business – divorces, debts, etc. – doing quite well, I imagine. He had a son-in-law working for him and he asked me if I would like a job with him. Now at that time I was on £2,000 a year, about the same as a Grade 1 Superintendent, and I doubted if George's business could have paid me that or anything like it, so I declined gracefully. Shortly after my appointment as a member of the Staff College, Patterson asked me if I would like to be a senior instructor at Taymouth Castle. A senior instructor did not appeal to me, it meant less lecturing, programme preparation, handling instructors who could be difficult, to put it mildly, and the pay was only about £150-£200 a year more. In any case, to go back to ordinary training, after the kind of work I had been doing, had no attraction at all. I wanted to prove I was capable of holding down a Staff College job – it was a matter of pride. I politely refused. He then got Brigadier Pennycook to work on me, but he too failed, so he tried to sell the idea to Rose. Now I had sensed something like this happening much earlier – so much so, I went on holiday to Scotland, and stayed a couple of nights at Taymouth Castle with Rose and the girls. They liked the place, but the idea of living there was out of the question, it was far too remote and lonely. I told them I might possibly end up there, and the prospect did not suit Rose at all. She told Pennycook so, and pointed out that another DS, Colonel George, had worked at Taymouth, and his wife had told us she nearly went mad. Living in, she had no housework or cooking to do, and nearly died of boredom. Finally, she left Colonel George and went to live in Brighton, where she started a business. The separation was only by distance, not marital. Rose also pointed out to Pennycook that she had only been at Sunningdale about six weeks, surely she wasn't expected to pack up and move on again. Pennycook, and I suppose Patterson, accepted this, and the subject was never broached again. Patterson could not, I think have had any misgivings on my ability, as on 30 July 1957 he had sent me a note congratulating me on my appointment as an established instructor, and saying how delighted he was to welcome me after the completion of distinguished service in the Police.

He also congratulated me on my demonstration of the 'Clearance Operation' the previous week, to members of the County Civil Defence Committee. I was always a bit puzzled by the whole business – perhaps they thought they were doing me a good turn – they were not moving me with any bribe, this was the job I could do well, and I loved the work. So I turned down the Senior Instructor offer.

Finally, the Moral Rearmament Movement. During a course given for WVS representatives, I gave my new talk, 'Morale'. One of the members approached me afterwards and brought up the subject of the movement. I had heard of it, but had never gone into what it meant, or was hoping to achieve. This lady was obviously a member, and made a few tentative enquiries about my beliefs and so on. A few days after the course had disbanded, I received a letter inviting me to a buffet meal at an address in Berkeley Square, London, and later in the evening a visit to a theatre. It was then hoped that I would understand what Moral Rearmament was all about. I asked General Matthews what he thought, and he said, 'Go and find out, it can't do any harm.' I accepted and duly arrived at a large house in Berkeley Square. There I was met by an elderly lady who took charge of me. There was a gathering of youngish people, some of whom were obviously Americans. We had a stand-up meal of what seemed like chicken supreme, very nice, and beautifully served. My companion was gently probing my attitudes, and giving me information on what the movement meant, had achieved, and hoped to achieve. It appeared that the play we were to see later was to portray and exemplify what Moral Rearmament was all about. During our long conversation, I was told a lot about Buckman, the founder, and the college in Switzerland to which promising recruits to the movement were sent before being despatched to their duties in the field. It appeared that I was being vetted for such a job.

We went to the theatre and saw the play. It was well acted, but at the end I felt that it, and all the conversation I had listened to, had not in the final analysis convinced me that it was practical politics. Perhaps as a policeman I was a little too pragmatic for such an idealistic movement. Part of me would have liked to respond – the other and stronger part said, 'It will not work.' I left my companion and returned to the College with no kind of commitment other than her assertion that I would hear from her. A week or so later, I had another invitation to a repeat performance, more or less. I pleaded inability to comply, and that ended my prospects in that direction. Interesting – who can say what might have happened had I gone on with it!

Outside Lectures

Meanwhile, my new presentation 'Morale' was attracting attention in Civil Defence and Armed Forces circles all over the country. Altogether, I gave the talk over sixty times outside the College, and hundreds of times inside. People would hear it and go back and persuade others to invite me to give it in their own locality. I went all over the UK in the next nine years, lecturing in many strange places. I will mention those which have some outstanding features. I began to feel like a stage artiste touring the provinces, with occasional London appearances. One of my first was at a biscuit factory in Reading. This was done as a tribute to Mr Darlow, the Town Clerk, and an old Wulfrunian, for the work he had done for the College. It went down very well to the audience of about 150 Civil Defence volunteers, councillors, and council officers. I met one of my old Ryton colleagues, now retired, and he said, 'You are as good as ever, Fred,' which was pleasing.

Caernarvon

The County Clerk of Caernarvon had invited me to speak to his council – there was difficulty in getting the Civil Defence estimates through – he thought my talk might help. I drove there in my Austin, and was agreeably surprised by the beauty of the scenery en route. I hadn't been to Wales for years; it always rained on my holidays there. I had phoned the Welsh Home Office contact at Civil Defence Regional Headquarters and asked him to give me, in phonetic Welsh, the last two pages of my script, so that I could pay my audience the compliment of speaking a little of their native language. He told me not to risk anything quite so ambitious, it was a difficult language, and the slightest mis-pronunciation could alter the whole meaning. He suggested I just conclude with 'Thank you very much, gentlemen, for listening to me', in Welsh, and this I did after going to some pains to learn it accurately.

I went into a crowded council chamber and was introduced by the County Clerk. I saw that all the notices around the chamber were in Welsh and English. I was occupying the Mayor's chair, which followed the normal practice of being on a raised dais. All arrangements for displaying my charts and slides had been made quite satisfactorily (this

Brigadier G. Wort, commanding 107 (Ulster) Independent Infantry Brigade (T.A.), who was in charge of the exercise held by the Territorial Army and the Civil Defence at Stranmillis Training College during the week-end, with Mr. W. R. Montgomery (left), deputy chief Civil Defence officer, Ministry of Home Affairs; Mr. F. Stonier, Civil Defence Staff College, England; Mr. C. C. M'Creight, chief Civil Defence officer, and District-Inspector J. B. Flanagan, R.U.C.

was always a gamble with outside lectures). During the impassioned part of my talk, I started to move about as is my way, and promptly fell down the steps of the dais, recovered none the worse, and resumed. There was no laughter – very serious folk, these Welsh. I concluded with my bit of Welsh, and there was a general grunt of satisfaction – no applause, which was unusual. Then an elderly figure arose and said in sepulchral tones, 'I never realised that the next war could be started with a press of a button, we should go outside and pray.' With his hand raised, and pointing finger, his grey hair and austere countenance, he looked like a prophet of old denouncing the devil. There was the usual vote of thanks, and that concluded an interesting experience. I parted from the County Clerk, who was delighted with all that had gone on.

Apart from 'Morale', I also gave several demonstrations of 'Clearing a Z Zone', in such places as the pavilion, Edgaston Cricket Ground, where I did a duo with John Batchelor of Training Division, and the same show at the Grand Hotel, Brighton, for the annual conference of

End of Police Service – A New Life Begins

From:- BRIGADIER G. WORT.

HEADQUARTERS
107 (ULSTER) INDEPENDENT INFANTRY BRIGADE GROUP (TA),
VICTORIA BARRACKS,
BELFAST.
TEL. BELFAST 32091.

Ref:- IBG/204/26/2/G

17 Feb 60

Dear Stonier,

Just a line to say "thank you" again for coming over.

From our point of view, your presence was invaluable and contributed a great deal towards the success of the Exercise. I was glad to be able to include your lecture as I am sure it has helped us a great deal "to sell CD" to the TA chaps. I am very grateful to you too for taking part in the discussions, and I am sure also that the civil side, particularly the RUC, very much appreciated having you at the week-end.

I trust you had a safe journey from the Airport and that your "drops" will catch up with you! If you have any further comments on the Exercise or set-up generally, I shall be glad to have them. And please be sure to tell the new liaison officer to call on me as soon as he visits BELFAST.

Again many thanks for all your help, and we thoroughly enjoyed having you with us.

My wife and family wish to be remembered to you.

With kind regards,

Yours sincerely,

V. Wort.

F. STONIER Esq. BEM,
Civil Defence Staff College,
Sunningdale Park,
SUNNINGDALE, ASCOT,
Berkshire.

the Industrial Civil Defence Officers, this with Doctor Black of headquarters, Scientific Advisors Branch. I worked a great deal with Black and Stanesbury of the Scientific Branch on regional studies. We went to Brighton in Black's car, and had a terrific argument on religion – he a disbeliever, and I a believer, all in good temper, and neither convinced the other. Previous to our presentation, we had spent many hours learning the topography of Brighton's surrounding districts as we had based our presentation on this territory, and it had to be accurate to portray the towns, villages and hamlets of the area represented on the floor map.

I gave a similar demonstration in Shropshire to a gathering of Midland Civil Defence personnel. Here I met several of my wartime colleagues who had still remained as Civil Defence officers with their authorities. Reg Reynolds was one; he had left the Police, and was now Civil Defence Officer for Worcester City.

In February 1960, I took my first trip to Northern Ireland, at the invitation of Brigadier Wort, of the 107 (Ulster) Independent Infantry Brigade Group T.A. I was to speak to his Territorial Army chaps, and take part in the subsequent discussions. He was combining this with the Ulster Constabulary.

I gave a mixed talk, part Civil Defence organization, and part morale, tailored to the course requirement. It was well received, and I have a picture of Brigadier Wort, McCreight, the Civil Defence Officer, Montgomery of the Ministry of Home Affairs, and District Inspector J.B. Flanagan of the RUC, taken by the local press. Flanagan often came to Sunningdale and so I knew him quite well; he eventually became Chief Constable of the RUC during the first part of the terrorist campaign from 1968 onwards, and became Sir James Flanagan.

I stayed the night as the guest of the Brigadier and met his charming wife and two children. He took me on a trip around Belfast in his car. I was struck by the slogans painted on the walls, the huge Union Jack paintings on the end walls of terraces, the obscene reference to the Pope. The part of Belfast I saw was squalid, and looked as I remember Birmingham looked when I was a child, particularly the public houses.

The Brigadier left Belfast with me by plane (it was my second plane trip), as he was going to see his father who was ill. Later I saw in the newspaper that he had died, and left the Brigadier a fortune.

He sent a nice letter of thanks; I was to visit Northern Ireland again, but more of that anon.

Sheffield

This visit is worth a mention. I was invited by the Commandant of the Special Police, with the concurrence of the Chief Constable, Mr G. Staines to talk to Wardens and Specials. We had lunch at a large hotel in Sheffield where my host was obviously well known. He, Staines and I lunched together. Whilst having a drink beforehand, I said to him, 'I hear you are a shrewd Stock Exchange investor, can you suggest a good investment?' He laughed, and said something about Woolworths, and that ended the conversation. We had a splendid lunch, my host making his own coffee at the table. During the afternoon I was looked after by Mr Staines and gave my lecture in the evening which went down very well, and my host gave me a lift back to my hotel in his splendid Bentley. During the journey, he asked me if I was serious about my Stock Exchange enquiry. I said I was, and had a few hundreds to invest, so he gave me a tip. On my return to Sunningdale, I told Charles Luce, who said, 'If he has told you that, have a go, I shall.' I invested a few hundreds, and sure enough a few months later, I nearly doubled my stake, as did Charles Luce. Inside information is now, I believe, unlawful – but not then.

Chapter XV

Changes

I must pause here to keep up to date on college changes. Leplar had gone, being replaced by Superintendent Howe, from Sussex. He was a quiet man, one of the few policemen I have met opposed to the Death Penalty for murder. He gave a good factual talk, with no frills. I had left the office I shared with the attached WVS DS, on my appointment, and now worked with four other DS in one of the main offices. Esme had gone, there were four other WVS DS during my period at the Staff College, but I was not working so closely with them. Our attached soldiers, Barton and Griffiths, had both joined the staff at the end of their period of secondment. I think Leplar tried, but no other civilian ever got on our staff after my appointment. It was obviously a job reserved for armed service personnel. I had been lucky indeed to break into this elite organization. I had to make sure I stayed there, and always felt I had to put in a little more effort than my colleagues, who felt they had nothing to prove.

About this time General Matthews went as part of a British team of observers to America, to witness a hydrogen bomb or nuclear explosion in the Nevada desert. One of our staff had previously witnessed an A-bomb explosion at Woomera in Australia. Neither he, nor General Matthews on their return, provided us with any more information than we had obtained from film and reports through official channels. It did, I suppose, give a certain authority to our teaching, the fact that members of our staff had seen an explosion. The only thing that remains in my mind was General Matthews' report of the effects that he felt. Despite the safety distance at which they were placed, there was an unearthly light, followed by the effect of an oven door being opened close to one's face, followed by a gale force wind. He also mentioned in passing, that his party had gone to Las Vegas, but were mostly too poor to indulge in gambling – a likely story!

While he was away, we had the annual garden party, and Colonel Butcher as Deputy Commandant had to officiate and receive the distinguished, and the not so distinguished guests. General Matthews' wife attended. She was beautifully dressed, and had been a very pretty woman from a distinguished family, but she had a problem. Esme and I took her home, and kept an eye on her until the General's return. His son Michael, a nice boy of about fourteen years was home from public school, and at a loose end. I took him under my wing, as much as I could, played tennis, and went swimming with him. I quite enjoyed my role of guardian. On his return the General was very grateful; he had Esme and I to his house for drinks and thanked us. He chatted to me alone later on, and spoke promisingly about a future post of senior instructor. I was pleased, but I had no great desire for the job – I had what I wanted. It is worth commenting on a strange feeling that had possessed me from the time of Doug Petersen's letter to me at Easingwold in January 1954, until well into the sixties. I felt I was being carried along by some irresistible force, over which I had little or no control. What was, and had happened to me seemed preordained. I was surprised at nothing that had occurred, feeling that I might have achieved anything I chose. I had never felt like this before, and I never felt like it again after about 1963–64. It made me think that this must occur to many people – how else did those immortal words, 'There is a tide in the affairs of man, which taken at the flood ...' ever get written? I suppose if one grasps the opportunities, success follows, if not, the chance has probably gone for ever. I think I grasped some of mine at least, but perhaps not all.

Back to Work

As I was the Z Zone Clearance expert, I was responsible for changes in presentation and scripts. We gave up the purely floor demonstration for a playlet with two actors, the moves being pointed out on the floor map by a demonstrator. This method went on for a long time.

I heard something one day, which gave me a new idea for presenting the subject. I had a stand-up map prepared of a section of the huge area covered by the floor map which leaned against the stage. I spoke from the floor, so that I could use the two maps, and instead of a lecture, I gave a soliloquy. I spoke my thoughts aloud, stating the problem, the courses open, factors to be considered – solutions.

It was a novel method and went down very well, even with CDOs, who were usually a pretty bloody-minded lot. It did, however, require rather a feat of memory, and some ability to act. I gave it successfully for quite a long time, until the snag appeared of the understudy. Every session presented had to have two DS capable of putting it on.

By this time Charles Luce had become Chief Instructor in place of 'Butch', who had been appointed Civil Defence Officer for Hampshire – a plum job.

Luce had difficulty with the understudy for this session, Colonel Thompson. I don't think it was the acting that worried him, but the feat of memory, or perhaps it was because it was new and unorthodox. Anyhow, Luce said it would have to revert to being a playlet, which presented no difficulty with understudies. I was furious, and Luce could see this, and apologized, but rather weakly asked, 'What could I do?' For such a usually strong-willed man to take that attitude was difficult to understand. He should have told Robert Thomson to get on with it, and not to 'belly-ache', a favourite expression of his.

I had a stormy scene with Thomson over this as I knew it was good, it was new and held attention – it was just a little too much trouble, or else, more likely, a bit of jealousy had crept in.

I recall long before this, General Bruce had told me to be aware of the jealousy of my colleagues, if anything I did went well. It was partly for this reason, and partly because I did not want my work acquired by others, that I never let anyone touch my 'Morale' presentation. This was one of the few occasions when I had trouble with other DS. Generally thereafter, I got on well with Robert Thomson and we did many presentations together.

One of these was a duo we gave to the WVS Transport Officers, at the WVS Headquarters in Tothill Street, London. We had a letter of thanks, part of which I quote:

> I was watching their faces, and you probably noticed for yourself, how, as the time went on, you lifted them from contemplation of the appalling task that would lie in front of anyone connected with transport, should the ultimate disaster occur, to an absolutely new conception of Civil Defence and our responsibilities.
>
> Everyone who heard you, told me later on in the day, how tremendously they had been impressed by Colonel Thomson and yourself, and the fact that we were able to spend two hours on Civil Defence, being kept utterly absorbed in the subject, by two such brilliant speakers.
>
> Yours, etc.,
> MARGARET TRIGGS

Robert Thomson had been a Territorial Officer in his younger days. He had been to public school, but had not been through Sandhurst and

Staff College, as had so many of his colleagues which he felt had greatly handicapped him in his early army days. However, he achieved full colonel rank in his Yorkshire regiment, and a CBE. He was tall, thin, wiry, and a glutton for work. He lectured well, and was the only other member of the staff who could sell emotion to his audience. Generally, all service lecturers that I heard avoided anything emotive or religious, like the plague. It may be the correct thing with any service audience, I am not sure, but to grip a civilian audience you need to appeal to their emotions to some extent. I suppose my many years of talking to civilians of all kinds and conditions had equipped me to do this – what I found surprising was that it went down very well with army audiences, too. Now Robert did this, and was all the better for it. I have spoken of the WVS at some length. They had a system of inviting to their Staff College courses, members from all the regions who had worked well. A week at the Staff College was a kind of reward. I was always invited to give 'Morale' to them. I did, therefore, see quite a lot of Lady Reading and her deputy, Frances Clode. Lady Reading always gave a final address to 'her girls' at the end of every course, and she was always well worth listening to. All this finally culminated in 'star billing'. I was invited to give 'Morale' to the Annual Conference of WVS County and County Borough Organisers at the Grand Hotel, Brighton, on 31 October – 2 November 1961. I was also invited to dine with them the night before. This was a great honour – the only other speaker at this function was the American Ambassador, Mr David Bruce, who was of course a friend of Lady Reading. He had given his address the day before and had left.

I made my usual arrangements, and had dinner sitting next to her Ladyship. We had a conversation in which I had told her that Carole, my youngest daughter, obtained a degree at London University, plus a Social Sciences or Welfare degree at Liverpool University, and was going to do Social and Welfare work, particularly Childcare. She enquired as to her age. I told her, and she thought that Carole was far too young to deal with the kind of woman she would have to encounter.

After dinner, I was introduced, and off I went to a very large gathering of WVS organisers from all over the country. I had been speaking for about twenty-five to thirty minutes, and was just reaching the climax, when to my utter astonishment and amazement, her Ladyship stood up and said, 'I'm sorry Mr Stonier, we shall have to stop there, we have been asked by the Home Office to watch a scientific programme on T.V., and give them our views.' I left the platform, maintaining as much dignity as I was able, and sat down in the front row. The TV sets spaced around the ballroom were switched on, and we listened for seven or eight minutes to a terrible dissertation on a most boring subject, by a man who never raised his head but spoke direct to his lecture notes. A hum of discontent arose. Lady Reading – no fool – stood up and said, 'I take, ladies, you wish me to turn this off and return to Mr Stonier?' The reply was loud and clear, 'Yes'. I returned to the platform and continued my talk. It was, although I say it myself, one of my best performances. The reception was heartwarming. After chatting for a time, it appeared they had forgotten to book a room for me and there was a great phoning around. I had one or two offers to share a room for the night – well, I guessed I was popular, but this was ridiculous! Eventually I was found a room, and retired for the night – alone. On 4 November I received the following letter:

Dear Mr Stonier,

I really don't know how to start to thank you for your wonderful contribution to our conference at Brighton. I do realise how much time and thought had gone into the preparation of such a talk, and I am especially grateful to you for showing what was needed.

I know you are always brilliant in putting across so many aspects of Civil Defence, and this I now realise is partly, at any rate, due to your sincerity, and your dedicated way of approaching the subject. I don't believe you can ever have been more brilliant than you were on Wednesday. I wish you could have heard all the nice things which were said about you, and your talk on the following day, because then I think you might have felt a little bit rewarded. I feel sure you will long remember that evening with the interruption to look at the truly awful television programme on 'Fall Out', and the way in which you finished your talk was an example to us all. I know that every single person went away from the conference feeling strengthened and encouraged by what you said to them, and for you I know this will be a very adequate reward.

With my personal very sincere thanks.

STELLA READING.

Mrs Clode also sent me a charming letter. I will not quote it all, but the last paragraph is illuminating:

I was the person at fault, and I do apologise. I shall take a long time to forget the expression on your face when you were stopped so abruptly.

Yours gratefully,
FRANCES CLODE.

Years later, on the death of Lady Reading, Mrs Clode became the Chairman of the newly titled 'Women's Royal Voluntary Service' – a very charming lady of a wonderful organization. I gave many further lectures to WVS audiences, they were always appreciative.

Relaxation

General Matthews had many contacts in the business world, as a result we had two very interesting and pleasant trips, of which one was to the BBC in London. Here we were shown around by the celebrated commentator John Snagge (his speciality was the Oxford & Cambridge Boat Race). The only things which I now remember were the large amount of technical apparatus everywhere, and being shown a small department in which, if I have got it right, there were facilities for newscasters to check on the pronunciation of difficult words and names, particularly foreign ones, before they broadcast – ingenious, I thought. The other trip was a visit to the Port of London Authority. We arrived at the headquarters, and were quickly shown around. Then to the large underground spirits and wine bond houses, or store houses. These seemed to stretch for miles, large underground passages lined with cases of wine and spirits. Over the years, hundreds I suppose, the fumes had caused large coloured stalactites to form, and these hung down from the low domed roof, giving a very strange effect. It was all most impressive, and on such an enormous scale.

After this we boarded the Authority launch, or yacht may be more correct, moored on the Thames. It was a magnificent craft, with catering facilities large enough to provide an excellent lunch for up to twenty, all told. Wine was served with the splendid repast, and cigars to follow. We felt highly flattered – this really was 'top brass' treatment, and recalled for me our trip to the Dorchester, which I mentioned earlier. After lunch we cruised to Gravesend, and returned, being supplied en route with quite unnecessary tea and cakes, served by uniformed stewards. Finally, we disembarked and returned to the Staff College. It had been a lovely day out.

We had a trip to Scotland Yard with Superintendent Howe as the

My mother at 90, she went on to make 97.

moving spirit, visiting the 'Black Museum' with all its macabre exhibits, and being shown the working of the information room.

During the summer on Sunday afternoons, there was polo to watch on Smith's Lawn in Windsor Park. The Duke of Edinburgh often played, and the Queen and some of the family as often as not attended. Between chukhas, the crowd were invited to tread in the divots caused by the horses' hooves. Whenever we had visitors at home, they all thought this a great treat to be part of a crowd, among whom was the Queen, treading in divots.

Sunday mornings were devoted to golf, usually at Sunningdale Ladies' Course. We had a foursome of Luce, Alldridge, myself, and sometimes Edwards or our attached policeman. We were all about equally competent, dependent on how you look at it. Occasionally we took enthusiastic course members, but usually the golf enthusiasts on courses preferred to try the proper Sunningdale or Wentworth courses. It had a certain cachet back home for them to say they had played these famous courses. I found it pleasant just to walk around any of them even if they were too difficult for me to play, the scenery was so beautiful. All the country thereabouts is great for rhododendrons, and in season the flower display is marvellous. It is also largely composed of heathland, which, too, has its own charm.

I occasionally saw a show in London. Carole, while at London University, queued up for, and obtained four tickets for *My Fair Lady*, at Drury Lane, with the original cast of Julie Andrews and Rex Harrison. It was greatly enjoyed by us all. In retrospect, it is amazing how seldom we went to London, although it was only forty minutes by train. Whenever we did go, we always came home exhausted physically and financially – it hardly seemed worth the effort. Usually, about once a month, Rose would buy a shopping ticket at 5/- (old money, return fare) and meet either Norah or Carole in London, shop in Oxford Street, lunch at Lyons' Bacon and Egg Grill, tea and cakes somewhere else, and return on the 4.50 p.m. train, financially ruined, and with aching feet!

The family were now living in Folkestone, and occasionally Rose and I would drive there to see them. Sisters Edith and Florence were engaged in a bit of aggravation with each other, into which they tried to drag us to take sides, but it all seemed rather childish at their advanced age. Mother was still going strong, often going out alone to Bobby's restaurant, and having lunch there, also to have a bet occasionally at a nearby betting shop.

Change of Abode

There were two lodges at Sunningdale Park, one at each end of the long drive, known as North and South Lodge. George Armour, the Catering Officer, lived in South Lodge from the opening of the College

North Lodge – my home at Sunningdale for over 8 yrs.

in 1949 until he retired in the 1970s. When the North Lodge became vacant, I asked General Matthews if I could move there from our council house in Park Drive. He agreed and we quickly moved. The Lodge was an almost circular building with two bedrooms, a large lounge, smaller dining room and kitchen – there was a small bathroom tucked away under the stairs. The garden was all around the house, with a crazy paved area, and a small lily pond, the whole enclosed by a wall and fence. It was a draughty house, but otherwise very pleasant, certainly an improvement on the council house. We lived there for about eight years. Opposite was a large estate and house belonging to Peter Cadbury, of Keith Prowse, and later bought from him by one of the Beatles. Just along the road from us lived Diana Dors. She had a visitor on Sunday mornings who arrived in a helicopter, landing in a field next to her house. This went on for several weeks, until the neighbours' complaints put a stop to it. To digress for a moment, it was surprising how many show people we saw while living at Sunningdale – Michael Medwin, Bryan Forbes, Glynis Johns – on the railway platform. Marilyn Monroe stayed in Ascot while filming *The Prince and the Showgirl.* Allan Cuthbertson and Marius Goring we saw often in Kingston, also George A. Cooper, Vera Lynn in Selfridge's and Jack Hedley in Fortnum and Mason's. Rose met Keith Barron in a cake shop in Richmond and congratulated him on his performance in a recent television play in which he had starred. He seemed genuinely pleased.

Change of Commandant

It was time for a change at the top, and General Matthews transferred from the Staff College to his previous role of Regional Director, not of Wales as before, but of South West Region. He was replaced by Major General R.B.B. Cooke, who had been acting as Regional Director for Wales. General Cooke was tall, very thin, with rather hawklike features, always beautifully dressed. He had the most perfect manners. He spoke well when giving the opening address to courses, and taking over the Commandant's speciality 'The World Situation', he made it an even better talk. He was just as keen on efficiency, and the College continued to run like a well-oiled machine.

The comparison between the three commandants I had so far worked under was interesting – Bruce was outspoken and forthright, a bluff man not greatly blessed with finesse. He kept an eagle eye on everything, particularly the instruction, as I said before. He would quickly learn of any deviation from the approved line; he was not particularly smart in dress, could better be described as a 'tweedy man' in that respect. I always remember his classic quote of a pessimist: 'A person who is not happy unless he is miserable, and then not too pleased about it'.

General Matthews was a more casual man. He adopted the classic public school attitude of not seeming to take anything very seriously, but underneath the pose, he was shrewd, quietly working hard on what was necessary. Nothing escaped his notice if it was important, either on the administrative or instructional side. In dress, he was again casual, but always well turned out. He was prepared to take risks if he felt justified, as he did with my presentation of 'Morale'. He and Bruce could, however, be quite ruthless with inefficient staff – Major Andrews, dismissed from the instructional side to DS Co-ord was one example of Bruce's attitude to inefficiency. Matthews, too, got rid of several instructors who were not up to Staff College standards, not by getting them discharged, for that was too difficult to prove, but as they reached sixty, and became vulnerable, they had their applications for extension refused.

General Cooke was a stickler for decorum. He had been in a crack cavalry regiment, Lancers I think, and although he commanded tanks in the Western Desert, according to photographs I saw at his home,

Rose and me in the 1960s, with our Triumph Herald.

he still retained all the habits of a cavalry officer. His dress was almost dandified – he was never anything but beautifully turned out. He was far more the polished gentleman than the other two. Nevertheless, despite his obvious kindness of disposition and gentlemanly behaviour, he had a streak of steel in his make-up. If he had made up his mind on something, nothing would budge him. I saw him on the occasion of his own Regional Study, when he was Director for Wales, give Major Clun, our Chief Demonstrator, a savage dressing down during a rehearsal. Clun could be a difficult cuss when he liked, and because he was so good at his job, he often got away with it; but not with General Cooke. After a blistering attack, he had poor Clun nearly grovelling – but this was very rare, I never saw him do anything quite so drastic again. I can say this, that I worked better, and was far happier with these Commandants, than I ever was with any Chief Constable I worked under.

Shortly after his appointment, General Cooke interviewed all the DS separately in his office, and to me he said what good accounts he had heard of my new talk.

I was invited about this time of the changeover, to go to Ilkley in Yorkshire, and give 'Morale' to north-eastern controllers. I had permission from General Matthews, and away I went to fulfil the engagement for Mr Watson, the ex-Sudan judge who was Director. I had to stay overnight, having driven there in my car – now a Triumph Herald. I took the opportunity of going on to Ilkley Moor, which was just behind the hotel. When quite alone on this beautiful wild moor, I took off my hat, so that I could say with truth that I had been 'On Ilkley Moor Baa-t-at'. On my return I put in for my expenses, and the use of my car at the approved rates. The new Commandant refused to authorize it as I had not asked his permission to use my car, so I had to accept the price of the rail fare. I could have argued that his predecessor had authorized it, but as it was verbal, I thought it not worth the trouble – there was about four pounds difference actually. This was the only time I was out of line with General Cooke. Looking back, there is no doubt that the last year of Bruce's reign, and the two periods of Matthews and Cooke, marked the high water mark of the Civil Defence Staff College. We had thousands pass through, from all walks of life, and from many different countries of the world. All our important ministries held studies there, examining their problems in war. The Armed Forces, too, had close connections with the College, either attending as a course, or using our lecturers to visit their establishments. Industry was a frequent customer, and local authorities probably used our facilities more than anyone. It was the peak of my career too, I was on top of my job, known in CD circles throughout the country, a phase that not everyone experiences. I revelled in it. I had never encountered quite such recognition before, although I had been popular in Wolverhampton during my Civil Defence days, except apparently with a couple of vital exceptions. I was affectionately known for years after I became an Inspector as 'Sarge'. But appreciation at the level I was now working was far harder to earn and maintain – to have achieved it was my greatest triumph.

I was working like a man possessed – any success always encouraged further effort. Whilst 'Morale' was a best seller, I was drafting a new extravaganza called 'Survival'. I again used the United States Strategic Bombing Survey reports as a basis, and extracted information on repair of services, factories, and civil organizations generally. I built up what I considered was an excellent talk, which I hoped would form the basis of a stage forward in our Staff College presentation and study, and which I will return to later.

Chapter XVI

Warning Signals

It is a strange irony of life, that when things are going splendidly, something always seems to occur which brings one smartly back to earth. I have encountered this so often, I have got to expect it. This is not unique to me, it happens to most of us.

It was nearing Christmas 1961 and I was walking in our grounds with Rose and the two girls. We found a large branch broken off a tree in the woods, so I went back home to get the car and a saw to cut it up for firewood. I noticed a shortage of breath as I climbed the hill back to my house, but I got the car and returned to the wood. On sawing the branch, I felt a tightness around the chest and a shortage of breath, but I put it down to an attack of bronchitis. I came home, and during the next few days the shortage of breath got worse – I went to the doctor.

I remember when I got out of the car at the surgery and started to walk, I had hardly enough breath to even walk slowly. The doctor examined me, and booked a visit for me to Windsor Hospital. I duly attended, and after lengthy examinations, I was told that the circulation around my heart was not very good – the arteries were getting restricted. I was told it was the usual ageing process, this hardening of arteries. I was told, 'Take it easy, and use these Nitro tablets under the tongue if you get distressed – never go over the threshold.' I felt quite shattered – we tend to take good health for granted, this really brought me up with a jerk! I was still able to lecture and do my job, but I did find that any protracted study and writing eventually brought on angina pains.

Fortunately, I had company, there was a 'Coronary Club' of heart cases in Civil Defence – both Luce and Edwards had the same trouble, as did many of our outside contacts – it seemed to be an occupational hazard. I never had time off for the trouble, but I had two years of great distress. I had difficulty in digesting food; I had, and still have indigestion, all my life in fact, but this was worse, I could hardly digest anything! Any physical exertion would cause me to get short of breath, and I would go grey in the face. I began to think I was about to completely crack up. I naturally lost weight and began to look gaunt. I am only about eleven stones stripped, in weight, but I went down to just under ten stones. People commented on my changed appearance, and this did not help. It was some comfort, however, to exchange symptoms with Luce and Edwards. I reorganized my workload, continued to polish up 'Survival', but undertook no new work. I considered I had made a fair contribution, and was now entitled to 'rest on my oars' as it were. I still had six years to go to complete my ten years minimum service to qualify for a second pension, which would be very small, but added to my police pension, would probably suffice. What I had to do was pace myself for these six years, fulfil my commitments, but slow down on the creative work – it is that which is so exhausting.

However, my weight loss worried me so much I went to the hospital again to find out why. I was given every conceivable test from thyroid onwards – the doctors who examined me said, 'You are a good figure, don't worry about it,' but they could find nothing wrong except the poor circulation around the heart. After a couple of years I suddenly regained my lost weight, and became much better, probably other arteries taking over and compensating. I don't know. I have survived a further thirty-eight years so far!

Scottish Command

In the spring of 1962, I had three commitments, all falling close together. I was invited by the General Officer Commanding-in-Chief to address the officers of Scottish Command at Edinburgh on 10 March on 'Morale'. My Regional Director, Air Marshal Sir Lawrence Pendred, wanted me to give two talks to his region – CDOs, Police, Ministry officials, Local Authority, and goodness knows who else on 8 March.

In addition, my brother Walter had died at a hospital in Cardiff, and was to be cremated on 12 March. I was deputed by the family to represent them at the service.

This was some commitment for a fairly sick man. I took all my gear, and to the Midlands I drove with Rose. She was to stay at her sister's house in Wolverhampton while I headed north. The commitment to Sir Lawrence was first.

I went to the Regional Headquarters, a large underground complex which had been two shadow factories, and to a large audience, I gave two very difficult and complicated lectures on new subjects: 'Operational Control' and 'Social Aspect', another name for my 'Survival' effort. I knew many of the audience – Reg Reynolds, now CDO for Worcester was there, but what a change, for he too had suffered a heart attack and he looked a dying man. His great size was reduced, his spirit was broken. It is remarkable how our lives had run on parallel lines – at Falfield together in 1936, doing the same job all through the War, both awarded the BEM, both at Ryton. Had I not got the job at Sunningdale I should probably have been CDO of Wolverhampton, as he was of Worcester. We must have had our heart trouble at the same time, but his was obviously more severe than mine. I heard of his death not long afterwards – thank heavens the parallel had run out. I silently saluted a stalwart comrade, who had literally worked himself to death. He must have been my age, about 56 years, too young to go, really. And, of course, we were both 'Brummies'.

I had to leave Regional Headquarters in a hurry to catch my plane at Birmingham for Edinburgh. Rose, Carole and her boyfriend saw me off. I had all my paraphernalia aboard. As we approached Edinburgh fog made landing there impossible. I well remember the pilot giving us a commentary as he came as low as he dared, before giving up and heading for Glasgow, where conditions were better. This dicing with death was hardly the treatment for a tired heart subject. We landed at Glasgow and I then had to contact the Army, who of course had arranged to pick me up at Edinburgh, to come and collect me from Glasgow.

Eventually I was transported in an army car to Scottish Command Headquarters in Edinburgh. After depositing my baggage, I was taken to the Officers' Mess for a drink and sandwich. By this time it was getting late, and I was absolutely exhausted after a long, tiring day that would have tested a fit man, and I was anything but that. I was afraid I might not be up to lecturing next day. However, a pint of good Scots beer, and I felt much refreshed – it seemed to 'reach those parts normal beer cannot reach' to quote the ad. I went to bed in a large room, and was given every attention, even a kind of batman to look after me.

My lecture was to an enormous audience of about 300 officers, mostly dressed in the kilt – very spectacular. It was the usual army set-up with the audience sitting in tiers in a half circle. From where I lectured, in a room almost dark, with a spotlight effect on my notes and drop, I could not see my audience – a strange effect it had, which had never happened to me before. But I was in good form, and the response from the audience was heartwarming, so far as I was concerned, this was what it was all about. I was, I decided, a real theatrical on tour. I had a formal invitation to cocktails that evening, to be followed by some kind of a ladies' night officers mess function. I would have loved to have attended, as it was probably a sight and event to remember, but I was too exhausted.

I arranged to have a quiet meal in a room downstairs, and watch a little television before retiring to bed early – I still had the funeral to attend in Cardiff. I left next day to hearty thanks, and boarded my plane back to Birmingham. On landing, I picked up Rose, and off we set for Wales.

We arrived in the afternoon, and I did the usual things expected of a mourning relative. Walter and I had nothing in common, there was too large a gap in our ages, and we had seen very little of each other for years. I offered my nephew, Graham, who was about fourteen, any help in the future should he need it, but I never heard from, or saw him again.

We returned to Sunningdale feeling that all in all, the trip had gone well, and I had survived much more than I had felt physically capable of.

A Postscript on Walter

He was in his late sixties when he died, very painfully, I heard, of cancer in the bladder. He had many talents, too many perhaps, the result was that he had periods of intense interest in a subject, and then dropped it to take up another. He was an excellent artist, had been a fine gymnast and swimmer. He had a very keen brain – for example, he had no experience of house-building but his interest was aroused, he studied books from the Public Library, and with some labouring help from Father, he built and sold four or five houses with little or no technical assistance.

He was obsessed with being his own boss, and gave up several good jobs to pursue this course, more often than not ending in disappointment. In the end he did have a small factory near Cardiff which was shared with a partner, making I believe, spectacle frames. He left his widow reasonably provided for, but it took him into his sixties before he achieved in a small way his ambition. I would have settled for half his talents, plus my staying power.

As an interesting postscript to the above. A few years later we had an attached army DS, Lieutenant Colonel Brian Carson. He did his two years secondment, and on leaving he came to say goodbye to us all in turn. He told me that he had been present at the Scottish Command

Study, had heard me speak and thought it the finest lecture he had ever heard – praise indeed!

I received the following letters:

From: Air Marshal Sir Lawrence F. Pendred, K.B.E., C.B., D.F.C., DL
R.A.F.(Retired.)

Home Office
REGIONAL CIVIL DEFENCE HEADQUARTERS
DAIMLER HOUSE, PARADISE STREET, BIRMINGHAM 1
TELEPHONE: MIDLAND 6251

RD/EMV.   9th March, 1962.

My dear Fred,

You were in great form yesterday and you bore the burden of the day. To give two long and intricate talks before such a large audience in such a strange environment required exceptional endurance. But you did not wilt. You held 'em all the time. And, from what I have already heard, you impressed them. Some said that they have never heard a clearer exposition of 'Operational Control' and I am sure that the letters I will get will be unanimous in their praise of your "Social Aspect".

Personally, I liked your approach to the latter subject. There was nothing in the wide picture you presented which I thought had the wrong emphasis. Your examples from the last war were apt. I would say that it would be a most admirable introduction to any Course or Study designed to establish or teach C.D. doctrine in the survival period.

Fred, I so often have to thank you, but I am more indebted to you for your "Plexus" effort than I have been for the many other things you have done for me. It was a tremendous contribution and an outstanding success. A simple "Thank you" looks so inadequate on paper but I am sure you must know how I feel.

Yours ever
Laurie Pendred

F. Stonier, Esq., B.E.M.,
The Home Office C.D. Staff College.
Sunningdale Park.
ASCOT. Berkshire.

From: Colonel R. E. HOLDEN,

HEADQUARTERS,
SCOTTISH COMMAND,
P. O. BOX No. 85,
G. P. O., EDINBURGH, I.

13 March 1962.

Dear Mr Stonier,

By some peculiar experiment in physics, you managed to evaporate on Saturday night and I didn't get an opportunity of thanking you finally for being kind enough to come all the way to Edinburgh and talk to us at the Command Study Period. Where the hell you got to I don't know but you missed a fairly alcoholic party and as it was all champagne, you would have shown no signs of it the next day!

Many people have said to me during the last two days how very cogent as well as interesting your remarks were. The Army Commander personally told me to ensure that you were made aware of our appreciation.

I hope that your breakfast was cooked, that your transport arrived and that you got your aeroplane as arranged. No doubt one day our paths will cross again, possibly when I want a rest and decide to attend another course at Sunningdale.

Yours sincerely,
Raymond Holden

F. STONIER, Esq., BEM,
    Civil Defence Staff College,
        SUNNINGDALE,
        Berks.

Royal Observer Corps

The Civil Defence Staff College was closely connected with the Warning and Monitoring Organisation whose task in war was to track aircraft or missiles and report the same. The organization's ears and eyes on the ground was the Royal Observer Corps, which has a long history going back even to the First World War; while in the Second World War, they played a vital role in Home Defence. As a consequence of their involvement in Home Defence, we gave a lecture at the Staff College on warning and monitoring, and members of the organization, both ministerial and on the ground, were frequent visitors. As a result of hearing 'Morale', one of the leading lights decided it should be given to all the ROC areas who wished to hear it, and I was invited to go to the areas from time to time, and gave the talk. I did, therefore, visit a fair number of 1939–1945 Fighter and Bomber stations. The ROC were very proud of their association with the RAF, they wore an RAF type of uniform, and were permitted at officer level to share RAF officers' messes. I had many dinners in the splendid surroundings. It was at one, Leconfield, I think, that I first met Vernon Barry. He was a Home Office Principal Officer, attached to the Warning and Monitoring Organisation, which was really a Home Office responsibility. I was to meet him a great many times in the future when he became Assistant Regional Director to Sir Lawrence Pendred, and his successor at Midland Region.

I enjoyed my many trips speaking to the ROC officers at their Area Headquarters, one of which was as far afield as Edinburgh. They were always appreciative, and I have many nice letters from the commandants. Another change of scene took place at this time, about 1962, when I lectured to Police War Duties courses held by the Hampshire and Isle of Wight Constabulary at Winchester, and I also spoke to the Welfare Services of East Riding at Beverley, Yorkshire. I certainly got around the country.

Regional Studies

These still occupied an important part of our programme. Every one of the ten regions, plus London, had to hold a week long study at the Staff College. They dealt with problems particular to their region, and this required new floor maps and drops for every show. These went on for years, as of course, standard courses and studies also had to be fitted in.

Illustration

A word therefore on this vital branch of our establishment. It comprised a Chief Illustrator, Martyn Jones, a commercial artist, and two staff, also commercial artists. They were competent, hard-working and generally very obliging people. They particularly liked to be consulted by DS on future presentations, and ideas, often coming up with brilliant suggestions. They naturally got bored with the constant drawing of maps, and loved a change in which they could demonstrate their artistic capabilities. I often wondered how they got through their workload, as it was pretty formidable. They were a very good team.

Demonstrators

Major Clun, who I have mentioned, had two assistants. When I first arrived, one was a rather attractive girl named Maureen. She was very competent, but I often wondered whether a woman, wandering around a large floor map, before a generally male audience, and having to bend from time to time, was really the best way to keep an audience's attention on the matter in hand. When she left to get married, she was replaced by a man. Clun retired about 1963, and was replaced by Don Woods. He had been a London bus driver, and was smart, intelligent, and very competent.

When Major Andrews retired about 1964, General Cooke had no hesitation in upgrading Woods to the job of DS Co-ord in his place. He did this job equally well. We had quite a lot in common, and he knew, as I did, that we had to do so much better than anyone else to hold our own in the College. Whatever may be said to the contrary, it remains a fact, that at that time, if anyone came from a working-class background to work in such an establishment, one had to be outstanding to hold one's place. Don would have loved to become a DS, and made certain overtures, I think, but he was firmly discouraged from pursuing the matter.

Superintendent Howe came to the end of his secondment, and was replaced by Superintendent 'Tiny' Hodgson, from Monmouthshire. He was a genial giant of a man. He had played top-class rugby, and rugby league too, I heard, until he sustained an injury which finished that career. He told me that he had collided with the posts and badly damaged his shoulder. He was at home on the tactical side of our establishment, but his lecture on 'Role of the Police' on the senior officers' side was hardly up to the Staff College standard. He got away with it, however, for he was big, bluff, and very good humoured, and this helped. He joined us in our Sunday morning golf outings, and was good company. His wife was a great bridge player, and quickly established herself in the local bridge circles. She did very well at it, I believe.

Tiny used his time at the Staff College to advantage, and on concluding his two-year spell, he obtained the job of CDO for Scunthorpe, where from all accounts he established quite a niche for himself.

Further Changes

Things never remained static for long at the Staff College. General Cooke retired, and was replaced by Vice Admiral Sir Nicholas Copeman, at one time a Lord of the Admiralty.

Previous to his retirement General Cooke invited all the DS and wives in small groups to his house for lunch on Sundays. Rose and I went with Robert Thomson and his wife, had a very nice lunch, were entertained well and made to feel particularly at ease. The General and his wife introduced us to their family, two sons and a daughter.

General Cooke had built a beautiful new house in Hampshire at Alton. When he left the College, he invited all DS and their wives to a house warming at the new 'Poland House'. We all went there and found a large array of marquees in a field, or paddock is a better term, next to the house. The catering had been undertaken by George Armour and his staff, who had excelled themselves. Champagne flowed freely, and I should think every dignitary in Hampshire had been invited. I never heard such a plethora of upper-class accents – generals, admirals, air marshals, colonels galore, and high-ranking public officials – there must have been two to three hundred people present. The AA even took over car parking. It was a wonderful party. I knew many people there as one-time course members. We were all taken over the house in small parties by General and Mrs Cooke, who were obviously very proud of their new home, it really was a gorgeous house. Yet I had a feeling that he was better suited to a place with a historic background – a castle, or a moated grange – a modern house did not seem to fit his image. However, he knew what he was doing, and old houses are notorious for their upkeep expenses. He said goodbye to us all in turn as we left, ever so slightly drunk, but still the perfect gentleman. We were all sorry to see him go, he was an excellent commandant, and treated his staff well.

The new commandant settled in the house in the grounds. He had been a close colleague of Lord Louis Mountbatten during the War and was always reminiscing about 'Dicky'. After his retirement from the Navy he had been appointed Regional Director for North West Region, and now transferred to Sunningdale as Commandant. He had suffered a recent heart attack when he came to us, and was not a very fit man.

He walked very slowly, and it was surprising that he had been considered for such a responsible job, under the circumstances.

He was a poor speaker, and his opening address to courses was not very inspiring. Had we but known, the great days of the Staff College were over. The growing realization of the power of thermo-nuclear weapons, with no limit to their size, and the small size of the United Kingdom, was causing a reassessment of the situation at the top. Finance, too, was becoming a problem, it cost an awful lot to run an establishment like the Staff College. A Labour administration from 1964 onwards did not help. There was no sign at this stage of all this, but looking back, it was from this point onwards that our fate was sealed.

A Distinguished Visitor

Early in the short career as Commandant of Vice Admiral Sir Nicholas Copeman, we had a visit from Lord Louis Mountbatten. He gave a splendid address to a conference of scientists who had come to the Staff College to discuss Civil Defence problems. He spoke in neither of our lecture theatres, but in the lounge of the main building. His topic was the world situation, we were allowed to attend, and greatly admired him, his style, and the content of his talk. He was authoritative, as one would expect, with a slight touch of humour. The Commandant had at least proved his assertion that he knew 'Dick', and that they had been close colleagues – not everyone could have got him to attend, and give an address.

A Visit to London

Meanwhile, I still had a few more triumphs to savour. I went on two trips to London County Council Headquarters, at County Hall. Captain Harkness RN, the Regional Director of London Region, had persuaded the Chief Officers of the Council to attend a course specially designed for them at County Hall. It was an ambitious gamble, as they were not an easy bunch to convince that it was necessary, so there could be no compulsion, it was quite voluntary, and one presumed that if they were very busy, they would not leave their offices to attend.

The regional officers were anxious that the first session should go well, 'pour encourager les autres', as it were. Harkness, who I knew rather well, had asked that, after his opening of the course, I should start proceedings with a mixture of 'Weapon Effects' and 'Morale'. I was used by now to adjusting 'Morale' to suit different courses, for example, when in Scotland I omitted any reference to Elizabeth I and Cromwell, and replaced them with Bruce, Sir William Wallace, and a favourite of mine, the Duke of Montrose, when dealing with historic leadership. I did therefore work out an opening as requested, and took all my paraphanalia to London with me. There were over two hundred people present, so the regional boys were very nervous and apprehensive. Harkness opened in his usual smooth, efficient way, and introduced me. I started off on what was a rather complicated session as there was so much to display in charts and slides. It went off swimmingly, and was duly appreciated by the audience. Region breathed a sigh of relief, thanked me profusely, and I left them to the rest of the day's programme. I returned next morning for a repeat performance. Again, another large audience. When I had finished my spiel, the Clerk to the London County Council came onto the stage, and thanked me, asking the audience to respond, which they did.

A letter from Harkness to the Commandant said it all:

> I cannot tell you how grateful I am to you for allowing Stonier to come and address the Chief Officers Course at County Hall on the 28th and 29th.
>
> His presentation was exactly what was required to get these people thinking along the right lines, and was the perfect opening for the day. I am sure it was good for them to see the pictures of Dresden, horrifying as they were, and the Hiroshima film just to remind them of their responsibilities.
>
> The final figure was 224 on the first day, and 180 on the second, and I genuinely believe that the majority of them went away feeling that the day had not been wasted. Again thank you for having made Stonier available.

To which the Commandant added 'A fine effort'.

Whilst in London, I called on Mr Barr, who had, you remember, been Deputy Town Clerk in Wolverhampton during the War, and after that had been appointed as Town Clerk of Ipswich. Now he had left Ipswich to become First, or Leading Solicitor to the London County Council. We had a pleasant meeting, and I was sorry to learn a few years later of his death, again from the great killer of talented hard workers, heart attack. He was a very fine town clerk and gentleman.

Further Outside Visits

I had two visits to Northern Ireland. One of their Ministry of Health and Social Services officials had heard my talk, and wanted it for the hospital nursing staffs of their institutions. I obtained permission to fly there, and was booked into a hotel which gave a view down the long drive to Stormont, the seat of government. I was taken next day to the Downshire Hospital, Downpatrick, to give my talk, which was intended in time for me to visit the six counties – go to a centrally situated hospital to which staff could then be drawn in to hear my talk. In the event, I went on two such trips, I was booked for a third in January 1968, at Londonderry, but by then we had received our closure notice, so it was cancelled. On my second trip, I was taken by my host, a Mr W.L. Kean of the Ministry, on sightseeing trips to the Mountains of Mourne, which was very lovely, and to Stormont. I went into the Assembly Hall, and noted that the seating had all been supplied, or the wood anyway, from all parts of the Commonwealth, and there were inscriptions indicating from whence the wood came. Around the balcony was an inscription stating that this place had been the Headquarters of Coastal Command during the 1939–1945 war. It was quite impressive, and I was indebted to my guide for his kindness in showing me around.

All the establishments at which I gave my talk were mental institutions. They just happened to be centrally situated, I suppose, and would hate to think there was any other reason.

About the same time I gave the talk to the nursing staff of the Bethlem Royal Hospital and Maudsley Hospital, Denmark Hill, London, which of course was the old notorious 'Bedlam'. This coincidence of mental institutions was getting a bit much!

I was still going to Observer Corps Groups and Areas, the last being at Hove in 1967, just after the ninth anniversary of my first giving the talk. I had altered it, adapted it, but it was still fundamentally the same, and just as applicable at the end as at the beginning. Actually, this was my last outside lecture in any subject.

Not everyone liked my talk, General Matthews once told me – General Kirkman, for instance, did not think it was right for a Staff College. It may have been so, but he never made any attempt to stop it, and in fact at one stage he suggested to Colonel Butcher, when he was Chief Instructor, to *ask* me to alter one tiny part. Butch spoke to me, and hastened to add that it was only a suggestion, as if he had been told not to upset me. What really set the seal on the talk was in the early days of its presentation, General Sir Alexander Cameron, Regional Director of South East Region, had requested that it be included in his Regional Study. Now this was a very redoubtable officer, even Kirkman treated him with obvious respect. He was a formidable debater, a devastating attacker of any nonsensical ideas put forward – a man to be listened to when he uttered. His request for the talk set the pattern, all subsequent regional studies included it.

It didn't stop General Matthews asking me to give it to his regional people when he left us and went back to being a regional director – they all recognized a winner when they saw one. I was sorry when it had to be mothballed, as it was like parting with an old and trusted friend.

Aims not achieved

I visited the Police College at Bramshill on two occasions – both social. The first was with the newly appointed regional directors during their initiation course at Sunningdale. I remember as we entered the imposing entrance to the College, one of the party exclaimed that this seemed too good a place for policemen. One of the senior police officers in the party quickly took this up, and there were sharp words before peace was restored, and ruffled feathers smoothed. The fine old building and grounds were very impressive, and we enjoyed our visit.

I went once more when our secretary left Sunningdale to take up a similar post at Bramshill, and invited some of the DS to pay a visit.

I mention all this as a lead-in to what may have led to an open-ended commitment for me to give 'Morale' at Bramshill. Colonel Lemon, the Chief Constable of Kent, and a Regional Police Commander-designate, had often heard me speak, and he wanted me to give my talk to the students at Bramshill. He did not approach me, but went directly to Charles Luce (whom he knew socially), when he was Chief Instructor, and asked if it could be arranged. Luce told him that most senior police officers had heard me, and there was really no point, so there the matter ended. Luce's objection was not valid, the type of policemen who came to Sunningdale on senior officers courses were older and more senior than the promising young men who attended Bramshill – they would never have had the opportunity of hearing me.

I was very sore about this when Luce naively told me about it – any police lecturer would feel honoured to speak at the Service's highest training establishment.

I always liked to have some reserve material in my locker, as it were, which I felt might have a place in future presentations. To this end, I swotted up on the NATO set-up, as we hardly mentioned this at the College, and I felt that this was wrong – it was, after all, an integral part of Western defence. There was no lack of suitable material easily available. I studied all this and extracted what I thought was germane, and drafted out a lecture on the subject. When it was ready, I dropped the idea to the Commandant during a coffee break. He expressed interest, and after consulting Luce, he arranged for me to go to his office and present my paper, which I did with Luce present. The Commandant was quite enthusiastic over it, yet Luce said he thought it was not the kind of presentation to be given by a member of the staff, but only by the Commandant. I left them arguing about it. Later the Commandant told me to let it lie in abeyance for a while – Luce had obviously persuaded him. It never came to light again – a good session thrown away. I felt that Luce was impelled by a bit of jealousy, as I thought back to his comment to me when I was writing 'Morale', 'What do you know about Morale?'

I got on well with Luce generally, we were quite friendly, but I know that Charles, like most of his service colleagues, was at heart a class snob. I felt there was always an underlying resentment of the fact that I, an ordinary policeman, was doing their job as well, if not better than they. Was this the Ballance syndrome rearing its ugly head again?

The last of my three untried efforts was a lecture on the 'Siege of Leningrad'. A book on this heroic resistance of a large city's population to bombing, shelling, starvation, and a terrible winter climate was in our library at my request, so I extracted what I felt was appropriate to our new trend towards survival. To show what a population of ordinary people – not soldiers – had been capable of achieving for years, not days, was in my opinion, one of the Second World War's greatest epics, even more so than Stalingrad.

I am sure it would have gone down well. I got it into lecture form, and even rehearsed it once or twice, but we closed down before I had an opportunity to exploit it. I kept the full lecture notes of my untried epic.

Chapter XVII

Random Recollections

Every course held a guest night which were unimpressive events. The 'bread and butter' courses, like Senior Officers and Sector Controllers, usually including port for every table, the loyal toast, and a get-together in the bar and lounge afterwards. But special courses, like the steel and oil concerns, GPO, Electricity Boards, Gas and Coal, Scientists and CDOs' conferences, army courses, and hospital matrons, usually paid a little extra on their mess bills, and had a 'slap-up' meal and wine in addition to the usual port.

I remember, in particular, the Oil Company Study – they ordered oysters, which George Armour supplied (in small barrels), cigars, and a splendid meal. All our staff except the Secretary suffered attacks of sickness and diarrhoea afterwards – probably the oysters – but nevertheless it was a grand night. The hospital matrons were a revelation – a really splendid body of women, and we loved having them. They were so attentive and appreciative. On their guest night, we were astounded, as they really let their hair down, singing and dancing on the tables – great fun. I have noticed this with all disciplined bodies – Police, Army – when the discipline is relaxed they really go mad.

When I first went to the College in 1954, General Bruce was a great one for guest nights – he returned to his subaltern days, arranged rugby scrums and other hard physical playing about. On one army course we had the officers doing climbing feats around the high balcony over the main hall. I have witnessed the damage that can be caused by officers' mess guest nights in Wolverhampton. They used to periodically wreck the room in the Drill Hall. This is quite in order if they pay for the damage, which they did, but in a Home Office establishment, with a middle-aged crowd taking part, it was hardly the thing. If one of these highly paid men was crippled, there would have been hell to pay. It died the death after a brief life, and our guest nights became more circumspect. Nevertheless, funny things still happened. I recall one chief constable, who shall be nameless, falling into the rhododendron bushes, quite drunk, and going to sleep there – he came to no harm. On the tactical side, guest nights often took the form of impromptu concerts. There was always some talent available – this never happened on the senior officers' side.

Cocktail Parties

These are a must with all armed services persons, they love them, probably a throwback to the Indian Army life, when such social gatherings were necessary as far as the Army were concerned; I don't know what excuse the other two services offer. To me, and a few others, they were an unmitigated bore. We had dozens of such parties, which were always pink champagne that was served, to which I am not very partial. To try and talk over the hubbub after a day's lecturing was a trial, as most of those invited were complete strangers and I detested them – the parties, I mean. However, we all had to attend, and put a brave face on it. I can see that the parties inviting local dignitaries were useful to help maintain an acceptable face to them – the local doctors were always invited, and this certainly helped when we needed their services. I could also see merit in inviting the Ministry officials – we had to work closely with them, and it helped to foster good relations. When I look back and try to assess what we achieved by so much expenditure of money and effort, I cannot for my part think of any tangible reward. I realize I am biased – a quiet sit down with a few congenial companions, a drink, a smoke, and a discussion is what I enjoyed in my evenings at the Staff College.

Invitations to Visit

At an establishment such as the Staff College, with the thousands who attended from all walks of life, it was to be expected that the DS would be the recipients of many offers to visit course members at their homes. Most of these offers occurred whilst drinking at the bar, and so far as I was concerned, meant nothing, although some of my colleagues made quite a point of taking advantage of their offers. Occasionally, people would really mean it, and invite us by letter. I had quite a few of these, two of which I took advantage of.

The first was Air Commodore Geddes, CBE of Seaford, Sussex. I took Rose and the two girls to visit him and his wife at their home. We stayed two nights, and had a lovely time. His accommodation was limited, so he erected a huge tent in the garden, equipped it with beds, and Rose and I slept quite comfortably in it. He took us in his old car to visit all the nearby beauty spots, and treated us to a splendid dinner at an hotel in Alfriston. His speed around the country lanes of Sussex was hair-raising. He was a most remarkable man – tall, well built, fair, and very talented. He kept bees, spun his own yarn on a loom, made his wife's clothes, was an excellent cook, and had countless other gifts. His great ambition was to retire and live in a bothy in a Scottish glen. His wife, a quiet lady, had, I think, different ideas. He was an Assistant CDO for Sussex at the time, and on a subsequent visit to lecture at Lewes, I stayed with him again.

I was also invited by a charming lady from the WRVS, Mrs Phillips. She lived with her husband and three girls in Suffolk, where her husband ran a Ministry of Agriculture farm project. We stayed two days and one night with them, just Rose and I. It was a lovely part of the country, the visit was very pleasant, and they made us very much at home. I was invited, too, by a colonel from Perthshire to visit him on his estate in that beautiful part of the world. I should have liked to have gone there, but never quite found the time or opportunity.

These were the only invitations that I accepted, to visit people at their homes – usually I was booked into a good class hotel when 'on tour'.

I don't count John MacIntyre, an Assistant CDO for Kent. I often called on him at Faversham, where he had a bungalow, while on my way to visit Mother when she lived at Folkestone. Mac had a charming wife, Rosslyn, and two lovely young girls. We always got on splendidly, and enjoyed each other's company. He was pretty hard up, I think, but though much older than his wife, they seemed very happy together.

Mac was considered a bit of a 'bolshie' at Sunningdale. He was inclined to be argumentative and belligerent during sessions. A number of CDOs and assistants were inclined that way. It may, in Mac's case, have held him back from occupying a higher post in Civil Defence. I never saw or heard of them after Civil Defence folded; I hope they have prospered.

The Back-Room Girls

Just a few words of appreciation. Rhoda ran the typing pool; her father had been the local policeman. She had an often changing band of assistants, never more than four. They got through an enormous amount of work, never letting the side down, deadlines were always met, if sometimes a close-run thing. We DS, and myself in particular, were always dreaming up some new presentation, which inevitably ended in a mass of typing being required. I owed these girls a lot, as I did those in the long past Civil Defence days at Chubbs, when Miss Sonia Caswell and 'Midge' May carried the same kind of burden for years – not the same exacting level, but vital nonetheless.

Then there was Gwyneth Davies. She had sustained some injury which left her partially crippled. She was highly efficient, if a bit bossy. She had to prepare the course folders – every incoming course had to receive its folders on arrival, as they reported to the reception desk. The folder was usually full of papers on the various subjects to be considered, details of administration, a map and local guide – some of the papers were constant, others had to be specially written to suit the particular course. Miss Davies' job was exacting, and on a tight time scale, but she never failed to deliver. Both these girls were still working at the new Civil Service Staff College in 1979. I hope they know that at least one of their 'customers' appreciated their efforts and hard work.

Suicides

I was involved in two cases of suicide whilst at Sunningdale. The first involved the hall porter of the time – about 1958–9. His name was Cliff – a friendly, obliging type of man, single, of good appearance and quite efficient at his job, although with hindsight a trifle excitable. He came of a fairly good family as became apparent at the inquest. I was always on very friendly terms with him.

One morning I was walking up the drive from my home in Park Drive, when I saw Cliff hurrying down the drive from the opposite direction; as I passed him I spoke, but he did not answer. I noticed his fixed, set stare as he gazed straight ahead. I was so struck by his strange attitude, that I stopped and watched him walk quickly out of sight. What on earth is wrong with him? I thought. Later that day I heard that his body had been found on the railway line just outside Sunningdale Station. It appeared that he was a heavy gambler on the horses, and owed a fair amount of money, some, I believe, to Donald Addison. I attended the inquest as probably the last person to see him alive, and gave my version of his strange behaviour. The verdict – suicide whilst temporarily insane.

The second case was about 1966–7. I was out one evening taking a gentle stroll through the grounds at about 7 p.m. I was walking along the drive from North Lodge to the mansion, and it was quite dark. Suddenly from the car park on my left was a flash and the sound of an explosion. I thought that one of the cleaners was leaving in her car, and had had some kind of backfire. I went to the car park, and there saw someone screaming, clothes on fire from head to foot, standing by a small car, also ablaze. I was not very fit at the time, still having circulatory trouble around the heart – my every inclination was to disappear into the anonymity of the nearby woods, but as at Rhyl, all those years before, my sense of duty made me do the right thing. I took off my short motor coat and smothered the flames on the victim, whom I now recognized as a man. By this time he was on the ground, and moaning pitifully, the car was blazing furiously, the horn still blaring away. I was afraid of an explosion, so I dragged the man away from the car and went to the house for help. It was all very horrifying and no good to me in my condition. On the way to the house I met the porter who was coming to see what was the matter. He went to phone for the Fire Brigade, Ambulance and Police. I returned to the scene of horror. The man was now quiet, but still moaning distressfully. After what seemed an age, the Fire Brigade and Police arrived. The car fire was quickly extinguished, and the poor burned man was taken away in an ambulance. He died a few days later.

At the inquest it appeared that he was a Cypriot, married, with a family in Cyprus. He had met and fallen for one of the Spanish waitresses at the College, and had been seeing her. She had that evening given him his marching orders, whereupon he had gone to his car and self-immolated himself by pouring petrol over his clothes, and setting fire to them. It came out that the Spanish girl was watching in horrified silence from the bushes which surrounded the car park during the whole of the tragedy, but I never caught sight of her. The incident seemed to raise me in the esteem of my colleagues, and the staff at the College. It was all very distressing, and not to be recommended to heart subjects.

I shall never forget that eerie scene, blazing car, blaring horn, crackle of flames, the screams of the victim, with a canopy of tall trees overhead, and the stench of burning flesh – horrible!

Erysipelas

This is a peculiar form of blood poisoning to which I am rather prone, and my father had had an attack during his early married life. In those days, when suitable drugs were unavailable, he spent sixteen weeks in bed with it, and was dangerously ill. He had to learn to walk again, when he finally left his bed.

I had my first attack during the Second World War. I had a pain behind the right ear, my head swelled (physically I mean), and I was confined to bed. In those days M & B was the drug prescribed, and I remember the hallucinatory effects it had. It was a painful complaint, requiring in those days frequent poulticing. When I got out of bed, my face looked like that of a fox, as the swelling had made my eyes appear tiny, and with a fortnight's beard growth, I was not a pretty sight. It took me about three weeks to recover. My second attack was whilst at Ryton. Again I had the pain behind the ear, and the head swelling, which was very painful. I was sent to Warwick Hospital. Penicillin was now the drug administered every few hours, by injection in the legs and buttocks, not very pleasant, but very effective – I was up and about in a week. The last occasion was about Christmas 1967, at Sunningdale. Again I had the pain behind the ear and head swelling, so I was packed off to an isolation hospital at Maidenhead, where I spent Christmas. This time the treatment was penicillin, but by oral method, much more civilized. I was out in a week. While in hospital I had a pleasant time as there were only two patients. We had a visit from the Mayor on Christmas Day, and arranged for a box of cigars and a bottle of port to be brought in by Norah and her husband Ted.

Rose had gone to stay with Carole and Ken in Axbridge, to help Carole, who had just come out of hospital with her new baby; I joined them later for New Year.

In all three cases I was run down with overwork, had pricked myself, and speedily shown the symptoms. I believe the illness can be quite dangerous, and requires isolation – not recommended!

Exploits with a Cabin Cruiser

During the early and middle sixties, Ken, my son-in-law, bought a rather nice small cabin motor cruiser with an outboard motor and moored it at Teignmouth in the river estuary. We all went there at weekends in the summer, Ken, Carole, Rose the two children, Chris, Lucy and myself. We went for gentle trips up and down the River Teign, and occasionally a short way into the sea. We picnicked, and generally had a very pleasant time. On one occasion we took sister Florence and her daughter Ann with us for the day.

But what I must record is the alarming experience which happened to Ken and I when trying to moor the boat in the middle of the estuary after one of our outings.

Mooring a boat, whether sail or engine powered seems to be something I have great difficulty in accomplishing.

On this day we had left it rather late, the tide was racing in, we got to the mooring, and were trying to secure the boat without damaging others already moored. Unfortunately, a large piece of cellophane had wrapped around our propeller, and we lost our ability to manoeuvre. The tide caught us and swept us downstream at speed. It was possible to steer to a limited extent, but that was all – the speed of the tide race was quite frightening. We were the only couple of idiots afloat by this time, and that was not by choice! As we approached the large stone bridge which joins Teignmouth to Shaldon, we tried to steer between two of the stone supporting pillars. We were now going quite fast, and crashed with a sickening thud against the right-hand side pillar; fortunately we had a large rubber dinghy strapped to the side of the cruiser which took the main force of the collision. We were then flung across, and struck the opposite pillar on the rebound. There was no possibility of fending the boat off, although we had a boat hook, the weight of the boat and the speed would have knocked anyone trying this ploy overboard, or impaled him.

I remember at the time no feeling of panic, but rather a feeling of resignation, we were going to sink, and that was that; fortunately we didn't, I hate to think what might have happened if we had – heavy clothing, knee-length wellington boots, a racing tide.

The strange feeling of resigned acceptance of what comes next, I have felt several times in my life, those seconds before a motorcycle or car crash, the branch of a tree breaking, and the fall down, going over the handlebars of a cycle or motorbike. I suppose it is better than getting panicky – funny though! I imagine Ken's feelings were much the same, we didn't say much.

After we had shot the bridge, we came into more open and calmer water, and the boat slowed down. We removed the offending cellophane, and pigheadedly under the circumstances, revved our engine and went back against the tide, through the bridge gap the way we had come. We managed it alright this time. There were a number of spectators watching our efforts on the banks of the river and estuary and we eventually ran the boat aground and safely disembarked.

Meanwhile Rose and Carole with the two children had noticed with alarm the speed of the tide race, had been unable to see the boat, and fearing the worst, reported to a police car crew the fact that we were missing. All ended well, and things were soon straightened out, but it was an alarming experience.

Ken and I on one other occasion, fell foul of this Teignmouth tide, when we were again trying to moor the boat, but had again left it too late, the tide racing in made mooring well nigh impossible. We persevered, and at length got attached to our mooring buoy, and waited to be taken off. After a short while the owner of the mooring came out in his rowing boat. He was furious, we had moored the wrong way round (virtually impossible – but we had managed it), and threatened to pull his mooring away from the river bed. All *too* complicated for me! We apologized, and came ashore – nothing further could be done then.

The last episode with this boat was when after a stormy period, Ken went down to Teignmouth to see if everything was alright. As he crossed the stone bridge, he looked for his boat, and found it just showing its mast, the rest was under water.

It cost quite an effort to later rescue, repair, and restore it. Altogether an exciting time!

Visitors

There were several visitors of interest who came to the College during these years. Ballance came as Chief Constable of Barrow. I usually invited my old Wolverhampton or Ryton colleagues home for a drink, and chat, but not in this case – I still felt too bitter. Anyway, he saw me perform at my best.

A member of my very first class at Ryton also attended, who was now an inspector in Exeter. He had been a flight lieutenant during the War, and was quite an outstanding police recruit; he had, I recalled, automatically taken over as class leader at Ryton. We had long chats in the bar. He bore out what I always told our ex-officer chaps in Wolverhampton, 'Be patient, work hard, with your advantages you must get on.' Evans, the Wolverhampton CDO was often on courses, and was, I'm afraid, a bit of a bluffer. I did not realize this until he was in charge in one syndicate during a 'telephone battle', when he acted as sector controller – he was quite hopeless, it was almost pathetic. He did not last long before a heart attack saw him off. His replacement I never really got to know.

Then during my period as Police Staff Officer, we had a day visit from the then Home Secretary, Major Gwilliam Lloyd George. He visited all the buildings, saw the courses in action and was introduced to the staff. The press were there, and had been tipped off concerning the link between our respective fathers. The Home Secretary spoke to me for about five minutes on this long ago exploit, and told me that some of Father's uniform was on show in Criccieth Museum. The papers also published the incident.

Midland Diary 'Bystanders who had been primed looked on with interest as two men shook hands at the Sunningdale Civil Defence Staff College yesterday. One of the men was Major Gwilliam Lloyd George, the Home Secretary, who was visiting the College, and the other, Superintendent F. Stonier, who is the Police Staff Officer Lecturer there, and son of the Birmingham policeman who helped Major Lloyd George's father to escape through the mob at Birmingham Town Hall in 1901. What did they talk about? "Little enough to do with that occasion," Supt. Stonier said afterwards, "there was no time for reminiscing".'

So now I had met and spoken to three Home Secretaries, Chuter Ede, Butler and Lloyd George. I still had Sir Frank Soskise to come.

Several Members of Parliament spent a day with us, and were given a special serving of appropriate material. For some reason I had to speak on the Police together with other services in a short recital. The only two members I recall attending were Herbert Morrison and William Deeds. Morrison, of course, was the most famous of London County Council leaders, as well as one-time Minister of Transport, and Home Secretary. William Deeds was, among other things, a one-time Editor of the *Daily Telegraph*.

I wanted to speak to Morrison because when I first became a motor patrol officer back in the thirties, he was the Minister of Transport, and the *Police Review* had a jingle going at the time, to the tune of 'All the King's horses, and all the King's men', it ran.

> The King's speed cops, Morrison's men,
> They wuffle up the hill, and they wuffle down again,
> The King's speed cops, Morrison's men,
> They're in mufti, they're in blue,
> If you've got a hot stuff bike, they're after you,
> The King's speed cops, Morrison's men.

He had also formally recommended me for my BEM. I met with him at the bar, and we had quite a chat. He was quite approachable, and amused at my reference. I noticed that he had tea or coffee stains on his waistcoat; it could, I suppose, have been snuff.

After lunch, there was a session in the Hodsall Hall, where Herbert quietly went to sleep. Still, he had been a power in his day.

Mr Deeds was a sharp, alert man. I told him during our chat that I would have liked to have said in my police bit, what most policemen felt about the abolition of the death penalty; he said, 'I wish you had.' Shortly after this visit, about ten members of the House of Lords came on the same basis. The only member that stands out in that gathering was Lord Longford, not for any contribution that I remember, but for his appearance, with that funny hair, or lack of it. Among course members I had a Watney in my syndicate, and on one occasion a Mrs Lethbridge. She was the wife of Major General Lethbridge, who had been the first commandant of the College, from 1949, when it opened, until 1953, when he retired due to illness. He had really laid the foundation of the fine establishment the College became. He returned on recovery to a job as Regional Director, and often came to the College on studies. He had been a distinguished Army officer, and held a position in Intelligence at the War's end. He was a charming, kind and intelligent man. His wife was in my syndicate on a WRVS course when the syndicate were set a problem, and she was the spokesman for giving the solution. Lady Reading sat in during the discussion. Mrs Lethbridge gave a solution of outstanding clarity and precision. I had by this time got used to hearing splendidly phrased answers to syndicate problems, both in syndicate rooms and in the theatre – after all, in studies some of the top brains and best-educated men and women in the country were speaking. I have never heard a solution given better than Mrs Lethbridge gave that day, so much so that Lady Reading was moved to say as she left the room, 'Mr Stonier, these girls are too good for me.' No wonder their daughter, Nemone Lethbridge, the authoress and Queen's Counsel, was so talented – from stock like that she could hardly be otherwise.

The Home Secretary, Sir Frank Soskice came in 1965 and inspected the College. It was arranged that he should conclude his visit with a short spell in the Hodsall Hall between 1400–1445 hours whilst a course was in session. It was also arranged that he should sit in on the final part of my talk on 'Morale' before addressing the course. He duly came in quietly with the Commandant and others, and sat down, while I continued without interruption. At the end of my remaining fifteen minutes I sat down to the usual applause, and Sir Frank was then introduced to the course by the Commandant. He gave a short address, and referred kindly to some remarks in my talk that had taken his fancy.

Lord Stonham, his deputy, also attended on several occasions. I remember chatting to him with Rose at a cocktail party. He was rather interested for some reason in my name, which is, of course, uncommon. He struck me as a kindly man, with the shrewdness acquired from his trade union negotiator background. At our fairly frequent cocktail parties, I met Chris Chattaway, when he was a minister – Postal Services I think – Sir Hartley Shawcross, and of course, armed forces dignitaries, both serving and on pension, too numerous to mention.

A fairly frequent visitor was Dame Evelyn Sharp, the permanent Secretary of the then Ministry of Housing and Local Government. This Ministry was concerned with the homeless problem of post-nuclear attack, and was therefore involved in most of the studies we held. She was slightly built, quietly dressed, and carried an obvious air of authority. All the Permanent Secretaries I saw at the Staff College carried the same aura – as in fact do most people who have held high command in whatever field. Dame Evelyn was the lady mentioned so often in the 'Crossman Diaries'.

Sir John Hunt, the Everest climb leader, came on a second visit, and this time he heard my 'Morale' talk. He made a point of coming to me in the passage between the syndicate rooms, and during a discussion we had, warmly praised my talk. I found him rather a quiet man, kindly, with the typical stamp of an English army officer in the finest sense of that term.

I must have spoken during my Staff College days to every town, county and district clerk in the country. For years we held controllers' courses, to which they all attended as time went on. They were all

At Sunningdale outside Lethbridge Theatre with Course Members, 1962.

controllers-designate, so there was an implicit compulsion to equip themselves for the task. I always concluded their course with 'Morale', it always went like a bomb.

A typical letter:

Council House, Halesowen.

Dear Mr. Stonier,

As I did not have an opportunity on Friday, I feel I must write to tell you how very much I appreciated your inspiring talk on 'Morale'. It was well worth going all the way to Sunningdale just to hear that alone. I know many others felt the same.

Thank you for all your help in syndicate.

With kind regards,
Yours sincerely,
JOHN MCCOOKE – Town Clerk.

So after seven years it still went well! But I must retrace my steps to about 1963 to other important events.

Transport

I had a good relationship with the Ministry of Transport officials from my earliest days at Sunningdale. Noting my interest and knowledge of road traffic, I was quickly roped in to present the Ministry papers on all the many studies that were held over the years. I worked closely with the Assistant Secretary Brian Davies, and his assistant Miss Allen of the Department's training division for years until, in fact, Davies retired late in 1966, when he handed over to a Mr Poole, with whom I worked equally well. The first purely Ministry study was held late in the fifties, and I was made Staff Officer for it. The study had gone well, and from then on our relationship was most friendly.

In July 1963, the Railways Board had their first study, in association with the Ministry of Transport, and other government departments. The object – to study problems that would face the railways in conditions of thermo-nuclear war, and to examine what instructions and guidance should be given to staff to enable them to cope with the situations in which they might find themselves.

The study was conducted by a Directing Staff working under the supervision of General Wansbrough Jones. It was of necessity a very technical course involving complicated engineering techniques. During rehearsals we had the usual 'nit picking' criticisms from the highly qualified audience. Anyone presenting any kind of paper, demonstration or whatever, had to expose himself to this ordeal – it required patience, good temper, and the ability to quickly respond and defend one's material. I had received the full brunt of this years earlier in 'Study Zeta'. As Staff Officer in this study, called 'Common Carrier', I did not have other than standard staff college material to present, so I escaped it this time.

The course went well, when towards the end there was a time gap. I can't imagine how it happened, it should have emerged during rehearsal, but there it was, thirty minutes to fill. I suggested putting in a talk on 'Warning and Monitoring'. It was a forty-five minute presentation, but I thought I could reduce it to twenty minutes, and retain the essentials. Could I really do this at the drop of a hat? I consulted the demonstrators, got their script and marked what I required presenting, altering my copy accordingly. We had no time to rehearse it, it was 'off the cuff'. In came the audience, and I went into action. Now I liked 'Warning and Monitoring', it was not my subject, but I had learned it 'just in case'. It went off very well, much to my surprise, the audience were most enthusiastic. I owe the demonstrators a debt here for they responded splendidly! After the study had ended there was an official report published – not to me, I hasten to add, but for general dissemination – it read:

Part V Acknowledgements

The Directing Staff are deeply indebted to the many people who contributed so much to the success of 'Covered Wagon'. Where so many have been so helpful it would be invidious to single out names for special mention, with one exception – Mr. F. Stonier, B.E.M., of the Civil Defence Staff College. Not only did Mr. Stonier give us invaluable help in preparing and stage managing the study, and deliver an interesting and illuminating address on the effect of thermo-nuclear weapons, but at very short notice, he gave a talk on the 'Warning and Monitoring' system which was little short of a tour-de-force, and was by common acclaim, one of the high spots of the study.

Signed on behalf of the Directing Staff,
BRIAN DAVIES – Ministry of Transport.
JOHN COULTHARD – British Railways Board.

It is a funny business – you can never quite be sure what will be a winner, and a cut-down version of a reasonably interesting lecture had proved a winner. I had nice personal letters from Davies and Coulthard.

The Italian General Staff

They were programmed to visit us as part of our link with NATO. We had some time to prepare; it was intended to give a brief description of the overall plans and organization in the UK to combat the effects of thermo-nuclear attack from the civil point of view. The staff of the College were to deliver the information from prepared scripts, which would then be translated to our high-level audience, sentence by sentence, by a representative from the Foreign Office.

I was instructed to give a fairly lengthy paper, as was Donald Addison. I studied my script and decided, without saying a word to any of our staff, to give the last three pages in Italian.

We had an Italian couple who worked on the College domestic staff. The wife was a very capable young lady, who spoke excellent English, and had lived in the UK for many years; she was in her thirties, I guess. Her husband's English was not quite so good, but he was quite an intelligent man; they lived in a flat in the stable block, next to my garage. I was friendly with them, and I told them of the proposed visit of their countrymen, and what I proposed to do. They co-operated splendidly – she translated the three pages into Italian, and I rehearsed it; when I was satisfied, I spoke it to them; they corrected faults in pronunciation, and we got it right enough to satisfy them.

Robert Thomson knew I was up to something, and was quite nervous as he was Senior Instructor for the show. Came the day – I spoke quietly to the translator, who was delighted to be relieved of three pages of script. Donald gave his performance first – it is pretty dreary to speak sentence by sentence, pause, have it translated, and then continue.

The audience were quiet, resplendent in their uniforms representing the three armed services, and must have been of high rank.

My turn came, and I did as Donald had. It was not my first experience of speaking in English and having it translated to an audience – I had done the same thing to a Polish audience in Wolverhampton just after the War, warning them not to settle their quarrels with knives – a bit different. When I came to the last three pages, I looked across to my translator, nodded and plunged off into fluent Italian – all learned by heart of course. When I stopped, there was loud applause from everyone

– Commandant, translator and our new Inspector General, Air Chief Marshal Sir Walter Merton.

The show closed at that point, General Cooke came across and congratulated me, and called me, 'Signor Fred'. Sir Walter, on our walk back to the house said, 'I didn't know you spoke Italian, Stonier.' I came clean with him and he laughed – it had been a great success and well worth the trouble. I bought my Italian helpers a large box of chocolates and they too were highly pleased. So perseverance paid, I had not managed Welsh a few years before, but my Italian was impeccable. I had much for which to thank my retentive memory during my Staff College life.

Midland Region

After Sir Lawrence Pendred retired, he was replaced by Air Vice Marshal H.A.V. Hogan, CBE, DSO. Vernon Barry had been established in Midland Region as the Director's No. 1, and so was able to show the new man the ropes. I never achieved the rapport with Hogan that I had with Sir Lawrence. Barry and I got on very well together, so my liaison duties were not in any way impaired. I did a number of jobs for Region before the end, in particular to the TAVR who held a show at Shrewsbury. My contribution to this was appreciatively received by the new man. I also did what I felt was a good, almost final show at Worcestershire County Headquarters, on the role of the Local Authority in the survival period. Barry and I did a duo effort here, which was well received.

We were, at this stage, jut beginning to get 'Survival' as a subject off the ground, and things were starting to 'gel'. A pity we were not going to be able to pursue it much further!

Wolverhampton Borough Police – Valedictory Function

Things were changing fast as small police forces were being absorbed into larger units – Wolverhampton merged with surrounding forces, and eventually became the West Midlands Police Authority. Mr Goodchild was to be the first Chief Constable of the new large force. Later, after his retirement, the force became even larger, merging with Birmingham City and others.

It was decided to hold a social function at the Victoria Hotel in Wolverhampton to celebrate, or commiserate, depending on how you viewed the change, the end of a long, long era. I received an invitation and duly attended, accompanied by Rose and Jack Crofts, who was by then the eldest surviving member of the old force. We had a splendid night, and met many old friends and colleagues, both in the force and among the town councillors who had been associated with the Force as members of the Watch Committee. There were also many absentees, people I would have expected to attend.

I had been away from the Force for over twelve years, many men had left, and others promoted. I was amused to note the reaction of some of my old colleagues. I was made much of by the now senior officers and the Chief Constable, so that I had the happy feeling of 'local boy makes good'. A few of my old colleagues, like Llewellyn and Gwilliam, were decidedly cool. Rose and I were whisked off to a committee room reserved for the top brass, while poor Llewellyn and Gwilliam had to use the common bar – this may have been the reason, but who can say what deep thoughts they may have had. Joe Dineley was there in great form; we spoke briefly, but had little in common any more. The lower ranks who still served and knew me were very friendly – in the words of one PC Appleby to Rose, 'He showed 'em, didn't he?' Jack Crofts enjoyed himself immensely, and was made much of by everyone – altogether a happy and memorable night. So ended an era that had lasted for over a century. One could not help feeling rather sad.

The Death of Charles Luce

For some time Charles Luce, who was Chief Instructor and living in the Commandant's house in the grounds, had complained of severe pains in the head. The doctor eventually ordered him to hospital at Paddington in London. I took him there with his wife Joyce, and Rose came along to keep her company. As we left the house, Charles gazed around the lovely garden and grounds, as if for the last time – which in fact it was. On the journey he carried a bowl in case he vomited, as he was now tending to do. We arrived at Paddington and got him comfortably installed, with no idea what was wrong; we never suspected a fatal illness. However, Charles did not last long, and died of a tumour on the brain. Strange, Colonel George, whom I have previously mentioned, had died shortly after his retirement of the same thing. A funeral was held at Sunningdale Church. Many important people attended – as I have said before, Charles came from a distinguished family, and the church was full of high-ranking service people and their wives.

After it was all over, poor Joyce, who was a little inadequate at facing life's problems, was left almost alone. Rose helped her pack Charles's masses of dress clothes and uniforms, as she prepared to leave the college house. It was remarkable how little help was offered to the poor widow from all her well-connected 'friends'.

I noticed this in other cases – these people do not help each other in trouble, as working-class people do, or did. Rose remained helping her until she left. We visited her once in her new home at Malmesbury, where she had settled in quite comfortably. She was a nice, kind, vague kind of lady, the very opposite to poor Charles.

Commander Ted Edwards took the job of Chief Instructor. He, too, was in a poor state of health, and it was not helped by the attitude of some of our DS who seemed to be as difficult as possible. Some of them could be pretty awkward when they chose and Ted was in no shape to combat this. In no time at all he collapsed after a theatre show he attended, and died. It was heart failure, I suppose. We buried poor Ted, and his widow was left distraught! She was not a likeable person, Robert Thomson helped her for a short time, straightening up her affairs, but he did a fair amount of grumbling about it before relinquishing the task to Ted's brother.

Our next Chief Instructor was Colonel Robinson. He was a crusty old stick, had been one-time Commandant of the School of Infantry at Hythe. He dressed in good old-fashioned clothes, highly polished boots, and was a stickler for standards. He was the bane of our drivers, Mick and Ron. 'They ought to wear caps and look smart,' said Robbie. Neither liked wearing caps, and removed them at the earliest opportunity. It is fair to say that all the domestic staff hated Robbie, who was trying to maintain standards in a world which no longer accepted them. He was a nice enough chap to work with – I had, before his appointment, had heated arguments with him on politics. I have no great belief in any party. I had been, when young, a rabid socialist, but when I became more mature, I was equally strong on conservatism – it seems to me to be a case always of the haves and the have-nots. What always gets me going is to listen to firm adherents of either side tearing the other to pieces, or in the case of our staff, making sweeping statements about working men of whom they can have had little or no knowledge – or on the other hand, to listen to working men condemning out of hand a system which despite its faults, gives us some freedom, choice and opportunity. The result is that I can argue as a staunch Tory if in Labour Party company, or staunch Labour if in Tory company. After a bit Robbie rumbled this, and his judgement on me was, 'Fred, you are the best Socialist in the Tory Party,' with which I am inclined to agree.

There had been other changes in our staff over the years. Bill Griffiths went as a CDO for ICI. The other Robinson went as a senior instructor to Falfield to complete his last few years before retiring. Tony Barton secured a position as a Civil Defence Adviser to the Ministry of Health. Gordon Laverick went to join the staff of Training Division at the Home Office.

Family Matters

Carole, after obtaining a Welfare degree at Liverpool carried on this work with various authorities in the North, and finally in Wolverhampton, where she met her future husband, Kenneth Kent. He was in the construction industry, and an expert on concrete. They were married while we were at Sunningdale. Carole did not want a church wedding, so they were married at Windsor Register Office. I gave a reception at the White Hart, Windsor, to which I invited Robert Thomson of our staff, and his wife Jeannie; my sisters and niece came. Mother was too old at over ninety to travel. Rose's sister Nell, husband Alf, daughter Val and her husband came. Norah's future husband, Ted Hobbs also

Carole and Ken's wedding.

Norah and Ted's wedding.

came. Ken, as an only child, whose parents were killed in the Blitz, had no relatives to invite. Before obtaining his present job, he had served as a Sergeant Pilot in the RAF. After the wedding, he and Carole went to live in Bristol, as he had a flat there, but he sold this quite soon, and bought a nice little cottage in Axbridge, going to his job at the Oldbury Power Station near Bristol each day.

Norah had moved from RAF Medmenham to the RAF Staff College at Bracknell; from there she had moved to RAF Kidbrooke, and then to Queen Anne's Mansions and Admiralty Arch in London. She came home most weekends bringing Ted with her; he worked in the Post Office Foreign Section in London. They were married in September of the same year as Carole and Ken. This time the ceremony was held in the Methodist Church in Windsor – Norah at that time was following that persuasion, and Ted did not mind. The reception was again held at the White Hart Hotel, but on this occasion, in addition to our family, there were Ted's relatives as well. This necessitated asking for College accommodation to sleep them, but this was no problem. All went off well, and Norah and Ted lived with his widowed father for a time in London.

A few months elapsed, and a vacancy fell due in the Demonstration Office. I had noticed that Ted had a bent for handling electrical gadgets, and demonstration work now required a good knowledge of this. I asked him if he would like a job of demonstrator, and he thought he would, so I sent him to see Don Woods, who as DS Co-Ord had to make a selection of suitable candidates. Ted eventually got the job, and transferred from the GPO to the Home Office. I took a risk, but Ted took to the job like a duck to water, soon had it mastered and performed it to the satisfaction of General Cooke, who was quite a stickler in such matters.

Once his appointment was confirmed, he obtained one of the College council houses on the nearby estate. Norah got a transfer to the Meterological Office at Bracknell, so they were well set up.

College Personalities

Let me give a brief account of members of the College staff, who in their own way helped to keep the place ticking over.

We had five or six gardeners, it varied; in charge was Wal Smith, who lived with his wife in one of the estate cottages. The grounds were kept in beautiful conditions; no money was allowed for seeds or plants, but Wal managed to produce his own. As time went on, the team of gardeners, due to government economy measures, had to take on another Ministry establishment nearby. Wal's brother leased the 'Home Farm', kitchen garden, and an acre next to it. Like similar establishments, the estate had a long walled garden for producing food for the 'Big House'. This was now worked commercially, the produce being sold to Covent Garden, the College kitchens, and flowers to course members.

Rose and I became friendly with Wal and his wife Renee. They were great home wine producers, and had a storeroom full of all manner of wines in bottle and barrel, some eight or nine years old. We often went to their cottage for an evening of winetasting, accompanied by homemade crusty bread, cheese, and crisp Cos lettuce. Wal never drank his wine, he had whisky, but we were quite taken with the idea, and later made a hobby of it ourselves.

Wal and Renee occasionally returned the visit, and came to our lodge. It was strange, in their cottage they were quite at ease, and quite natural with us, but at our house they both seemed a bit constrained; it couldn't have been our lavish home – our furnishings were no better than theirs. We took along Carole and Ken, and Rose's sister Nell and her husband (when they came on visits to us) and we all enjoyed ourselves hugely. Wal got on well with Ken and Alf. We all used to get quite tiddly supping the various wines, but there was never a hangover next day.

Then there were the two drivers, Ron and Mick. Ron was a melancholic type of fellow – a bit of a gambler. His wife was a housemaid, looking after the course members' bedrooms; she too was a pretty miserable sort of girl. They had no reason to be so as they had a nice cottage in the grounds – no children, regular work in beautiful surroundings – they might have been happier with a family.

Mick was very different. He had been a jockey, but either because of weight problems, or because he was no good he had given it up. He was jolly, sharp as a razor when it came to making a few pounds extra, obliging – he always drove us to the airport, and picked us up on our return when we went abroad. I knew both drivers well because they took me out so often when I lectured within reasonable distance of the College. Mick had a family and lived in a council house at Ascot.

Mr Crump and his Wife

Crumpy was getting on a bit, he had, like so many of our older staff, worked for Cunliffe Owen, the old owner of Sunningdale Park. He was the general odd-job man: boilers, lights and so on. His wife, a tiny hard-faced little woman, but kindly withall, was the head waitress in the mansion. They were there when I came, and there when I left.

Roger

I never knew his other name. He was the 'works' carpenter, and did all the many jobs requiring joinery skills. He was a good craftsman, and had a workshop just behind my garden.

Mr Groves

He was the barman, was there when I first arrived, and remained for five or six years until advancing age caused him to retire. He was a most dignified gentleman, and had been butler to Cunliffe Owen. He had in his time mixed with very high society, and would tell interesting tales of the great parties that had been held in his younger days, and the famous people he had served. No one ever treated him with other than respect from the Commandant down. He added a sense of dignity to the place.

Andy – the Cook

A huge woman – pleasant, and a very good cook. Communal meals at an establishment like ours did not give a good professional very much scope. The meals were good quality, but repetitive. There was a strict budget laid down, and it could not be exceeded except if courses made an extra contribution, as they did when guest nights were held, of which more anon. Also on special occasions if the College drew on its Welfare fund for some particular function, like the Garden Party. Or if an outside organization used the College for some purpose like the CDOs' Annual Conference, which ended with a formal dinner. On such occasions as these, 'Andy' could really show her skills, and some of the items served – boars head for example – were quite marvellous to behold. Our many cocktail parties, too, had the titbits that go with it beautifully prepared and served. In her kitchen she could hear me in my early days rehearsing in the room above, and made quite a thing of Mr Stonier pacing the room for hours, talking to himself. She had a brother who had been an inspector in the Metropolitan Police, so we had common ground for our frequent chats.

George Armour – the Catering Officer

He was there when I arrived, and when I left. He did a difficult and purse-restricting job in a masterly fashion. He had to purchase all the food and wines, keep within a strict budget, and keep a critical clientele satisfied, which I thought he did very well. Having two messes made his job more difficult – two lots of cooks and waitresses, two barmen, all the stock to watch, difficult staff to keep happy. In the past, and still to some extent in the fifties and sixties most of the working people in Sunninghill village worked for big establishments like ours, and there were many scattered about in this part of the world. Towards the end of my stay this was fast dying out, the young people no longer accepted this kind of work, and the influx of foreigners was quite noticeable – mainly Spaniards and Italians – which hardly made the Catering Officer's job any easier. George was a bit inclined to exaggerate his knowledge of wines. At Christmas, when we went into his cellar to order our wines and spirits, he would air to us a knowledge which I am sure was only superficial. Still, we all have our little weaknesses, and generally he did a first-class job. Before he retired in the seventies, he was awarded the MBE, and then shortly after retiring to Wales, he died suddenly, like so many of our staff.

Survival

Immediately after the death of Charles Luce, the Commandant and DS all returned to the Hodsall Hall, where I presented my lecture on 'Survival'. I did not expect it to be accepted, as it was, into the programme. For some time now, as the size of weapons increased in megattonage, the life-saving stage on which most of Civil Defence was based, was now giving way to an acceptance of huge casualty figures, with a hope that something could be done for the survivors on the fringes of damage, and the restoration of some of life's necessities in food, water, power and transport. I had planned my talk to cover this in general terms, but hoped it would stimulate further thoughts along the general lines. In the event this is what happened – Baxter was told to prepare a floor demonstration based on Southampton, illustrating a survival stage. This was to be for senior officers, and no more than an introduction to this vast subject.

Robert Thomson and I were deputed to prepare an exercise for controllers, giving a heavy damage picture in North East Region, and to prepare from that syndicate problems and possible solutions. We locked ourselves away in the loft over the Gloucester Hall, and with maps of North East Region, we started on this massive task. After about three weeks hard but enjoyable graft, we emerged with an exercise, syndicate problems, and solutions. This was presented to assembled DS and members of Training Division for the usual 'nit-picking'. It was eventually approved with some alterations, and was used for the remainder of the life of the Civil Defence Staff College. Robert and I enjoyed our work, and had put together a rather good exercise which went from strength to strength. I kept my 'Survival' talk, and gave it quite often outside the College, in particular at Falfield, in a series of Sunday morning study sessions to CDOs, while still fully engaged giving 'Morale' all over the UK.

Instructional Staff

I have mentioned many of our staff, but there are a few more I should not forget.

Rupert Caswell

He had been well educated at Sedburgh Public School, and served as a civil servant in India for a time. Then I think he was a regional officer of some kind, although it was difficult to find out exactly what he had been – he certainly had not been in the armed forces. He was a good lecturer, but his real forte was the stage, he was excellent in playlets, and had a 'feel' for theatre, which is what he should have been – an actor. He was not a smart dresser, living with his wife in a fine house on the main A30, just outside Sunningdale. I went with Rose and the girls to dinner at his home once, when his wife served a beautiful meal; his home was expensively furnished, so either he or his wife must have had money. He became a senior instructor, but no-one took much notice as this was a futile rank – apart from allocating DS to tasks there was really no authority with the job, and with a staff like ours, all of whom had held command of men, it was not worth the trouble of trying to keep them in order as they were a self-willed lot. Cas saw his time out and retired in due course in about 1967, and went to live in Wiltshire.

John Baxter

An Indian Army Lieutenant Colonel. He was tiny, very much like Ronnie Corbett, the actor. He was a bit of a humorist, and gave his lectures with a certain 'tongue in cheek' attitude that audiences loved. He was able enough – when he joined the Indian Army from Sandhurst, they only took the men who had achieved high marks. His family history was Indian Army – his father had marched into Damascus in the First World War with Allenby, as one of his staff officers. He told us that his ancestors further back had been in the siege of Lucknow. He also told us the surviving orphan white children of the officers and wives, killed or dead during the siege, were adopted by the adult survivors. His ancestor had been such a surviving child, so he was not very certain whether his origins were Baxter or not. It was a good story – it could have been true – these service people could be strange folk. I remember how surprised I was to hear that the widow of a naval officer is as often as not married to another eligible brother officer. But to return to John, he had an unfortunate marriage that had broken up in India, and had returned to England after partition, more or less broke. Money in India could not be taken out of the country, so that all he had was a pension which was reduced after commutation. He had married again, and kept his two children from the first marriage with him. They all lived in a large house on the A30 in Sunningdale, which he leased. He was a naturally idle man; we both had seats by the window in our office, and could gaze out on the beautiful view down to the lake, which John often did. He never to my knowledge, initiated any new presentation on his own, but would work to order, as he was not an originator. A college like ours lives on original ideas being thrown up; without them it cannot properly function and might as well be a training school using a syllabus. When he set his mind to work he could turn out excellent material.

After the College closed, he obtained a job of Fire Prevention Officer at the BBC where his brother had some influence, and eventually retired to live in Dorset.

Donald Addison

He had been a Lieutenant Colonel tank officer in the Western Desert, where he saw a great deal of action and won the MC. His tank had been hit, and Donald sustained severe wounds, losing an eye, and was in hospital for months. Whilst there, he said he had perfected a system for betting on horse racing which guaranteed success. He did not try to sell us the idea, in fact he kept it very much to himself. He and Mick, the driver, carefully laid their bets, and due to his success, bookies were not anxious to take his bets, so he had to lay the money around, and Mick, with his knowledge of the Turf, could do this. Occasionally, Donald would give the other DS a tip, but the horses never won for us. He was a small man, and his missing eye was quite unnoticeable. He was a joker, full of fun, and a very good lecturer.

After I had launched my 'Morale', General Matthews gave me a huge pile of literature on 'Disasters', and suggested I write another winner based on that, but I was feeling rather spent after my efforts on 'Morale' and backed out. He gave it to Donald, who made a good talk out of it. This was turned into a great success by the following experience. At Frejus in southern France, a dam burst its banks and flooded the village, drowning and rendering homeless many people.

The BBC went there with a team, and General Matthews got permission for Donald to go as well, and see what he could bring back to bolster his 'Disaster' lecture. He came back with excellent information and pictures. His lecture became a 'best seller' like my 'Morale'. Donald and I were always out on circuit with our respective productions, but he paid a price. His health was always precarious after his war experiences, he picked up a germ at Frejus, and was ill on and off ever after. Shortly after the College closed in 1968, he died. He was a good colleague, and generally liked by all, the only DS with whom he had cool relations was John Alldridge, who he referred to as 'Jolly Jack'. Aldridge in turn referred to Addison as that 'Brown Job', a naval reference to army types.

There were other DS but none with whom I had close enough relations to take more space.

The Final Stages of the Civil Defence Staff College

The New Commandant, Vice Admiral Sir Nicholas Copeman, invited Rose and I to drinks one evening at his home. We met his wife, a charming lady. During our chat, Rose mentioned that her father, Dick Lander, had been in the Royal Navy in the last century, and had sailed around Cape Horn in one of the last of the windjammers. The Commandant could not see how this could have been and he and Rose had quite an argument. I was quietly intrigued at this clash between a representative as it were of the lower deck, and a late Sea Lord and distinguished officer of the quarterdeck. Rose was correct, however, I myself have seen pictorial evidence of her father's ship, which was in fact a sailing ship.

I noticed a photograph on the table of a number of Japanese officers being escorted by British officers, so I asked about it, and the Commandant told us that when the Allies recaptured Singapore, they captured the senior Japanese officers, some of whom had been responsible for atrocities, and brutal conditions in the notorious Changi Jail. To punish them in a rather subtle way, they were escorted to their trial by the tallest officers that the Royal Navy could find. Copeman was one of these, and he flanked the Japs on one side, while another tall officer flanked them on the other. The Japs, of course, looked incongruous between these two tall men, and this must have caused them great 'loss of face'. I have since seen the same picture in newsreels of the time – rather clever, I thought. Towards the end of December, 1967, we began to feel that something was brewing. Rumours that some of the Home Office training establishments were to close, were voiced.

In January the Commandant, on his return from a visit to the Home Office, called a meeting, and broke the news. Taymouth Castle, Falfield, and the Staff College were to close down. Easingwold was to be retained. Staff would be recruited from the younger members of the other establishments, to enable a composite type of course to be held covering essentials from the training schools and staff college. Only two of our staff survived – John Alldrigde and Alastair Fennell – they were to join others from the schools to make up the Easingwold staff. Most of the DS would leave in March, with Robert Thomson and I to go in

June, after winding up the College's two outstanding courses, and disposing of the silver and valuables owned by the Mess Committee.

In the event, to accommodate a late police course, we hung on to the end of September, which enabled Robert and I to complete a further full year which helped to slightly increase our pension.

Some of our staff had insufficient service to qualify for pension, but most got other jobs fairly quickly. The Commandant hoped, unsuccessfully, that he might be retained as Commandant of the new Civil Service Staff College which was taking over the establishment. He hung on for a time, but was eventually retired. Our last two courses were uneventful – the police course was for a week only; Ron Chapman, the police officer ran it, Robert and I helped. The other course was a two-day affair for senior police officers from Thailand – Robert and I ran this. I remember they were very interested in our planned police mobile columns, and asked a lot of questions on this. When they left, they presented us both with a Thai gold brooch with their police crest thereon, in a neat little box. It was very nice of them, and is a treasured possession, together with my 'Phoenix' statue, which was given to all departing members of the Directing Staff. The 'Phoenix' was the Staff College insignia, depicting a 'rising from the ashes', which is, I suppose, what Civil Defence was all about. Our last few days were taken up with disposing of our mess property and funds, all of which went to Easingwold.

I sold off an amount of furniture from home quite easily. It is surprising what people will buy – it was all done by word of mouth, so no need to advertise; we just mentioned it to our domestic staff, and they soon found customers.

Of course, the domestic, gardening and other such staff were all kept on if they so desired. My son-in-law, Ted Hobbs, was transferred as Chief Demonstrator to Easingwold, where he remained quite happily until he transferred to the United Kingdom Warning and Monitoring organization on promotion to Executive Officer, some years later. Another Civil Defence related duty, he retained this post until his retirement. His daughter Rosemary became a volunteer 'foot soldier' as a woman observer in the Royal Observer Corps. She was selected to represent the Corps at the Annual Festival of Remembrance at the Royal Albert Hall in November 1993.

Within the next twelve months Admiral Copeman died in Hasler Hospital, Portsmouth. Colonel Robinson died of cancer. General Bruce and then General Cooke, and finally General Matthews, all passed on within a few years.

General Matthews spent his last few years happily as Joint Master of Foxhounds somewhere in Wiltshire, going every year to Italy to ease his arthritis sufficiently to allow him to hunt the following winter. I pay a tribute to all my ex-army commandants – it was a privilege to work with such men, as it was with Kirkman, Merton, Pennycook and the numerous principals and assistant secretaries of the Home Office, Transport and other Ministries. My colleagues too added much to my enjoyment of life at the Staff College. I knew at the end that I had passed my peak, but I had for many years taken part in work for which I was particularly gifted. It had taken me a long time to find my vocation – I was, I believe, a good policeman, but I know I was a first-class lecturer. I was for years enabled to perform a task I loved and did well – not everyone is so fortunate. Incidentally, it set me up reasonably comfortably financially.

A Look at the Future

In 1966, I began to look for a place to which to retire when my Staff College days came to an end. I did not wish to return to Wolverhampton, and Sunningdale, though a lovely place, was too expensive for my liking. Rose and I kept our eyes open for a suitable place. For a time

Our cottages in the 1960s. A big headache for over 2 years with the builder, but it turned out quite a profitable investment in the end. Daughter Carole in forefront.

The garden at Redhill 1960s, before my occupation late 1960s.

Completed cottages at Redhill, Avon.

we were on the East Coast, but the cold winters eventually turned us from it. Carole and her husband had settled in Somerset, and on our visits it seemed a nice place.

When Carole had her first child, a boy, this made the prospect of living near them very attractive. Eventually, Ken, her husband, found a site that seemed promising. About six miles south of Bristol, two old cottages, with partially built extensions on each, with three-quarters of an acre of land. I liked the look of it, and bought it for just over £2,000. It needed a deal of construction work, and Ken hired a newly started local builder to complete the job. We agreed a price and he started work.

The estimate was sadly out and the job dragged on for over two years. I hired a solicitor, and so did the builder. Letters passed back and forth and there was still £1,000 of work to be done for completion. Stalemate was reached. I changed my solicitor in Sunningdale for one in Bristol. He eventually settled the matter to my satisfaction, but not, I fear to the builder's who promptly went bankrupt. I had to seek further estimates to complete the job. After more trouble than I care to think about, the job was finally completed.

About this time Wal Smith, the Head Gardener, was selling a cottage he had bought in Wiltshire. I bought his furniture and some carpets and kitchen utensils, and after a period in storage, I moved them to my cottages.

Rose and I had great fun attending auction sales around the Bristol area until we had reasonably furnished both. I decided to let them as furnished cottages until I was ready to live there myself, when I would occupy the one and keep letting the other. I quickly found tenants for both cottages, which was very satisfactory.

My retirement came, and we went to live in Somerset, now Avon; and for six months I worked getting everything in order in the cottages and gardens. After that I became a little bored. So I wrote to the Chief Constable of Bristol and through his good offices, I obtained a part-time job as a cashier. I held this post for thirteen years until I reached the age of seventy-two when I finally retired after working for sixty-two years. I am still going strong, if a little rheumatic, but I feel I have earned my retirement.

My thirteen years at Parkers Sunblest Bakeries in Bristol was quite a change. There were huge amounts of cash to take from the large delivery force – cheques, notes and coins. I never counted the annual take but it must have run into millions of pounds and most of it paid in on Saturdays, which was a long, tiring day. Although there were, of course, long and boring days as well which gave one the opportunity to write.

The staff were all very friendly once they got to know you as the years rolled on, and when I left in 1982 I was taken out to lunch by the Accountant and his deputy. Later the Manager presented me with a £70 tool kit, to which all the staff and roundsmen had contributed, in a touching speech at a farewell ceremony at which I had made my farewell speech.

Rose and I carried on quietly at Redhill until 1986 when she had a sudden heart attack and died before the ambulance arrived. So ended our 54-year marriage and I lost my loving and steadying partner, still sadly missed. She was a great wife and mother.

I carried on alone for another three years when I had a second hip operation. It was quite successful and after a couple of months recovery in a nursing home I sold my remaining cottage, having sold the other in 1974, and left to start a new life in Scotland. As both my daughters' husbands had also retired and both had chosen to live in the Highlands, I went there so they could keep an eye on me.

As the millennium approaches I am fairly fit at ninety-two, still drive my car, look after my garden and myself, and have my memories of an eventful life to look back on and watching my four great-grandchildren grow up.

My three grandchildren have turned out well. Chris, my grandson, is now a chartered accountant. Lucy my Kent granddaughter is a highly qualified lecturer at York University. Rosemary has an important post with a business firm of national repute. I am proud of them all; they too are now parents.

In conclusion. If my reader has patiently stuck with me so far let me conclude by saying: From 1937 until 1968 I entered a stage when I found my natural gift. I worked hard developing it through life's ups and downs. It finally blossomed at Sunningdale. After my long search I had at last achieved my long held ambition – to be a good teacher, the ability to prepare important material and expound it to a variety of audiences in a dramatic manner. 'The Brummy had after a long search found his talent.'

My Bungalow in Alness, my home since 1989 with its garden and view of Cromarty Firth

*Granddaughter Rosemary Ward
(The Hobbs child)*

*Lucy Sitton-Kent
(The Kent child)*

Grandson Christopher Kent and wife Dominique after their wedding in the Bahamas.